Kahlil Gibran
A Biography

Kahlil Gibran

A Biography

MIKHAIL NAIMY

With a preface by Martin L. Wolf

Quartet Books
London   New York

Published in the UK by Quartet Books Limited 1988
A member of the Namara Group
27/29 Goodge Street, London W1P 1FD

Copyright © by Mikhail Naimy 1934

Published in the US by Philosophical Library, Inc., New York

British Library Cataloguing in Publication Data

Nu'aymah, Mīkhá'íl
Kahlil Gibran: a biography.
1. Gibran, Kahlil. *1883–1931* — Biography
2. Authors, Arab — Lebanon — Biography
3. Authors, Arab — United States — Biography
I. Title   II. Jibrán Kahlil Jibran. *English*
892'.78509   PJ7826.I2Z/

ISBN 0-7043-0036-2

Printed and bound in Great Britain by
The Camelot Press plc, Southampton

Some Notes for the Reader

This book, originally written in Arabic, had its first printing in Beirut, Lebanon, in 1934. It is now offered in English with very slight changes in the text. The following notes may prove of help to the average reader:

Lebanon, which meant so much in Gibran's life, is a narrow strip of picturesque mountainous land stretching a little over 100 miles along the east coast of the Mediterranean between Palestine to the south and Syria to the north and east.

The name means "The White", so called because the Lebanon peaks are snow-capped a good part of the year.

In the Bible, Lebanon is often mentioned as a symbol of purity, beauty and immortality. Its famous cedars are spoken of as denoting strength and endurance.

Lebanon was the home of the ancient Phoenicians who, centuries before Christ, had sailed the high seas, established colonies in North Africa and Europe, fought Rome, and are said to have been the first to invent the alphabet and to discover the way of making glass.

Of all the countries of the Near and Middle East, where Islam is the prevailing faith, Lebanon is the only country with a Christian majority.

The *Maronites* to whom the Gibran family belonged are a Catholic sect named after its patron saint Maroun who lived in Northern Syria and died about A.D. 400. They are the largest Christian denomination in Lebanon.

Lebanon is to-day an independent republic with a population of 1,200,000.

Arabic became the language of the country after the Arab conquest which swept from the heart of Arabia, far to the south, soon after prophet Mohammed's death, spreading as far west as Spain, and as far east as India.

Literacy in Lebanon is higher than in any other Arabic-speaking country, reaching in some sections 85% and more.

The Arabic-speaking world comprises, in addition to Arabia proper, all of Iraq, Syria, Lebanon, parts of Palestine, Transjordan, Egypt, Lybia, Tunisia, Algiers and Morocco. Its estimated population is between 60,000,000 and 70,000,000.

M. N.

Apologia

It was after much hesitation that I decided to write this book. For I believe that no man can faithfully, accurately and fully describe a single instant of his own life in all its intricate meanings and its infinite connections with the universal life. How, then, is one, no matter what his talents, to put between the two covers of a book the life of another man, be he an idiot or a genius! In that respect everything that men relate of men under the name of "History" is, in my judgment, but so much froth breaking over the surface of that sea which is human life; the depths remain too deep, and the horizons too distant for any pen to plumb, or any brush to paint. Until this day we have not been able to write the "history" of any man or of anything at all. Had we written the history of but a single man *in full*, we should be able to read in it the history of all men; and had we recorded *faithfully* the story of but one thing, we should discover in it the story of all things.

Another reason for my hesitation was the fact that my long and close association with Gibran enabled me to learn of some intimate sides of his life which he jealously kept secret from others. I say "some" advisedly; for most of Gibran's "secrets" went down with him to the grave. Would it be proper for me to speak of some of that "some"? And if I keep it out of my book, what would be the sense of writing it? Shall I be a traitor to Gibran and to myself and draw of him a picture with no balance between its lights and shadows to please those of his readers who have no taste in art and no power to pry deep into life? Shall I hide from the reader's eye what I know to be an open page in the book of Life? And how can there be anything secret from Life which contains all things? To the blind only are all visual things secrets.

A third reason was that I could not write of Gibran without at the same time writing something of myself. How could I do otherwise, with that close spiritual kinship that existed between us? Would the reader understand that in speaking of myself I had no other purpose but to make the portrait I am drawing of Gibran clearer, more complete and more life-like? Would the reader know that I am reluctant to speak of myself, especially in a book I am writing of another?

These were some of the reasons that made me hesitate to write the book. But when I returned to the East a year after Gibran's death I found that my friend had already become a mythical personality. He was not the Gibran I knew for fifteen years, whose dreams and pains, whose strength and weakness, whose bitter fight with himself and the world I had come to know and to observe at a close range; who shared with me his longings and his thoughts as I shared with him mine. Besides, many of the literati and semi-literati of the Arab world began to press me for a book on Gibran. Some said it was a debt I owed my friend; others called it a sacred obligation toward modern Arab literature which no other could discharge; still others asserted that my silence in the circumstances was an unforgivable sin.

The result was this book. I wrote it in the hope that the reader, as he turns the pages, would come to see and to know Gibran as I saw him and knew him, rather than read the "history" of his life which no man knows. It is also my hope that the reader will find in these pages certain helpful reflections on life in general in which all men are partners and co-actors.

As I send this book on its way, I am fully aware that certain outspoken passages in it, while pleasing to some, will be displeasing and startling to others, especially to those who did not know Gibran and who have come to form their own picture of him out of the pages of his books, or from his drawings. I would be untrue to myself and to my subject, if I were to sacrifice my frankness in order to win the cheap plaudits of hypnotics. Without this frankness the book would not have been worth writing. Without it the best and the noblest in Gibran's life should have remained under cover. And the best and noblest in his life was his stubborn, incessant struggle with himself to cleanse his soul from all impurities, and to make it as beautiful as the beauty he glimpsed with his imagination and so generously spread in his books and drawings. For art, no matter how highly regarded by its own creator and his fellow-men, is of little value save when translated by its creator and by men into a power capable of leading them from the bounds of limited existence to the boundlessness of Life — from the man in God to the God in man. And literature, no matter how absorbing, has little meaning except that it reveal to us the meaning of Life which is more enduring than the earth, and more lasting than the sky.

MIKHAIL NAIMY.

Biskinta, Lebanon.

Contents

PART THREE

APPENDIX

Preface

Mikhail Naimy, leading literary figure of the East, is the logical (if not the necessary) biographer of Gibran, great Lebanese mystic, for so close and so understanding was the fine relationship of these friends, these two poet-author-philosophers, that for all purposes of accuracy, inner knowledge, and utter truth, this volume may be considered as much Gibran's autobiography as it is Naimy's biography of Gibran.

Naimy, now leading an existence of "active seclusion" atop his hill in Lebanon after a varied career in many parts of the world, is the person who possesses more facts on Kahlil Gibran than does any other; it was to Naimy that Gibran confided his deepest problems, secrets, and anxieties, personal and otherwise, seeking the wisdom of counsel and consolation that only Naimy was equipped (and entrusted) to offer; it was with Naimy that Gibran sought association with the influential *Arrabitah* (Pen Bond) movement that revolutionized and gave impetus to the previously neglected and unrecognized Arabic contribution to world literature; it was to Naimy—almost exclusively—that Gibran penned his countless letters and inquiries, opening his heart and his experiences to the last detail; it was for Naimy that Gibran deliriously called on his deathbed, and it was Naimy who responded in breathless haste, comforting the *Prophet of Lebanon* until the end.

Both were born in the shadows of the famous cedars of

Lebanon; both sought and found fame in the fields of literature and philosophy; both won honor and acclaim in America as Americans; both returned finally to Lebanon, Naimy to the contemplative observation of nature from his hilltop at Biskinta, Gibran to the permanent reunion with his beloved homeland.

Born in Biskinta, Lebanon, in 1889, Mikhail Naimy received his early education at a small, primitive parochial school in the village, and at the age of nine was received at the school, newly opened and conducted by the Imperial Russian Palestine Society, one of the many schools set up in the Near East by many Western nations for the purpose of enlisting sympathetic support to their aim at plucking the remaining feathers and meat from the crumbling Turkey, fast falling in strength and influence as a world power at the time. Naimy was selected therefrom to attend the exclusive Teachers' Institute at Nazareth, and in 1906 was awarded a scholarship to the Seminary of Poltava in the Ukraine, where he mastered the Russian language in short order and wrote poems and treatises which provoked wide admiration. Prepared to matriculate at the Sorbonne in Paris, he was prevailed upon by an older brother to pursue his advanced studies in the United States instead, where the University of Washington quickly accepted him, qualifying him to take a difficult six-year course in four concentrated years; two degrees were conferred upon him at his graduation in 1916.

While at the university, he wrote critical articles and stories which were reprinted by leading Arabic periodicals throughout the country and the East. His heart was set on a literary career, and he determined that the Arabic literary *milieu* in New York, with Rihani, Gibran, Arida, and others, was his field.

Although not yet a citizen, he enlisted as a private in World War I, serving at the front with the AEF in 1918. After his discharge in 1919 he rocketed to literary fame, but at the height of his popularity decided to return to Lebanon in 1932, perhaps in consequence of the death of his dearest friend, Gibran, a year earlier. He is still in Lebanon, writing, lecturing, and meditating upon the basic problems of life and the beauties of nature.

Among his many works published (parts of which have been translated into French, Russian, Portuguese, Spanish, English and German) are *Two Generations*, a well-received play; *The Cribble*, a series of critical essays; *Stages*, an excursion into inner and outer life; *Once upon a Time, a collection of short* stories; *Food for the Godward Journey*, his famous discourses; *Eyelid Whisperings*, a group of philosophical poems; *Encounter*, a novel; *Threshingfloors* and *Light and Darkness*, poetico-philosophical contemplations; *Pitted Face*, the portrait of a bizarre personality; *Vineyard by the Road*, aphorisms and parables; *Present-Day Idols*, an analytical lecture; *The World's Voice*, meditative views of life; *The Book of Mirdad*, a "lighthouse and a haven" for seekers after spiritual emancipation, and many other publications of varied, interesting, and helpful theme.

Since youth he grappled with such questions as Good and Evil, Life and Death, the Here and the Hereafter, and the like. The story of creation, fall, redemption, resurrection, and final judgment, as taught by the church, satisfied him but temporarily, for his thirsty mind stubbornly refused to accept things as they appeared on the surface. He shunned the beaten path, the commonplace, the conventional, the traditional; to this day he continues his solitary quest.

Of the many superlative comments throughout the East regarding Mikhail Naimy and his impact on world literature and thought, perhaps the most expressive is that which appeared editorially in the literary supplement of *Al-Misry*, the most influential and most extensively read Arabic daily newspaper in the world, and the organ of the WAFD party in Egypt. By way of introduction to a full page reproduction of one of Naimy's chapters on Gibran in its issue of December 24, 1949, it stated:

If the Arabic language—nay, if the entire East—were to boast of its thinkers and take pride in its philosophers, poets and writers, then it would be the right of the Arabic-speaking nations to place Mikhail Naimy at the very top of their spiritual and literary glories of the present.

Mikhail Naimy is a unique humanitarian school, and one of the truest and noblest creeds of the human mind. This is not the place to speak of him as a school, or as a creed. This is but a kind of call to the readers of Arabic to draw more and more from the treasures of this genius who bestows so liberally the fruits of his mind on men.

Mikhail Naimy gives and does not take. Sufficient for him to give, and sufficient for men to take, if only they knew how to take.

*   *   *

Naimy offers here the first truly un-aureoled picture of the life of Gibran, dissipating much of the myth built around him in the last few decades. Here, through the unimpeachable eyes and words of his closest friend and associate, we meet Gibran the philosopher—the man—the artist.

Many of Gibran's hitherto unpublished writings and sayings are included, throwing a new and interesting light upon this unique figure.

Martin L. Wolf

New York

Kahlil Gibran
A Biography

PART I

Twilight

DYING

Death-rattle!

How often I had heard of it before I heard it. But since that night—the night of April 10, 1931—I scarcely hear anything else. I hear it in my heart-beats; in my voice and every voice; in the stillness of the night and hubbub of the day.

Blessed be Life whose passing wizardry presses eternities into a wink where antonyms appear as synonyms, and things unequal stand as perfectly equal. Bless it because it mocks our human standards, drawing no lines between essences and shadows; between things that amuse and things that instruct; between business offices and graveyards; between the rattle of death and the rattling of a telephone bell!

The day is Friday. The hour about 5:30 P.M. I am making ready to leave an office where each day I slaughter a number of virgin hours of my life to placate an equal number of prostitute dollars, and where I seldom hear any talk except of buying and selling, of rising and falling prices, of profit and loss. The telephone rings, and I am called to answer. Is it a customer wishing to order some goods, or to complain of some goods, or to offer an excuse for delaying the settlement of an account?

"Hello! . . . Yes . . . Speaking. What do you say? Gibran in the hospital?"*

"In St. Vincent's Hospital, and in coma. The doctor does not think he will live beyond midnight. Not one of his friends is near

---

* Gibran's full name was Gibran Kahlil Gibran, the middle being his father's name in keeping with the traditions of the Arabic East. He always signed his full name to his Arabic works, but dropped the first name in his English writings.

3

him. Since I know you to be his closest friend I considered it my duty to call upon you."

"Taxi! St. Vincent's Hospital. And hurry if you please."

How can that poor soul hurry in streets so choking with humanity a-foot and a-wheel? And where are all those men, women and children hurrying? — Each to his hospital! And one is the hospital for all.

And who is this St. Vincent? And what has he done to be sanctified? There is but one mile between me and his hospital. Yet is it the longest mile I have travelled in my life. Gibran is on his death-bed. Will I reach him alive? "Hurry, driver, hurry!"

"I am to-day a well man, Mischa."* Those were the last words I had heard from him when I telephoned him a few days before, in-quiring about his health. We then agreed to dine together soon and to spend the evening in my apartment. And here I am, dashing to eat with him the dinner that Death has spread for us at St. Vincent's restaurant!

"I am a well man to-day, Mischa. I am a stranger in this world, Mischa.—I love this world, Mischa."—Health and sickness. Life and Death. Homeland and foreign land—Who can show me the difference between them?

"Hurry, driver, hurry!"

* * *

"In what room is Kahlil Gibran?"—I hurl the question at a man sitting behind a desk at the foot of a long staircase. The man begins at once to fumble his index cards under letter "G" much like one looking for a word in the dictionary, quite unconscious of the fact that the voice of the man speaking to him choked with the throes of death.

---

* "Mischa" is the Russian diminutive for Mikhail, and the name by which the author was known in a small coterie of close friends.

"We have no patient by this name, sir." When I insist that they have a patient by that name, the man politely refers me to another entrance from another street. There I learn that Gibran is in room number so-and-so, on the third floor. I ascend many staircases. I make many turns. I stare at many doors before I come to the door I am looking for. Behind each door I pass lies some human body on a bed of pain; some human soul caught in the claws of Fate. Lord, Lord, Lord! Here is a portion of Your creation begging a hand that would set their broken bones, or darn their torn skins, or piece together the fragments of their hearts and livers. What do they get instead?—Drugs, more drugs, and yet more drugs! Where is Your healing ointment? Or is it Pain—the forge of Love—Your priceless Love—and the gate of deliverance—Your deliverance indescribable . . . ?

Nuns flit by like shadows from another world. Their dark, flowing robes spread darkness in the heart. And nurses walk into one room and out of another. Their dazzling white raiment hurts the eye.

"Where is ward so-and-so, sister?—To the right?—Thank you."

In front of the ward I see a man surrounded by four women. As I approach, one of the women detaches herself from the group and walks toward me, her right hand extended for greeting. She is tall, bony, sallow of complexion, with deep-set eyes and a prominent nose. She is an American poetess nearing her sixth decade. She met Gibran some seven years before and made herself quite useful to him in transcribing his manuscripts. I had met her once before in his studio. As I put my hand in hers she sighs and says,

"Thank God, thank God you are here."

One question fills my heart and floats in my eyes and upon my face. Yet my tongue hesitates to articulate it. But the woman answers it without waiting to hear it:

"There is no hope. There is no hope."

"Tell me what happened."

"I was with him in the studio last night. He had an attack the like of which he had never experienced before. I called the physician and asked him if it was necessary to move him to a hospital at once. He thought it wiser to let him spend that night in the studio. To leave him alone was unthinkable. So I spent the night with him. In the morning—this morning—his pains became unendurable. So we brought him here between 10 and 11 o'clock."

"Why didn't you call me yesterday, or early this morning?"

"Yesterday we thought it a passing crisis. But this morning, when we brought him here, you were the first to come to my mind. I did not know where and how to get in touch with you. Then occurred to me what was like an inspiration—to telephone "The Syrian World" magazine and ask them to pass to you the sad news; and they did. Thank God you came."

"How is he now?"

"He fell unconscious soon after we brought him here, and is still unconscious."

"Did anyone ask him if he wished to confess and to commune?"

"One of the sisters asked him, 'Are you a Catholic?' His answer came loud, almost gruff, 'No!' She left him and went her way. Soon after he fell into a coma; and a Syrian priest came —a short, thin fellow—perhaps you know him—and he began to shout at Kahlil at the top of his voice, 'Gibran, Gibran!' but Kahlil was no longer conscious. I was so provoked with that priest and his harsh manner that I almost wished to throw him out of the window."

"Did the priest do anything else?"

"That was all he did."

"Where is the doctor?"

"There he is." And she pointed out to me the man standing in front of the door.

"What is his ailment, doctor? Is there no hope in medicine . . . in surgery?"

"A cancer in the liver.* I don't think he'll live to midnight. He is now unconscious, and I don't believe he'll ever wake up again." He said it in a cool and matter-of-fact manner, as one speaking of the weather. No wonder; that was not his first encounter with death. Will he encounter his own death in the same cool and matter-of-fact manner?

Ah, medicine, medicine, medicine! The God of the aching world and, perhaps, its greatest ache.

"May I go in and see him, doctor?"

"Certainly."

*   *   *

Gh-r-r. . . . Gh-r-r. . . . Hm-m-m. . . .

Weird and ghastly sounds rush into my ears the moment I open the door slowly and gently, and as slowly and gently shut it behind me. The feeling comes over me, as I cross the threshold of that room, that I am crossing from a world where nothing is mystery into a world where everything is mystery. And I forget that the two worlds are locked in one, and that there are no thresholds and doors between them excepting those which ignorance creates and eyes perceive through the thick veils woven on the crude looms of the crude outer senses.

I approach the white bed behind the door and fail, at first, to notice the intern standing at its head; my eyes become glued upon a face they had long known and loved, yet now scarcely recognize. They have always known it to be the color of sand flushed with the blood of life; now they see it ashen under the breath of death.

There is the straight nose with its full sensitive nostrils. It

---

* An autopsy revealed cirrhosis of the liver with incipient tuberculosis in one of the lungs.

has become thin, pale, lonely. The straggling drops of blood still animating it are scurrying away before the spectre of breathlessness. The nostrils barely twitch, barely breathe, as if clogged with a catarrh, and as if Death—the master physician—were treating them with a breath from an earth other than ours, from skies beyond our skies.

There are the eyes, shaded with thick, long lashes. But yesterday they brimmed with dreams and mirrored shadows of many, many worlds. How often I had seen them light up suddenly with a flash of inspiration, or with a burning longing, or with an innocent twinkle of an innocent delight. How often I had seen them flow with tears, or sparkle with laughter, or peer into the faces of men and things in search of what lies behind the veil. How often they would look afar, oblivious of everything about them, as if chasing the ethereal shapes of some thoughts and emotions which did not frequent men's haunts and temples. But now . . . now they neither laugh nor weep; they neither peer nor sparkle. They lie tightly shut under their thick, arched brows, jealously guarding all their secrets. Yet there may be many hosts of mystic shadows flitting behind their eyelids this very moment. For who knows all the lights and shadows that flit through that void which stands between the consciousness of Life and the unconsciousness of Death?

There are the lips, but yesterday so crimson and so sensitive; now ashen and insensitive. How often they parted with a smile, or were glued with pain. How often they kissed and were kissed —mother's kisses, lovers' kisses. And that upper lip—how frequently I saw it twitch with anger, and with joy or sorrow. Now it is so tightly pressed against its lower sister as to form with it a straight line which is, perhaps, the seal of silent wisdom, or the dividing line between what may and what may not be uttered. The seal is broken now and then to offer escape to a groan which is more like the groan of one being butchered than the groan of an unwell man.

There is the high, noble forehead which retreating and grey-ing hair has made higher and nobler. The few soft wrinkles drawn upon it by the years give it a touch of majesty. It is the very forehead which seldom hid from my eyes the thoughts, visions, purposes, or difficulties that shaped themselves behind it. But all that is now beyond my reach.

And that chestnut hair which the comb and brush have thinned to less than half of its former amplitude—how lifeless and devoid of sheen it has become! Small wisps of it lie on the pillow as if they were of cashmere.

"Gibran!"—I hear my heart and everything in me calling him. But my tongue does not move, and my lips do not open. For when I look at his face so tortured with pain, and when I hear that awful gurgling in his throat and those heart-rending groans escaping from his chest, I say to myself, "Perhaps he will hear me if I call him and will be the keener pained because he can return no answer." Then in a flash, "Perhaps he sees me. And why not?" The thought becomes a conviction; and I am comforted.

I drop to a chair by the bed and listen long to that ghastly hubble-bubble in my brother's throat and to the moans and groans that accompany it, and I almost shout at him, "Spit it out! Throw it up!" not knowing that the moment he spits it out he spits with it his last breath. At last I surrender to the will of Fate being carried out under my very eye, and lose myself in an ocean of meditation which is my refuge and retreat in times of heavy trials. And I feel as if Gibran and I were engaged in conversation. How frequently we had conversed before in utter silence! And I also feel that he is conscious of my presence, and conscious of the fact that a friendly heart is here to see him off this shore and on his way on to the other shore.

* * *

Every now and then the intern, in a white jacket, would feel the dying man's pulse and inject something into his arm, whether to stimulate his heart, or to dull his pain, I did not know.

"Does he feel any pain?" I asked.

"None at all."

"How long will this struggle last?"

"It's nearing the end."

My conversation with the intern finished, I return to my conversation with Gibran, with Death, and with myself. I say to Gibran,

"What food have you stored, my brother, for this journey?" And Gibran answers,

"Ghr-r-r . . . Hm-m-m . . ."

And I say to Death,

"What are you doing to my brother, Death?" And Death responds, "Gh-r-r . . . Gh-r-r . . . Hm-m-m . . ." And to my soul I say,

"What see you and what hear you, my soul?" And my soul replies,

"Gh-r-r . . . Gh-r-r . . . Hm-m-m . . ."

My heart then jumps to my ears and begins knocking violently, impatiently, insistently. And when I ask it of its pleasure in knocking, it gives me no other answer but "Ghr-r-r . . ." For a moment my mind becomes clouded. My horizons narrow and tighten about me. But soon the cloud lifts and the horizons broaden and flare up with many meteors and lightning darts. Faces, events, vistas, thoughts, emotions, names, hopes, long buried in the memory, now jam the avenues of consciousness in their helter-skelter rush to occupy the foreground. Some would come and go times without number; some would barely lift the corner of their veil; others would parade in majesty and leisure. An old memory would flare up much more quickly and brightly than a recent one. And by the light of those memories the life of the comrade now slowly yielding his breath passes before my eyes in loose, disconnected pages. Yet, I know that one and the same hand has written those pages with one and the same pen and ink. And I further know that the hand that wrote them wrote not a page more nor a paragraph less than was necessary; nor did it put a comma or a dot except where the meaning would not be clear without them. Because I know that, I try to perceive the connection between this word and that, or between the first page and the last: Bisharri and New York; The Cedars of Lebanon and St. Vincent's hospital; Kahlil Gibran and the women standing outside the ward; between him and all men, women and children whom he met in his life; between him and all those who have read, and may now be reading, his books; and those who have looked, or may this very moment be looking at the products of his brush; between him and the people he made happy or unhappy, and those who gave him joy or sorrow; and finally between him and myself; why have we met and become friends at a certain point of time, and not before or after; and in a certain place, and not in another? Why has it fallen my lot to attend the last and the most meaningful spectacle of his dramatic life, and to see him off this shore? Will he be waiting on the other shore to receive me when my time for sailing comes? Does he know, does he feel what he is passing through?

How often we have talked of Death—Gibran and I—and called it the twin of Life—another birth. Would he now, if given the power of speech, say what he said before? If he thinks neither of Earth nor of Heaven, neither of Life nor of Death, what, then, does he think of? Or is the unconsciousness of death a state much deeper than thought, much more distant than dreaming and imagining? Perhaps it is a short release from the sensation of being to the Being that transcends all sensations. Perhaps it is a foretaste of the eternal freedom from that sense of being which is yet a plaything of Time and Space.

Barely do I pass out of the world about me when the rattle of Death brings me back to it sharply and imperiously. Through

the small window opening on the street rush at me wave after
wave of the clamorous life of the city—a great jumble of voices,
tongues, passions, lusts, schemes, aspirations, fleeting joys and
abiding sorrows, all resolving themselves into that awful
"Ghr-r-r- . . ."

Then I feel the walls of the ward recede away into the distance, and the roof lift as on wings, and the huge metropolis lie
open and naked before me. I walk into its bedchambers; into
its temples and brothels; into its courts and prisons; into its
factories and stores; into its palaces and hovels. I stride over
the whole earth, seeing all and hearing all. I stroll with kings
and tramps, with soldiers and generals. I see the babes being
born, men and women being married and unmarried, or dying,
dead and being buried. Yet one is the melody I bring back with
me from every corner of the earth—Ghr-r-r- . . . The melody
sinks deep into my soul until I feel that it has ever been there;
and I wonder why I never heard it before. I also imagine it to
be the song unique, eternal, universal which the whirling stars,
the burning sun, the effulgent earth, the babbling men and howl-
ing beasts are perpetually chanting. The feeling becomes sharp
and clear that even the "wow-wow" hurled at the world by a
babe at birth is but a variation of the "Ghr-r-r" issuing from the
throat of a human being about to pass from this to another
world.

BISHARRI SHADOWS *

— 1 —

"Waah-w-a-a-h!"

The voice is issuing from the selfsame throat that is now being choked before me with the gurgling of another birth. But the midwife who hears that voice does not hear this gurgling. Therefore her face lights up with a broad smile as she turns to the mother and proudly announces the glad news:

"A boy! A boy! God be thanked for your safe deliverance."

The muscles of the mother's face, taut with pain, relax in a smile as soft and tender as moonbeams passing through a cloud; and she answers in a barely audible whisper, "May God accept your thanks, dear sister." Instantly the small, modest room becomes filled with one magic word that goes fluttering about like a bird escaped from a cage. It is on the tongues of the women gathered round the brazier near the mother's bed; it is in the walls blind of every sight except the door; it is in the ceiling painted black by smoke, and in the cold wind outside— the wind of December, weaving a white *burnoose* for the gorge of Kadisha, for the great-grandchildren of Solomon's cedars, and for the peaks jealously guarding the cedars since eternity— A boy! A boy!

The women congratulate the mother and each other as if the babe just born belonged to each of them: "Bless him who has been given to us."

---

* Bisharri is a small town in Northern Lebanon situated at the foot of Cedar Mountain.

13

With the baby crying, the mother sighing, the midwife mumbling and the women neighbors and relatives babbling, the door suddenly flies open letting in a wave of the frosty breath of December. In the door appears a medium-sized man in his forties, well-built, fair complected, blue-eyed and with a chestnut mustache. The midwife shouts at him in horror,

"May your mother bury you soon. Shut the door. You will freeze the babe and us."

The man slams the door and in two or three leaps reaches the side of the mother's bed, and there he stands silent and breathless for a space. Then twisting his mustache proudly he shouts in glee, "A boy! A boy!"

The wicked midwife answers half in jest and half in earnest, "Too good for you. You don't deserve him."

"No, no, Oum-Hanna. You don't mean it. Kahlil Gibran deserves more than that. I may be drunk; but I have the fear of God in my heart." Then to his wife, "Kamileh! I swear I shall wash your feet and drink the water thereof. Bless him who has been given to us. Do you know what we shall call him? He shall bear the name of the founder of the family—Gibran! Record it, my woman, record it."

"What is the date to-day? The sixth? Record that Gibran Kahlil Gibran was born on the sixth day of December, Anno Domini 1883, in the town of Bisharri of the autonomous province of Lebanon."

A thin veil of sadness is drawn over the soft, gentle face of the mother, and she turns away from her husband to hide the two tears imprisoned by the long eyelashes.

"Kamileh, Kamileh! What a shame. Weeping? If I don't drink on a great occasion like this, when then?"

"As if anyone ever saw you sober." This from the midwife.

"Oum-Hanna, Oum-Hanna! Don't overstep your boundaries. Your business is to draw babes from their mothers' wombs, not to draw men out of wine-barrels. Kamileh, what a shame! Allright, allright. I shall divorce the bottle. I swear it by Gibran and by this mustache." And the man puts his hand to his mustache; then he jumps to a cupboard in the wall whence he takes out handfuls of raisins, almonds and walnuts and begins distributing them to the women present saying, "Eat, eat a hearty welcome to Gibran."

The women take and eat and pray aloud for the mother and the babe: "May he be a child of health and safety. God be thanked for your deliverance." Soon afterward they light their lanterns and walk out into the December darkness, each to her house; all save the midwife who stays by the mother's side.

With the women threading their ways to their homes, and by the light of their lanterns, a new life begins to thread its way in the earth; a life of whose many mysteries they knew nothing beyond the fact that it was "a boy"; and of whose many voices they could hear but "waah-waah."

— 2 —

The mother sleeps that night with the lump of flesh she calls her son sleeping at her side—that lump of which she knows no more than does a water-tap about the water flowing through it: what it is, whence it comes and whither it goes, and what the purpose is of its coming and going.

Were it given to Kamileh Rahmeh that night to see the link connecting her bed at Bisharri with that bed in St. Vincent's hospital, and to see the drops of life that issued of her womb sink forty-eight years later into the sands of Time, and in a land so far away, how quickly her delight would have turned into a chill, and the pains of travail without its hopes would have re-gripped her heart! Were it permitted her to touch the hidden threads of the spirit that tie her babe to thousands of men, women and children then walking the earth, and to thousands yet unborn—and this writer among them—the wonder and the shock of it would have surely overcome her.

But Life—the all-Mother—is too considerate of her children. She puts no more light in any creature's eye than is commensurate with that creature's need. Nor does she lend any man's feet more speed than that man requires to traverse the distance she has set for him.

— 3 —

With the dawn the news spread from door to door in Bisharri that Kamileh Abd-es-Salaam Rahmeh, Kahlil Gibran's wife, had given birth to a baby boy. A woman neighbor of the Gibrans, separated from them by a wall only, repeats to her husband what she had said the night before:

"Believe me, Kamileh quite deserves it. There is no use arguing. She has a lot of goodness, and to spare. Intelligent, poised, soft-spoken. So quiet, even the earth does not feel her weight. But God—praised be He in His kingdom—allowed her no success in marriage. She married first Hanna Abd-es-Salaam Rahmeh. He was a good man; but he took her to Brazil and died there leaving her a widow with Boutros (Peter) yet a baby. Now she married this drunkard. Do you think she'll bury him also after having given him this boy? He does not deserve her. Her small finger is worth ten like him."

"Why don't you say that she does not deserve him? Didn't he marry her a widow with a son?"

"What if she be a widow? Is she not yet young? She is no more than twenty-five."

"You are ashamed to say thirty-five. If she be young he is not an old man."

"Old, yes, old. He is every bit of forty-five and over."

"It's a lie. He's no more than thirty-six. Yet tell me, please: In what way is she better than he? Is it her long rosary? Or is it her drawn, dark face? If it comes to talking, there are few who command as clever a tongue as he. If it comes to looks, how many do you know in Bisharri who are better looking than he? If it comes to sociability and joviality, I know no one so sociable and so jovial as Kahlil Gibran."

"In that you are right—just fill the cup, and let the world go hang. Away with people like you and him!"

— 4 —

The following morning the small Gibran household is awakened by the lusty "waah-waah" of the new born. A six-year-old boy, sleeping in a corner on the floor, sits up with a start and rubs his eyes. Kahlil Gibran lying near-by quickly takes the boy in his arms, and kissing his rosy cheeks and his large sleepy eyes, says to him laughingly,

"Boutros! Did you know that your mother brought you a baby brother? Do you want to see him? Go, my soul, and ask your mother to show him to you."

The boy walks timidly towards his mother's bed, his little heart fluttering, his sweet face alight with joy. He piously kneels by his mother who tenderly strokes his silken curls, and bending his head to her mouth presses her lips to his bright forehead and asks him softly and lovingly:

"What do you wish to call your brother?"

"Antar!" comes the quick reply.

The mother smiles at the answer; the father bursts into a roaring laughter that wakes up the neighbors. He takes the boy's head into his hands, and presses hard his flushed cheeks, saying,

"Gibran shall be his name, after the founder of the family. Gibran is greater than Antar."

* * *

That same hour the clock strikes midnight in the town of Columbia, state of South Carolina. A ten-year-old girl by the name of Mary sits up in bed and rubs her eyes with her two hands as if trying to see in the darkness about her what she had just seen in her dream. She dreamt that she was on her way to school. As she walked the familiar path several dogs, snarling menacingly, sprang at her from behind a bush. Terror-stricken, she began to shout for help; but her mates, instead of coming to her aid, began to mock her, saying, "Just open your beautiful mouth, Mary, and the dogs will be scared away." Crying in desperation, she decided to run as fast as her little feet could carry her. Presently she came to a thick wood overgrown with brush and bramble. As she stopped to catch her breath she looked back and saw neither dogs nor mates, nor even a road. Fear so gripped her that she fell to her knees and began to pray.

While praying she felt a force drawing her forward so hard that she almost fell to the ground. She looked and, lo! A white silken thread was tied about her waist as thin as the thread of a cobweb. But when she tried to break it she found it stronger than a hempen rope and stretching through and beyond the wood as a ray of light. Instantly she forgot the fearful dilemma she was in and her main concern became the silken thread; she wished to reach its other end and to find out to what it was tied and who tied it. Slowly and carefully she began to wind the thread about her wrist, following it all the while through the thick wood. She walked and walked until she finally came to a far-flung, turbulent sea, over which she saw the thread stretch to the distant horizon and beyond. Then she sat her on the soft sand of the shore, and the only picture that came to her mind was that of an acrobat she once saw walking a wire. And she wished she were that wire-walker. The wish so possessed her that she arose fully determined to walk the silken thread as the acrobat walked the wire. But as she lifted her foot to put it on the thread she woke up, her little heart fluttering like the heart of a fawn chased by a coyote, her hands feeling all about her waist in the hope of touching the thread. Failing that, she dropped back to her bed, pulled the cover well over her head, and sank into a sound slumber.

— 5 —

It is Thursday evening of the Holy Week. Kamileh Gibran is sitting on a mat in her house. In her lap is her year-old daughter Sultana, sound asleep. Stretched on the floor, and also sound asleep with her head on her mother's thigh, is Marianna, two years older than Sultana. In front of the mother sits the first-born of her second marriage, his dreamy eyes glued upon his mother's face, his sensitive heart drinking avidly his mother's simple narrative of Christ and His Crucifixion.

That night the five-year-old Gibran went to sleep with queer, fantastic shadows dancing behind his eyelids: A hill with a huge wooden cross planted at the top. On the cross is a man with a fair beard and long hair falling on both shoulders. The man is nailed hands and feet to the cross, his only crime being that he came down from Heaven to make all people good. Milling around the cross are multitudes of people; and they hold spears with which they stick the man on the cross, spitting at him and making fun of him. While up in Heaven is a great armchair firmly fixed upon four stars. In the chair is "The Lord" with a thick white beard reaching to the earth. He sadly looks at His only son and from time to time spits fire upon the heads of the Jews. At the foot of the cross stands a woman called the Virgin; she weeps and cries in agony, "My son! O my son!"

The morning of the following Friday, appropriately called in the East "Sad Friday," Gibran wakes up to see his half-brother Boutros with a number of chums standing at the door, all barefooted and ready to go somewhere. To his query "Where?" Boutros tells him that he and his chums, in keeping with the ancient traditions, are going to the mountains "to suffer with Christ" on His day of suffering, and to gather flowers with which to adorn Christ's shrouds at the dramatization of his death and burial that takes place on "Sad Friday" in every church in the East. Gibran implores the boys to take him with them, and Boutros is inclined to gratify his half-brother's wish,

for he loves him dearly. But one of his mates pulls him by the
sleeve saying that they had no time to coddle babes and to wipe
their tears. And so the little boy is left behind.

Hurt to the quick Gibran bursts in tears and would not be
consoled by all the sweets and delicacies his mother proffered
him. His father sipping his morning black coffee and puffing a
cigarette becomes unnerved and gives him a cuff on the ear.
That leads to a quarrel between the father and mother which
only adds to the boy's grief and tears. Infuriated, the father
takes the boy by the shoulder and pushes him outside the house,
shutting the door behind him and mumbling, "The sniveller!
Away with you. You have spoiled the taste of my coffee and
cigarette."

The time for the "funeral" service at the church comes, but
Gibran is not to be found. Thinking that he may have gone ahead
alone the mother and the father, together with the neighbors,
wend their way to the church. There they find Boutros and his
friends, their hands full of flowers, but they find no trace of
Gibran. To his mother's question Boutros replies that he had not
seen Gibran since he left the house. The services over, the mother
hurries back to the house hoping to find her younger son there.
Disappointed and very much alarmed, she chides her husband
bitterly holding him responsible for any ill—God forbid—that
may befall their son. Finally she takes Boutros and some of his
friends, and all go on a search for Gibran. Just before sunset
they come upon him in the cemetery behind the church with a
neat bunch of cyclamens in his hands. The mother, fully intent
on giving her son a severe reprimand, finishes by hugging him
close to her heart and by covering his face with kisses when she
hears him relate how he went out to the country "to suffer" with
Christ, and how he brought the cyclamens to put on his "bier",
but finding the church doors locked, he went to the cemetery
to look for Christ's grave among the other graves.

— 6 —

Of a certain noon Gibran came home from school with his mouth bleeding, his ears badly scratched and his "ghumbaz" * torn. After a thorough questioning and cross-questioning by his mother he confessed that he had a scramble with one of his mates who dared call him a "snivelling sissy." He would not accept the insult, therefore he returned it with a box. But the other was a much older and bigger boy. Had he been his age he would have "buried" him. But he shall become big some day and shall surely "bury" that fellow. Whereupon his mother gave him a lecture on how to behave and how to avoid evil and encounters with evil boys. Whereas his father called him a coward and "presented" him with two more cuffs in addition to what he had already received from his school-mate.

— 7 —

On another day Boutros came home from school at noon and, contrary to his custom, his half-brother was not with him. When questioned by his mother of the reason, he explained that the priest at school punished Gibran by locking him up in the class-room and denying him luncheon for two offenses: The first was that he did not read well his Syriac lesson; the second, that the priest, as a punishment, ordered him to write that lesson ten times over; but when he came to examine his book he found that Gibran had, instead, drawn what looked like a sleeping donkey with a priest's cap on its head, and a book dangling from one ear and a feed-sack from the other.

It happened that a few days before Gibran's father caught his son drawing with a charcoal on the wall of the house what looked like a house with a sad girl sitting in front. The drawing was not clear, but that was what it suggested to the father who gave his son a severe reprimand saying that he had better study

---

* *Ghumbaz* is a tight-fitting robe formerly worn by men and boys in the Near East; now almost entirely discarded.

his Syriac than smear the wall with charcoal. When he, there-fore, heard of how the priest had punished Gibran, his only comment was, "Serves him right."

— 8 —

Gibran was playing near the house when he saw a stranger driving a mule with two skinbottles on its back, and heard the man shout at the top of his voice, "Pure olive oil." Presently an old woman with a long rosary in one hand walked out of a house near-by and asked the muleteer to give her a little of his oil to taste. Having tasted the oil the woman dickered long with the stranger about the price. When an agreement was finally reached the woman slipped into the house and came out with an empty bottle asking the man to give her a pint of oil. Before the oil was emptied into the bottle the woman turned to the man and asked him of what denomination he was. "Greek Orthodox," said the muleteer. No sooner did the woman, who was a Maron-ite, hear that answer than she snatched the empty bottle from the man's hand, and crossing herself profusely she turned round and walked into her house mumbling indignantly some inco-herent words.

Gibran was puzzled by the spectacle. He ran to his mother and asked her,

"What is our denomination, mother?"

"We are Maronites, my son."

"And who are the Orthodox?"

"They are Christians like ourselves."

"And why are they called Orthodox and we, Maronite?"

"Of that you must ask the priest, my son. He can enlighten you better than I."

"Would God choke us if we bought oil from an Orthodox man, mother?"

"Of course not, my son."

Barely had that colloquy between Gibran and his mother been finished when Gibran's father ran into the house and called to his wife to hand him an empty bottle. Whereupon he called the muleteer and asked him to fill the bottle with oil, paying him the price on the instant and in full. Not content with that he insisted on the man to eat supper with them that evening and to spend the night at their house. Gibran was filled with joy at his father's behavior. But when the stranger gratefully declined his father's invitation and went his way, Gibran wept soft and silent tears.

— 9 —

"Have you made up your mind to go to-morrow, God willing?"

"I have."

"And have you hired a horse for the trip?"

"I hired two."

"For whom is the other horse?"

"For Gibran."

"For Gibran? Are you joking? If not, you must have lost your wits."

"I'm quite earnest."

"How is a boy of eleven years to roam these rocky mountains on horseback, to sleep in nomads' tents alive with fleas and lice, and to spend days and nights with flocks of goats and sheep? Or is it your wish to train him from now to carry on your work of contracting with the government for the collection of taxes from poor goatherds and shepherds, earning their hate and enmity with their shekels and remaining withal as poor as we are poor?"

"Rather do I wish to teach him from now that a flea-bite is but a sweet caress when compared with the stings of his mother's tongue, that sheep's and goats' manure is more precious than the jewels of men, and that a nomad's tent is nobler by far than a nobleman's castle. Besides, if you know of an easier and more profitable road for him to follow, please show it to him."

The parents' wrangling grew so hot that even the children were drawn into it—Boutros siding with his mother, and the two girls with their father; while Gibran remained neutral, for it pained him to take sides against his mother whom he adored, as it pained him to displease his father for fear of being denied the exciting trip on the morrow. The consequence was that the family supper which had been already spread on a round tray woven of wheat straw remained untouched. The bread was put back in the bread-bin, and the porridge poured back into the kettle. The father ended by emptying the better part of the contents of a bottle of *arak* * into his stomach and by not making the trip on the following day.

— 10 —

One afternoon Boutros came home and found his mother alone with tears coursing down her cheeks. Before he had time to open his mouth his mother lifted her head and looking at him tenderly, said,

"Let not this disturb you, my boy. Be not afraid. There are moments when the breast becomes too stifling for the heart, and the poor heart flows out of the eyes. When the breast is a mother's breast, pity her heart and pity her eyes. You insist on emigrating. It is right and manly on your part to think of your future. Heretofore I have blocked your way. How could I otherwise? But to-day I have thought long and prayed long, and came to the conclusion that you were more than right in your determination, and that I was wrong in trying to bind you forever to this house so as to keep you under my wing. Surely you have no life, no future in this land; and having come of age you are at full liberty to go wherever you may choose, and I, your mother, am

* Arak is a national drink in Lebanon, distilled from grapes; when mixed with water it turns the color of milk.

ready to bless you and to wish you Godspeed. But my foot shall touch the gangplank ahead of your foot, and the ship that shall carry you away shall carry me also and your brother Gibran and sisters Marianna and Sultana as well. While *he* shall remain behind. We shall do our utmost to make his life here easy and comfortable by keeping him well supplied with *arak*, coffee and cigarettes; for that, as you know, is of more importance to him than anything else."

"With God's help, mother, I shall earn enough to provide my step-father with all the things he likes; for I love him despite all the pains he has caused you to suffer. Gibran, Marianna and Sultana shall have a decent education. As to you, dear mother, you shall live the life of a perfect lady. Yes, with God's help we shall bury poverty forever."

"Bless your heart, my son. May God be your guide; may He guide us all. Truth to tell, my heart bleeds for *him*. He shall be left alone, all by himself, just like a tent peg with no tent ropes tied to it. What else can I do after my patience has been so thoroughly exhausted? Yet my heart is heavy about this whole business, dear Boutros. Who knows when we may come back here? We may never see this land again. Do they not say that whoever gives himself up to the sea is dead, and whoever is given up by the sea is born again? Ah, Boutros, Boutros! Let His will be done. I have put my trust in Him. Do you also likewise."

"Have courage, mother. In Boston where we are going is a goodly number of Bisharri folks. We know them, and they know us. They shall be only too glad to show us the way in the beginning."

The mother's eyes became dry; but the shadows of pains suffered in the past and pains to be suffered in the future hung upon their lashes. While Boutros felt the energy of his 18 years bubbling in his veins, his soft face flushed with the blood of innocent youth, his large eyes aglow with the light of budding hope. It flattered him to feel that his mother began to look upon him as upon a man fully capable of carrying men's responsibilities. Little did it occur to him, or to his mother, that even if they wished, they could not change a dash or a tittle in the plans they had just laid down for themselves; for quite unconsciously they were carrying in part the hidden plans for innumerable other lives intertwined with theirs, among them the life of the twelve-year-old Gibran of which they had glimpsed some unintelligible symbols only, some veiled lights and shifting shadows.

BOSTON SHADOWS

Boston, the city of buffalo-path streets, of high claims to antiquity, light and culture, and to the lion's share in the Pilgrim Fathers, received the five bewildered emigrants from the village of Bisharri in northern Lebanon as the sea would receive any five drops of rain. The haggard family slipped into Chinatown unnoticed except for a handful of men and women from Bisharri who came to inquire about their relatives in the "old country" more than to bid the newcomers welcome.

In the summer of 1925 I chanced to pass through Chinatown in Boston. In certain spots I had to close my nose against the odors rising from heaps of garbage left here and there in the streets and offering a rich banquet to flies and mosquitoes, as well as to dogs. On both sides of the street through which I passed huddled four or five-story buildings with murky walls and dark passageways. From the windows of most of them hung stockings, shirts, drawers, towels, etc., washed and left to dry in the air. In front of the buildings played little children of quite a cosmopolitan complexion: Chinese, Lebanese, Irish, Italian, Syrian, Polish and what-not. They spoke a delightful jargon of dialects, now exchanging pettings and compliments, now curses and blows. I leave it to the reader's imagination to picture that quarter of Boston in the year 1894 when Kamileh Gibran and her children settled there and began to plan their attack on the overfat New World—how to start and where to strike.

— 1 —

"Gibran, my son! Isn't it time you stopped studying?"
"What are you cooking for supper, mother?"

"*Mujaddarah,** my darling; you like mujaddarah."

"Everything you cook is delicious, mother; and everything you do is nice. God bless your hands."

"Your father never said that. And your brother and sisters complain of my cooking not infrequently."

"Never mind my father and the rest. You have Gibran; isn't that enough?"

"And Boutros also."

"And Boutros also. Boutros will make plenty of money for us. I went to his store after school, and while I was there he sold a pair of overalls for a dollar and a hat for two. He will be rich some day, and we shall all go back to Bisharri and build us a large, beautiful mansion, and you shall be the lady of that mansion with maids and all."

"God protect and keep you for me, sonny. So long as you are well your mother is well. Health is more precious than money."

"And I shall write stories like the one I'm reading."

"What is that you are reading?"

"Uncle Tom's Cabin."

"In English?"

"In Arabic then? Of course in English."

"May the cross of our Saviour be your shield, my son. In two years reading such a large book, and in English?"

"My teacher of English likes me very much. She calls me by my father's name—Kahlil—for she finds it odd that my first name is the same as my surname. It was she who gave me to-day this book to read. It is unbelievable how ugly and how hard-hearted some people can be, mother. I wish you could read the story of poor Uncle Tom and how he suffered at the hands of bad men. I shall tell it to you when I finish it."

"You have made me forget what I wished to say to you in the beginning, namely that you leave your book and go out and

---

* A kind of porridge made of lentils and rice.

play a little. From books at school to books at home—you shall ruin your health."

"With whom do you wish me to play? With Irish, Chinese or Syrian children? There are many of them with tongues so filthy, ah, so filthy—even among the girls. How I like a clean tongue and a clean heart! I am much better off with my books, papers and pencils. They, at least, are clean."

"Nevertheless, you should go out and take some fresh air."

"Did I not tell you what the teacher of drawing did to-day? No? She brought a man into the classroom who, she said, was a painter—a man that makes pictures with his hands, not with the camera. She showed him some of my drawings, and he said to me, 'You are a little artist.' He invited me to his studio to-morrow."

"Are you going?"

"Of course."

"Wouldn't it be better for you and for us, my son, if in your spare time you helped your brother in the store and learned his trade instead of making pictures and reading stories?"

"What a shame that Gibran's own mother should say that. The small finger of an artist is worth a thousand business men—excepting Boutros. A page of poetry is worth all the goods in all the stores."

"But we need money."

"You shall have money. If Boutros does not earn it, Gibran will."

"God save you all for me, my darling."

— 2 —

The afternoon of the following day, as soon as school was over, Gibran, excited and impatient, went looking for the address given him the day before by the visiting painter. He walked as if borne on a cloud, and as if behind the door which he sought awaited him a world full of charm and mystery, and the man who was to open that door for him was to be his initiator into that charmed and mysterious world. Had he not heard and read of famous painters whose first steps towards fame were guided by Fate through some chance acquaintance? Undoubtedly this painter whom he met yesterday at school was his guardian angel —the man who was to open up for him the gates of heaven and earth.

As he walked, Gibran turned over and over in his mind the conversation which was to take place between him and the man, and always ended by having the man so deeply impressed by his words, his looks and his character as to exclaim: "A young man of your talents should not be left to the care of people unable to appreciate his worth. I shall take care of your education, and you shall be a great artist." His unruly imagination kept painting the future in most attractive colors until he reached the mystic door and knocked.

The painter was very cordial in his welcome of the bashful youth from the ancient land of the biblical cedars, and straight-way led him to a lady whom he was painting, saying to her, "This is the young man from Lebanon of whom I spoke. I saw some of his drawings and was quite struck by the unusual power of imagination and the artistic taste they displayed."

The lady put forth her hand to Gibran. As he grasped it, Gibran felt his face suddenly flush and as suddenly pale. A tingling sensation went through his veins, pressing his throat tight and almost tying his tongue. He lowered his eyes in order not to see the lady's chest bare to the breasts, and her arms uncovered to the shoulders.

"You seem to be very shy, Mr. Gibran," said the lady softly and coyly. "Come nearer and permit me to stroke your lovely chestnut hair. You wear your hair long as artists do. You must be an artist already. May I kiss you on the forehead?—thus, thus. Your country must be very beautiful, and all its people artists. Is it not so? I love art. But so far my share in it has been no more than to pose and be painted. What do you think of my portrait? Of course, it is not quite finished yet." And the lady pointed to the canvas on the nearby easel with the paint on it still very fresh.

Gibran then lifted his eyes to the canvas and, as if wishing to avenge himself on the woman who dared treat him like a mere boy, said in great earnestness:

"No picture is ever finished even after its own author declares it finished. We draw and paint suggestions only. The full and finished picture God alone can draw and paint."

"You speak much beyond your years. How old are you, Mr. Gibran?"

"Fourteen."

"No more?"

"And two months."

"You have not given me your opinion of my portrait yet. Speak your full and honest opinion, and I guarantee that my friend will take it very impersonally."

Gibran began to shift his eyes from the woman's face to the canvas and back, but in fact he was not scrutinizing either; for he was provoked at himself for allowing the woman to treat him like a boy by stroking his hair and kissing his forehead. Had he been the man he took himself to be, she would not have dared to do what she did. He should have demonstrated to her by his words and acts that he was no longer a mere boy. Yet, by asking his opinion of her portrait she offers him an excellent opportunity to rectify his position. Should he or should he not give an answer? It would be wise not to answer, thus showing the woman that he had a will of his own to oppose to hers, and that he, as an artist, had the right to keep his opinion to himself.

On the other hand, wouldn't it be more telling to give an answer that would make the woman and the artist "sit up and take notice"? Most certainly, that would be the wiser course to

follow. But Gibran could not find the answer he wanted, for his
mind was upon the woman. How old was she? Twenty-five?
More than that. Thirty? She was nearer to thirty than to twenty-
five and of a most beautiful countenance. How becoming to her
brunettish complexion that gown of crimson velvet!

"I'm still awaiting your opinion, young man."

Again Gibran hears in the woman's voice the condescending
tone of an older person speaking to a lad, and it provokes him
the more against the woman and himself. Finally his tongue
moves against his will, and he answers,

"You shall have my opinion when the portrait is done."

"Splendid. The portrait shall be at my house to-morrow.
Will you not be good enough to come and see it there? Be sure
to come. I shall expect you at four in the afternoon. Here is
my address."

— 3 —

Gibran walked out of the painter's studio with the woman's
address in his pocket, and in his hand a small bundle of pastels
presented to him by the good painter "in commemoration" of
his visit. Thoughts quite different from those with which he came
besieged his mind. It was evident to him that the painter was
not the guardian angel he had hoped him to be. Was it not possible that the woman he met at his studio was that angel? But
she was so "untactful" with him at the beginning. Yet hers was a
new door to knock at. Perhaps it is the door that leads to the
paradise of his dreams.

That evening, while at the dinner table, Gibran related to
the family the happenings of the afternoon:

"The painter is not bad as a painter; and as a man he is
exceedingly kind. He asked me to sit for him."

"To sit for him? What does that mean, my son?"

"It means, mother, that I am to sit before him in the pose he
may choose for me so that he can paint me in that pose."

"Paint you? What need have we of being painted? And where shall we get the money to pay for the picture?"

"No, no, mother; not that. You seem to know of painting as much as I know of the Turkish language. A painter, you see, has need of men and women of all shapes and ages to use them as models for the different pictures he may wish to paint. If I, for instance, wished to paint the Virgin Mary whom I have never seen, I might take you for a model. But I would choose to dress you in clothes that suit my purposes. I might wish to paint you standing, sitting, or reclining; smiling or weeping, with or without a babe in your arms—just as my taste and imagination might require. Do you understand now?"

"May I never live to understand."

"So I shall sit for that painter who promised to give me paints for compensation."

"I wish he would give you money instead."

"The same thing. For with that money I would buy nothing but paints."

"Was that all you did during your long absence this afternoon?" The question came from Boutros.

"I haven't told you of the most important which is that I met there a lady of immense wealth and position. She insisted on seeing some of my drawings and invited me to her house to-morrow."

Whereupon Gibran was showered with questions. Asked Marianna:

"Is she young or old?"

"About thirty."

Mother: "Married or single?"

"I don't know, and I don't care to know."

Sultana: "Is she beautiful?"

"Very beautiful."

Marianna: "What's her name?"

"That is a secret."

Boutros and mother together: "Are you going to see her?"
"Of course."

A deep hush fell on all. Gibran felt bitterly hurt. He arose
and pounding the table with his hand said defiantly: "How
long shall you look upon me as upon an irresponsible boy?
I am no longer a boy. I am a man, and I have the right to do
what I please and to go where I please. Do you think me incapable of protecting myself and of differentiating between
good and evil?"

"God deliver us from the hour of temptation, my son",
came from the mother in a gentle, barely audible whisper.

"I'm mightier than temptation. I made a mistake in telling
you what I told you of this lady."

Had a stranger walked in at that moment on that small
assembly he would have been most amazed to see a lambkin
trying to look like a lion and to affect the roaring of a lion.

— 4 —

"Welcome, welcome, my Lebanese friend. Now that you
came I'm glad I had no way of sending you a note not to
come. I had intended doing that when I woke up this morning
with a terrible migraine and was forced to stay in bed. It is
because of that you see me still in my nightgown and kimono.
Please excuse me. Forgive me also if I receive you in my
bedroom, for I would feel much better if I recline in bed. You,
of course, want me to be comfortable. Besides, the portrait
which you came to see is now hung on my bedroom wall. Come
and see it and give me your opinion of it which you declined
to give yesterday."

The hostess led the guest into her bedroom where she
seated him in a broad Louis-Quatorze silk chair, he all the
while making an effort to apologize and take his leave.

"It may be better, madam, if I leave you to-day and come
to-morrow."

"Not at all. Now that you have come you must stay. Perhaps, with you around, my megrim will pass. It is already better. Besides we have many things to talk about. You are a man from the East, and I love the East; so full of charm and mystery it is. The charm of art suffused with the charm of the East must be quite irresistible. I should like, in honour of your visit, to burn some eastern incense. Do you like sandalwood?"

The woman brought a silver incense-burner in the form of a dragon together with some sandalwood to which she set a match. The fragrant white smoke, rising in delicate wisps, soon filled the room. Done with the burner, the woman hopped to her bed, sank her elbow in the pillow, her palm supporting her head, her long, black shining tresses falling partly on her chest and partly on her naked arm. Her eyes sparkled with a light which her visitor had not detected before.

"Forgive my behavior yesterday. To-day I shall neither stroke your hair nor kiss you on the brow. First of all I must hear your opinion of my portrait."

"Would that Leonardo were alive to do your portrait. I am sure he would give you the eyes of a wounded eagle rather than those of a contented ewe. He would shut your lips upon the smile of the rose from whose heart has flown the last gem of morning dew, rather than the smile of the rose greeting the rising sun with her petals yet moist with the breath of dawn. I see in your face a sadness which is not seen in the portrait, and a veil of false contentment which is caught in the portrait as a reality."

"How wonderful! Not only are you an artist, Mr. Gibran, but a poet and a sorcerer to boot. Who, pray, revealed to you the secrets of my life? Who made it known to you that my folks gave me in marriage to a rich business man more than twenty years my senior; that he failed and lost his fortune two months after our marriage; that he had no interest in anything under heaven except his business, and that I have been with him ten years which appear to me as ten centuries of pain and self-denial? Happy are they who can find in this world sympathetic and understanding hearts. That, to me, is the greatest blessing, my friend. Despite your tender years you appear to me as a man with an understanding heart. Believe me, this house has proved a grave for me. Come nearer, friend, and let me put my hand in yours; perhaps a touch of your poetry, charm and art will pass to me and help me, though for a moment, forget my troubles."

"Does your husband mistreat you?"

"He treats me as a concubine whom he had bought with money. In fact he had bought me with money, and if he dared, he would imprison me in the house. Enough of him. Tell me now of your beautiful East."

"Where is your husband now?"

"Within the last two years he has been able to reinstate himself in business, and is again a big business man. He is now in his office and has to-night some very important meetings which will keep him till midnight. How often I have tried to make a man of him, to soften his coarse manners and tune down his vicious temper; the result was pain, and more pain only—pain of the body and of the spirit. My suffering this morning was nothing else but the result of a quarrel . . ."

"Do you feel better now?"

"Much better. In fact the pain is almost gone thanks to your kind sympathy and deep understanding. Perhaps, if you just put your hand on my forehead the pain will entirely disappear. Come nearer; a little nearer."

The hostess let out a deep sigh as two large tears glistened in her eyes. Her interlocutor's eyes responded on the instant. Both fell silent for a while.

"I do not deserve your precious tears, my friend. I should have bridled my tongue and kept my sorrow buried deep in my heart as it has been all these years. Forgive me."

"From this day on your sorrow is my sorrow."

"How compassionate is your heart, how beautiful your soul, and how weak are women! Why do I feel now a weight upon my chest, a tightness in the throat and a giddiness in the head? Come nearer; a little nearer . . ."

— 5 —

It was about an hour before midnight when Gibran bade his "guardian angel" good-by and with her, the innocence and purity of budding youth. On leaving that house he felt as one coming out of a furnace, with each drop of his blood burning like a live coal. How to put that fire out, and where to flee from it—he did not know.

Having walked a distance he felt the heat within him turn to a shiver of disgust and repentance, and began to chide himself very bitterly. His mother's words "God deliver us from the hour of temptation" came back to him with a tremendous force; likewise his reply that he was mightier than temptation. "Yes", said he to himself, "I am mightier than temptation. Hereafter I shall not approach a woman except the one whom I shall choose for a wife; and I shall tell her of my sin. Sin . . . Temptation . . . What is sin? It is to turn a deaf ear to the cries of a heart in torture. What is temptation? It is to hear Love call on you to offer yourself a sacrifice upon his altar, and to refuse to make the sacrifice. Should I leave her a prey to a ruffian? How divinely beautiful she is! For her to pick me out of all the men in Boston—nay, in the world—is not that happiness too wondrous for words?"

Again Gibran felt his blood on fire, and again the fire turned to shivering. Between alternating bursts of elation and depression he finally reached his house, mounting the dark, squeaky, spiral staircase with muffled steps, and repeating at each step his mother's words, "God deliver us from the hour of temptation."

All the inhabitants of the small apartment on the fourth floor were sound asleep—except the mother. She alone sat wide awake in the small sitting-room, used also as a dining-room, awaiting Gibran's coming home. No sooner did she detect his steps on the staircase than she jumped to the door and opened it; and no sooner did her eye fall on her son's face than she sensed a strange barrier between him and herself the like of which she had never sensed before.

"You have been gone a long time, Gibran, my darling—much longer than usual. We waited on you for supper until eight; and I had prepared for you a dish that you like. In fact we all became quite worried about you. Have you had supper, my son?"

"Why the worry, mother? Am I a baby? I am a man, and I should no longer be made to account for every move I make—not even to my mother."

"Shall I bring you something to eat, my soul?"

"No. I had supper."

"At *her* house?"

"Yes."

"Were you alone with her?"

"There were others, mostly artists and prominent men and women of Boston."

"Her husband, too?"

"I did not see her husband, nor do I know if she has one."

"Is she very beautiful, my boy?"

"Oh, mother. If you have nothing else to talk about, let us better go to bed."

"Go to bed, my eyes; but try not to wake your brother Boutros, for he—the dear soul—was very tired to-night and went to bed unusually early having swallowed but a mouthful of food. Good night, my darling."

— 6 —

A year passed with frequent visits to the "mysterious" house. One night the silver dragon was busier than usual sending out columns of white smoke which twisted right and left as they ascended higher and higher, now thick, now barely perceptible. Gibran sat watching the quiet dance of incense smoke and the fantastic shapes it formed when mixed with the smoke of his cigarette. A heavy silence hung over the room which was finally interrupted by "the guardian angel":

"How much longer shall you torture me, Kahlil?"

"Don't call me 'Kahlil' any more. My name is Mr. Gibran."

"Never did I think you so vindictive. Just because I said that my oil portrait, which was the medium of our acquaintance, looked better than the one you did of me in pencil, you tear up your work and cast me out?"

"What I did was less than one percent of what I should have done. You know nothing of art—not even the ABC; yet do you dare to give opinions. I drew you as subtle as a spirit, as beautiful as a child of fancy, as distant as a dream. I drew you as I saw you with the eye of my love. But you failed to recognize yourself, because you see yourself with earth eyes; and he who is earthy had better not speak of art. I make no exception of your friend who painted the portrait you like so much. Go to him and let me be."

"What a shame that you should so speak of a man who has his weight and standing in the world of art. Perhaps, when you reach his age and experience you will be a much greater artist. But now you are still too young and at the beginning of your career . . ."

"There is more art in my small finger than his head ever contained. It is time you knew that I am much bigger than you and he. If you still consider me a boy, I shall show you how easily a man can discard a woman."

"But I would show you how a woman *cannot* discard a

man."

Saying that, the "guardian angel" spread her wings and enfolded her "charge". Silence, then tears, then recriminations, then sweet conciliation.

"What of your trip to Lebanon? That is now the thing uppermost in my mind. Can't you put it off?"

"It can't be put off. My folks and I are all agreed upon it. I must master my mother tongue, and know more about the country of my birth. For that reason I must go to some school in Beirut."

"I seriously suspect, Kahlil, that in sending you so far your folks mean only to tear you away from me. They have succeeded in their designs; for surely you shall forget me."

"Let my right hand forget me if I ever forget you."

"You have given me the flower of your youth, Kahlil. You have given me your manhood."

"Rather have you given me my manhood."

THE GIFT OF DEATH

There is a charm in the sun of April unknown to the other months of the year, particularly in crowded cities such as New York, London, Paris and the like where people spend the winter in a state of siege and armed resistance against the vandalism of Cold and his implacable armies of gales, rains, snows, frosts and cloud-veiled skies. Such a stubborn enemy and such a tricky strategist is general Cold! He is always on the offensive. Not thick stone walls, nor massive iron gates can keep him out. He sneaks on people at home, in the church and school, in the office and factory with all the doors firmly locked and windows tightly shut. In fact he attacks them wherever they may chance to be and in whatever position he may find them. No quicker does he breathe on them than they begin to shiver and to shake. Therefore do they fight him with fire, and steam and heavy woolen blankets. They do not dare meet him outdoors except with their bodies swaddled in heavy under and over-clothing, and their stockinged feet well wrapt in hide, or rubber, or both. Yet their complicated defense notwithstanding, Cold manages to clog their nostrils, to plant his vanguards in their throats and chests, to paralyze their muscles and to do a thousand mischiefs to them.

When people see the sun of April ride the sky, benevolent, warm and majestic, they at once feel that a strong ally has come to their rescue, and that their long siege will soon be at an end. Jubilant and bright-eyed, they fling their windows wide open to the sun; they swarm out of their stuffy dwellings to the streets to bathe their faces in the golden warmth and to

41

feast their eyes and ears on the sights and melodies of Spring slowly marching from the south. To cover his retreat Cold may now and then strike back with a bite or a sting. But people feel confident that he is "licked" and fast losing his claws and stings.

It is the fourth of April, 1902. The sun, gliding softly over the slowly flowing Seine, sends forth torrents of light and warmth over Paris, and the ancient city with its somber, winter-bitten buildings appears like a prisoner just set at liberty, or like a giant relieved of a lump in his throat. Human currents meet, mix and part in perfect harmony as if directed by a single will.

On a bench near Notre Dame sits a youth who appears in the mobile mass of Paris humanity as a drop of oil in a sea of quicksilver. His simple, neatly arranged clothes speak of many things but affluence. From under his brown hat emerge long tufts of chestnut hair. His dreamy eyes, as if half-asleep, cast a veil of sadness over his ruddy face—the sadness of one unable to project his dreams into the ugly reality about him. The youth is deeply absorbed in self-searching:

"The years are hard upon your heels, Gibran; and they are quite right in what they say: The slow of foot had better stand aside! And you are slow of foot. For what have you accomplished till this day? Behind you are twenty years—a long preface to nothing. Is it not time you stopped to be a spectator and joined the ranks of those who act and who create? Leonardo was not a spectator, nor was Michelangelo, Botticelli, Titian, El Greco, Rembrandt, Rubens, Velasquez and the rest of the galaxy of immortals. There is the Louvre. Hundreds of thousands of pilgrims come to it from every corner of the globe, yet those inside—the masters—move not an inch to meet the pilgrims' hosts, or even to nod them welcome. They do not go out into the ways and by-ways of the world to look at men, because they are greater than men. Ah, Michelangelo! Would I were fortunate enough to have been born in his days. I should have begged him to take me as an apprentice in his studio. How glorious was art in those days and how easy to approach its masters. To-day there is no end to the impediments in the way of one aiming to be an artist.

"How vast and how inordinate your dreams, Gibran! Where shall you find the money to study when you are still a burden to your folks instead of being a help to them? Your mother works, your brother works, your sisters work—all work to support you and your father. Poor father, how good of heart he is, how congenial, yet how very lacking in practical sense. An unscrupulous partner cheated him out of his money and property, yet would he not divorce his arak, coffee and cigarette. What a wonderful road-companion he was on those trips to Baalbek, Homs, Hamah, and the higher reaches of northern Lebanon. And that night you spent with him in a shepherd's tent on top of Cedar Mountain with the moon and stars above you, the peaceful sheep and grey hills about you, and the sea below—how very witching it was.

"Cedar Mountain and Eiffel Tower. The river Abu-Ali and the Seine. Notre Dame and Mar-Sarkees. The Louvre and the Cave of Kadisha. The Cedar Grove and the Bois de Boulogne. Beirut and Paris. Al-Hikmat School and the Sorbonne—how sharp and strange the contrasts!

"Four years on the benches of Al-Hikmat—what have they given you? Be thankful, however, that you are rid of the nightmare of Arabic grammar, syntax and prosody. Be thankful that you are no longer driven to church twice every day. Surely you have prayed enough to last you till the end of your days, and henceforth you shall not enter a church as a worshipper; for the Jesus you love so dearly is not found in churches. Many are the places of worship, but few indeed are those who worship 'in spirit and in truth.'

"*She* worshipped in spirit and in truth, for she worshipped with her heart, though her mind was left a prisoner and a prey to priests. How cruel is Death, and how horrible men's conventions! Would she were at your side this very minute. Just to see her innocent smile was to forget all pain; just to be touched by the tips of her delicate fingers was to be lifted on wings. With her you were delivered from the "hour of temptation," keeping her chastity unsoiled. Great, indeed, is Love when mightier than passion. And great the difference between *her* and "the guardian angel".

"What shall you say to your 'guardian angel' if you chance to meet her in Boston? What will she say when she finds out that you have deserted her for another? Let her think and say what she may please; after all she is not the guardian angel you have always been dreaming of. She is earthy, of the earth, and quite unable to grasp your dreams and to follow the least of your *other* longings.

"Yet who cares for your dreams and longings, Gibran? You persist in the belief that a guardian angel will yet turn up, somehow, sometime, somewhere. Is not that angel in your mother's heart so simple, yet so rich in love and so quick to sense your every whim? There is Boutros besides. He, too, thinks thoughts and dreams dreams not very different from yours; but he conceals his thoughts and dreams from the eyes of others—even your eyes—that he may give himself up to the business of providing you with a living and an education. If you had no one else but such a mother and such a brother— that alone were riches beyond computing. But you have two lovely sisters in addition—Marianna, already deft with the needle and able to earn some money, and Sultana—the pet of the family and now a "sweet sixteen." Would she recognize you to-day? Would the rest of your relatives and neighbors recognize you? How good it will be to see them all after such a long absence. But it would be a shame to meet them empty-handed. In your pocketbook is a small sum of money. With careful spending you should be able to spare a few dollars for gifts; and let the nicest gift be for Sultana."

Whereupon Gibran took out his pocketbook and counted the money therein. Then rising from the bench he started off not knowing where to go and what to purchase. Side by side and in step with him walked the angel of death who had just received, the other side of the ocean, Sultana's soul as a gift from the hand of Life. Gibran, however, neither saw nor heard his companion, being deep in speculation as to what kind of present he should buy for his beloved little sister.

— 7 —

Two o'clock past midnight; yet the darkness encamped in the room where Boutros and Gibran lay in their respective beds can testify that the two brothers' eyes have not tasted of sleep. Each pretended to sleep so as to give the other a chance to sleep. At last Boutros heard a tearful sigh issue from under his brother's blankets, and he said in a whisper,

"Gibran, my brother, my soul. Crying at this hour of night when you are so worn out after a long sea voyage, and so in need of sleep?"

"Tears take no account of hours, dear Boutros. You have shed your share; let me shed mine. Not Sultana do I bewail, but God; for He died to me when Sultana died, and His lungs have been eaten out by tubercular germs as were hers. And that is only right and just. Was it not said long ago that they who take the sword shall perish with the sword? Likewise should he perish with tuberculosis who afflicts the others with tuberculosis. My god was a tubercular god, and I endeavored to cure him with all manner of church drugs and theological amulets. But he died, and shall not come back to life until the day of resurrection. Aye, my god died when he caused Sultana to die. How shall I live henceforth without a god?"

"You are feverish, Gibran. You are drunk with grief and worn out by fatigue. Never deny the truth of anything simply because you haven't yet come to know it."

"Consumption—what sly and fearful armies sent by the Almighty's command to take by storm the lungs of one of his poor creatures and to force that poor creature after months and years of excruciating pain to give up the breath which He, the Almighty, took but a wink to blow, thus shattering in a wink a temple which He was years in rearing up. What has pure Sultana done for God to launch upon her such a ferocious attack? Why did He single her out from among the rest while she was the purest of us—a tender lily whose aroma was still locked up in her petals?"

"Death may well be a reward rather than a punishment. There may be dreams in the sleep of Death far surpassing in beauty the loveliest dreams of wakeful life. Who knows, Gibran, who knows?"

"Why was she made to die this death and no other?"

"You shall know the ways of God when you become a god."

"Why did He snatch her out of the light-flooded bosom of Cedar Mountain to bring her to die in a small, stuffy room— from Bisharri to Boston—from a nest perched on the edge of Saints' Valley in Lebanon to a house panting for light and air in the Boston Chinatown?"

"There must be reasons for all that which I do not know, and which have not been revealed to anyone I know."

"Why was she made my sister, and I her brother? Why did she die at this age and no sooner or later, and on the fourth day of April of this year and not on any other date?"

"Let *Why* alone, my brother. It has consumed many hearts before your heart."

"Ah, Boutros, Boutros! There are a thousand *whys* in my head, and they attack me with a thousand spears. Either they lay me low and bury me in one grave with my god, or I lay them low and rise strong and confident, and with me my God, mighty, just, beautiful and everlasting."

"Enough of that, brother. And now that sleep is far away from your eyelids and mine, come, tell me of Bisharri. How many times have you climbed Cedar Mountain and descended to the Valley of the Saints? Did you, while there, rise with the dawn and observe the magic procession of light moving from the sea upward to meet the rising sun at the summit? Did you say to the sun, though once, that Boutros sends you his greetings? Did you go to the monastery of Mar-Sarkees and pray in its chapel hewn in the rock? And did you steal some grapes from its vineyard and eat though one berry for your brother Boutros? How ignorant, how rash we were when we chose to exchange the roar of the Falls of Kadisha for the din of China-town! It was a bad exchange. Had we been contented to remain in our beautiful country, perhaps God would not have taken Sultana away from us. Six years—seven years—what have we accomplished in them? Neither wealth, nor knowledge. To be sure, you have received some education, and you shall atone for our failures. It always gave me great delight to read your letters which often reminded me of the Psalms, the Song of Songs, or the Book of Job, so much so that I often wondered whether as a writer you were not more expressive than you as a painter. Perhaps you shall win fame both as a writer and as an artist."

"People have almost forgotten the fine art of writing; instead they occupy themselves with the business of stringing words together paying little heed to the spirit and beauty latent in syllables and words. They should go back again and again to the Book of Job, the Song of Solomon, the Psalms of David, the flaming exhortations of Isaiah, the rich lamentations of Jeremiah and kindred outpourings of the heart and mind. Then would they realize that words, as moulds, were too narrow to contain the human heart and mind, and that their beauty was not in *expressing* man but in hinting at the inexpressible in man."

"Do you think we shall ever see Lebanon again, Gibran? I doubt. I, for one, am certain that I shall never feast my eyes on the purity of those snow-wrapt peaks; and I pray that you may not be denied that pleasure . . ."

At that point Boutros was seized with a fit of coughing that shook the darkness in the room so saturated with tears and grief.

— 8 —

"Verily, verily, I say unto you, Except a corn of wheat fall into the ground and die, it abideth alone: but if it die, it bringeth forth much fruit."

The January skies were blanketing Boston with snow when Gibran, unable to sleep, took the New Testament and, opening it at random, fell upon the above verse in St. John's gospel; and even though he had come upon it many times before, he felt as though he were reading it for the first time. He further felt as if a veil were drawn off his eyes. And lifting his eyes from the book, he fell to musing: Everything dies that it may be born again in another form. The rock dies to become stones and pillars in the temple; the candle dies to be transformed into light; a piece of wood dies to give birth to the fire within it; a fruit dies to give birth to the seed which dies in turn to give birth to the tree. Everything goes back to its origin. Life is a going forth; Death is a coming back. Life is an investment; Death is a dividend. Life is a thought embodied; Death is a bodiless thought. While God is both—Life and Death.

Having reached that conclusion, Gibran went straight to his easel on which was poised a piece of white cardboard. Taking his pencil, he began to draw on the board light lines, circles and semicircles. In a few moments there emerged out of those vague twisting lines what looked like a bent-down human head.

Gibran felt as if a hidden hand was moving his hand. His pencil shifted quickly from one part of the head to another, each stroke adding something new to the picture—an eyebrow here, a touch of a mouth there, or a strand of hair in another spot. Often the fore and the middle fingers came to the assistance of the pencil by thickening or lightening a shade. Now and then Gibran would move a distance from the easel, squint at the cardboard for an instant, and then rush back to it as a lover to his beloved, or an adorer to his adored. A cigarette he had lighted was left to burn out to the end in the ashtray. He did not stop to light another until he was done with the eyes, hesitating for a space whether to draw them open, half-shut, or shut.

In less than two hours the cardboard was no longer a mere cardboard; it became the living background for a magnificent head whose noble brow was bathed in soft celestial light, with delicate, warm shades between and above the eyebrows, and with eyelids apart barely the breadth of a hair as if careful not to pour forth all the light behind them for fear it may blind the looker rather than clear his sight. The lips, slightly parted, were infinitely tender, compassionate and loving, and seemed to speak softly of the bliss of Paradise. The hair, dropping in ethereal wavelets, framed the face in a circle of light that suggested two curved wings whose pinions almost touched below the chin.

From the bottom of the board rose a tongue of flame in the likeness of a human body, but without the flesh, bone and blood. Looking at it one would not think it simply so many lines drawn upon a flat cardboard, immobile and lifeless. The body, its back towards the looker, seemed to rise without any effort until its head touched the lips of the face at the top. Another look, and the hair of the person at the top takes on the appearance of two arms extended to the person rising from below, like the arms of a mother reaching down to lift to herself a most beloved child.

"A ray projected from the sun returns to the sun; a tree issued from the earth goes back to the earth; a spirit flowing from the All-Spirit rejoins the All-Spirit. Everything is eternally coming and returning. Sultana went back to God."

Gibran looked at the creation of his hands and found it very beautiful. But scarcely had he initialled the picture when Boutros walked in as one overtaken by the shadow of Death, and almost out of breath, he said to his brother:

"Quick, Gibran, quick. Go after a physician, and don't come back to this house. It is fast falling on our heads—ceiling, walls and all. The very floor is slipping from under our feet. Save yourself at least. Your mother's life is in danger. Your brother Boutros is also 'packing up'. Hurry."

— 9 —

The physician departed from the house leaving in Gibran's ear a fearful word which soon turned into scorpions, vipers and dragons, twisting, hissing and seething in the ceiling and the walls, in the windows and the doors. Gibran was overwhelmed.

"Tuberculosis, and in the third stage . . . Where is your justice, God? And who are we—five poor immigrants from distant lands—to withstand the mighty rush of your ferocious, invisible, hordes? But yesterday those hordes carried away beloved Sultana. Now they have come to strangle my mother and my brother, the dearest in the world to me. As well strangle me with them, rather than leave me bound hand and foot, with eyes veiled, wings broken, hands empty, and a heart bereft of hope and love. The physician says it is imperative that both my mother and my brother be moved to a hospital at once. Where shall I find the means to carry out his orders? Men would not treat my wounds with their drugs except I first 'treat' their pockets with money. Wherewith shall I treat You that You may condescend to treat my wounds? Lord, Lord, Lord my God!

Do not desert me. Do not punish my ignorance. Perhaps your invisible, mighty hordes are now encamped in my chest as they are in my mother's and my brother's chests . . ."

The thought sent a shiver into Gibran's heart, gripping his throat as with a vise. For a moment he felt as if every breath of air he inhaled teamed with regiments of "the ferocious, invisible hordes," and he became like a fish caught in a net. Soon, however, he recovered himself and began to buttress up his waning courage:

"How cowardly of you, Gibran, to shun an encounter with death when your mother and brother are with him face to face. Let God's will be done. It was His will that brought you from Lebanon to this land. It was His will that took away from you your sister Sultana. It was His will that drove the 'invisible hordes' from Sultana's chest into your mother's and brother's chests. Yea, it was the will of God. But why did God will what He willed? Why, why, why? Perhaps, because you have soiled your soul, Gibran; because you have sinned. But why should God visit the son's sins upon the mother, and the brother's sin upon his sister and brother?—'But I say unto you, That whosoever looketh on a woman to lust after her hath committed adultery with her already in his heart . . . Verily, verily I say unto you, except a corn of wheat fall into the ground and die . . .'

"But what is the connection between a corn of wheat and tubercular germs? Or between the silver dragon puffing sandalwood smoke and this horrible dragon now standing at the door and belching disaster and death? Or between 'the guardian angel' and . . . If she only knew how you suffer now. No, better if she did not know. You did well yesterday when you met her quite unexpectedly in the street and returned not her greeting. She was but a shadow that crossed your path. Not so was she whom you buried in Beirut.

"A good picture, indeed, was the one you drew to-day—

the Soul's return to God. A better one shall be 'The Dance of Thoughts' which has been haunting you for some time past. Where is the pencil? This is the thermometer . . ."

The pencil and the thermometer. The dance of thoughts and the dance of death. The museum and the hospital. The call of the muse and the cough of the tubercular. A heart on fire and a sky shedding frozen tears. What a jumble! At the thought of the snow falling outside Gibran rushed out of the house as one shot from a cannon. Soothed by the nipping air and the snow-flakes plastering his face, he went on and on with no definite goal in view, repeating at each step, "Where are you, my God, where are you?"

— 10 —

"Marianna! You'll ruin your eyes, sister, drawing this needle and thread at such dim gaslight."

"What else can I do when this needle and thread help to pay the rent and the light, and to keep us fed and clothed? Shall we go out and beg?"

"Marianna, Marianna! Your needle pricks my eye, and its thread is like a rope about my neck."

"What's the matter, Gibran? You are so over-sensitive of late that the slightest word sends your tears gushing. Have I said anything to hurt you?"

"Do not mind my tears, Marianna. When love overfills the heart it also overfills the eyes. Your needle and thread speak so loud and so eloquently of your love. What hurts is to see you bury your days and nights in the eye of a needle in order to help me live; whereas I should burn my days and nights to help you live. You spend your sight to spare me my sight."

"Have no anxiety about my eyes, but take good care of your own. You overwork them night and day with reading and drawing, and the least protest on my part upsets you."

"It is an obsession with me, dear Marianna. Were it not for that I should have joined Sultana and the rest. Do you know what people say about me? They say that death should have taken me and spared Boutros. Do you know what father said in Bisharri? He said he would have gladly exchanged his three children for Boutros alone. What seems right to men may not at all be right in the eyes of God. Were death a penalty, as people seem to think, I should have been penalized long before Boutros, mother and Sultana. It may well be that life is a penalty and death, a reward. You and I have been severely penalized by being made to taste the bitterness of orphanage. But with the penalty, though most severe, goes a rich reward—the reward of having known the gentlest and the most loving of mothers, the sincerest of brothers and the sweetest of sisters. It must be that the tissue of your life and mine has not yet been completed; that certain threads in that tissue are yet being woven into the life-tissues of many men and women, known to us and unknown. Whereas the tissue of the life which was our mother's and our brother's and sister's has been completed; and where? In Boston! And what were the fingers that wove the last threads of its web and woof? Those of tuberculosis! Therein lies a great mystery, and also in the time and place: Sultana dying at home on the fourth day of April, 1902; Boutros at home the twelfth of March, 1903; mother in the hospital on June 28, 1903; and here we are in the year of 1904 whose end we may never see. What grieves me, Marianna, is that mother was denied the loving ache of seeing Boutros at the hour of his death. In that also is wrapt a mystery."

"Why dig into the past, Gibran? To cry and to make me cry? Do you not know that a tear in your eye calls forth two in mine?"

"Pity the man and woman, Marianna, who greet death

with hands cuffed with lust and soiled with wickedness, for they shall find the hands of death colder than ice, and harder than iron."

"To-morrow we must pay the rent for a month and the gas-bill for two months."

"While they who die in the death of some loved ones even before they actually taste of their own death are to be envied. And I am to be envied; for I have died thrice, yet am alive."

"I have left you the money on the table in your room."

"The world is deaf and dumb, Marianna. Pity them who are driven by necessity to speak to the world."

"And don't forget to buy yourself a new hat to-morrow. The present one is no longer fit to wear."

"Life has a great book of accounting, Marianna, in which are kept most careful accounts of every man's and woman's life, which accounts are checked and settled every twinkling of an eye. What we have and what we lack this very moment is but our balance from eternity till now."

"For my sake and for the sake of our dear ones' memory, please go to sleep, Gibran."

"For my sake and the sake of our dear ones' memory, please, make me a large pot of Turkish coffee, Marianna, and go to bed and leave me alone; for I have work which must be done to-night. I am preparing to exhibit some of my works soon, and have been fortunate to find a small hall for the purpose at a photographer's studio. His name is Fred Holland Day. The regular art exhibition galleries would not accept me because I am not yet known; and if they did accept me, I would not be able to meet their terms."

"It seems that you are already walking in father's footsteps —I mean in smoking and coffee-drinking. Will you not cut that down to the minimum? I fear so for your heath, especially since you began to take a drink now and then."

"For that you have no one to blame but yourself; for you make excellent coffee. Furthermore, I find our new apartment, though in Chinatown also, more comfortable and more conducive to work than the one we had before. Should you divorce me from cigarettes and coffee, beware of driving me to the pipe of our Chinese neighbors."

"How horrible! Better a thousand cigarettes and a hundred pots of coffee than one puff from an opium-pipe."

* * *

Gibran kept smoking and sipping coffee till away past midnight. While looking for a certain drawing he came upon a long article he had written in Arabic on music. It was one of his first literary efforts written a year before. On reading it over he began to correct a word here and to change a sentence there until he came to a passage addressed directly to Music. That passage he read in a voice somewhat above a whisper, and with an evident feeling of self-satisfaction:

"Child of Love and of the soul; vessel of the honey and the gall of passion; dreams of the human heart; fruit of sorrow and blossom of joy; fragrance of the flowers of emotions; tongue of those who love and those who are loved; distiller of tears from pent-up sentiments; inspirer of poets and stringer of the pearls of meter and rime; welder of thoughts with words and creator of beautiful feelings from things that impress with beauty. O Music—the wine that lifts the hearts of those who drink it to the lofty regions where lovely shadows dwell; you that steel the spirits of warriors and purge the souls of pious worshippers . . ." As he read Gibran kept adding and changing, and as he reached the end he became quite convinced that the piece was well worth publishing in a separate booklet which would launch him as a writer among writers in the Arabic-speaking world. With that decision Gibran went to bed.

— 11 —

Between success and failure, as between life and death and
all the opposites, is an indefinite, shifting line which renders
it most difficult to label this act as success, the other as failure.
In fact it often happens that what appears now as a huge success
turns out a moment later to be a total failure; and vice versa.

Several days passed since Gibran opened his first exhibit;
but neither the press nor the public showed much interest in it.
One would say it was a flat failure.

One day Gibran sat alone in a corner of the small *salon*
where his pictures were on exhibit, and aimlessly turning the
leaves of a magazine in his hand, he mentally reviewed the
few visitors that had come to see his pictures, most of them
passing by those pictures as by some Chinese puzzles. "Childish
work, and quite unintelligible," was the prevailing verdict.

Gibran recalled in particular a man accompanied by three
women. The man discoursed expansively on art as if delivering
a lecture to his companions. He had some criticism to offer on
every picture but hardly a word of praise. Of him Gibran said
to himself, "What a jackass!" Quite the opposite was the case
of one woman who came accompanied by three men. As she
stopped to admire a touch of light or shade here, or a masterly
stroke there, she would exclaim, "What a daring! What an
imagination!" Of her Gibran said that she knew what she was
talking about.

Gibran was consoling himself over the failure of his pictures
to attract more admirers when a lone woman walked in and
stopped long before the first drawing her eye fell on. He cast
a quick look at her and turned back to the magazine in his
hand as if most absorbed in reading, and quite unconcerned
about who came in and who went out and what they said of his
exhibit. Meanwhile he kept watching the new visitor out of the
corner of his eye and was pleased to see her approach each
picture as one intent on understanding it. Recalling Marianna's

needle and thread, he said to himself, "Perhaps this lady will buy a picture." He arose from his chair, stroked back his long hair, and with a smile dripping tact and gentleness approached the woman and said:

"Would madam care to have some of the pictures explained?"

"I should be most grateful for some explanations, since these drawings are quite out of the ordinary. They are so different. While I love art, I am not an artist. Are you, perchance, an artist?"

"I have the honour to belong to that family."

"Do you happen to know the artist exhibiting here?"

"I am he, madam."

Surprised for a moment, the woman put forth her hand saying:

"I am very happy to know you, Mr. Gibran. My name is Mary Haskell. I own and operate the Cambridge School for girls, perhaps you have heard of it. The school was founded by my sister, and I bought it from her last year when she decided to marry."

"Of course I have heard of your school. It is a well-known institution in Boston. Believe me, it is a great pleasure to make your acquaintance, Miss Haskell."

"Forgive my curiosity—what country do you hail from? You look to me like a Frenchman or an Italian."

"I come from Lebanon."

"Lebanon? The land of the cedars and the Song of Songs?"

"Yes, the land of the cedars and the Song of Songs. In fact I was born near the Holy Cedar Grove, on the edge of Saints' Gorge, in a village called Bisharri."

"Did you study art in Paris?"

"Very little in Paris, but mostly with some Boston artists and through independent personal effort."

"How marvelous to have achieved so much at such an early age."

"Won't you sit down, Miss Haskell?"

"No, no, I haven't come to sit down but to study. Won't you please explain that picture?" And she pointed to a drawing on the wall opposite.

"This I called 'The Soul's Return to God.' Perhaps you agree with me that everything we see does but symbolize the life unseen, and that the purpose of art is not so much the faithful reproduction of the symbol as the revealing of that symbol by means of other, more suggestive symbols. The face you see at the top is the face of God. I know—and you know—that no human eye has ever seen God; yet many have seen Him with the eye of imagination. Had we all been imaginary beings, we should have no need of symbols. But we live in a sensory world; and it is quite impossible for imagination to make itself real to the senses unless it clothe itself in shapes and forms perceivable by the senses. Having seen this face with your eye, endeavor now to see it with your imagination. Perhaps you will then see some of the attributes of godhood which I aimed to endow it with. Perhaps you will see more than I actually aimed to put into that face. Looking then at that shaft of light rising from the bottom of the picture, you will, perhaps, have no difficulty in seeing in it a soul returning to God after death. Art must be a direct communication between the artist's imagination and that of the looker. For that reason I avoid, so much as possible, busying the looker's eye with too many details in order that his imagination may roam wide and far. As to the physical molds art is forced to create for expressing itself, they must be beautiful molds. Otherwise art defeats its purpose."

"Your words sound very reasonable and very beautiful, Mr. Gibran; I have heard nothing like that from any artist before. What about that picture over there? I have looked at it long, but was unable to grasp its meaning."

"What caught your eye in it more than anything else?"

"Those naked bodies twined together and shot upward by a hidden force as is a stream of water in a fountain, then falling down after making a curve in the air exactly as the drops of water in a fountain."

"What feelings did those bodies awaken in you as you looked at their forms and faces?"

"They are bodies in pain."

"Then you don't need me to explain the picture to you. I have called it "The Fountain of Pain," and wished it to speak of that hidden power which purifies the soul through pain. Pain is a greater reality than pleasure, and much more effective as a teacher. Life itself is but a fountain of pain."

"Why do you draw the bodies always naked?"

"Because Life is naked. A nude body is the truest and the noblest symbol of life. If I draw a mountain as a heap of human forms, or paint a waterfall in the shape of tumbling human bodies, it is because I see in the mountain a heap of living things, and in the waterfall a precipitate current of life."

"I also observe that the symbols of pain and death recur again and again in your pictures. Do you mean by that anything other than pain and death?"

"Until to-day I've had a very large share of both. Between April 4, 1902, and June 28, 1903, I lost my younger sister, my elder brother and my mother. All three were dearer to me than life itself, Miss Haskell."

"I can readily understand your sorrow, Mr. Gibran; and the tear I now see in your eye is well understood by the tear in my heart. I, too, have lost my mother recently; she was the dearest person to me in the world. You see, we have found two lines of kinship between us—that of art, and that of pain."

"The kinship of pain is stronger and more lasting than the kinship of pleasure and blood."

"You have been exceedingly kind, Mr. Gibran, and I know

not how to thank you for your kindness. Will you not be kind enough to come and see me at the school, so that the kinship we found between us will not end where it began? How thankful I am to the friend who told me to-day of your exhibit and insisted that I should not miss seeing it, saying that it was a rare and an unusual one which all lovers of art should see. Were it not for that friend I should have been denied the great pleasure of seeing your beautiful work and of making your acquaintance. I hope your exhibition is successful."

"O yes, in so far as the number of visitors is concerned; but sales have not been encouraging. Many offered to buy, but few would pay the price. I have, however, many promises which may materialize."

"I hope they do materialize. Good-by, Mr. Gibran. I shall expect to see you soon at the school. Meantime I wish you well and thank you again for your kindness. You have really offered me a cupful of delight."

"The cup of art is ever full. But few are the thirsty. Good-by, Miss Haskell."

Mary Haskell went back to her school entirely unconscious of the fact that she had touched with her hand that white silken thread she saw in a dream twenty-two years ago in the city of Columbia, South Carolina; and that she had tied that thread tight about her waist. She only thought of the friend who had told her of the exhibit at Day's studio, and of how she was to express her thanks and to describe the kindness and the abundant talents of that young artist from distant Lebanon. In her heart she wondered much about the wisdom of God in distributing His gifts so unequally among men.

Gibran, too, went home having no thought whatever that in touching the stranger's hand he had touched the wing of that "guardian angel" whom he had been expecting for years. In his heart he was grieved that God did not add two or more inches to his stature so that he would not feel so small alongside a tall woman like Miss Haskell.

It occurred neither to Gibran nor to Miss Haskell that the Great Weaver had again caught the two ends of the threads of their lives, and that His shuttle was again busy weaving the tissue He started in eternity upon His mysterious loom.

— 12 —

Miss Haskell was pouring the tea for her guests, addressing most of her attention and words to the young man at her right.

"You have obliged us indeed, Mr. Gibran, when you accepted our invitation to exhibit your drawings at our school. For that we are indebted to my assistant, the young lady sitting opposite you. When she heard me speak of your exhibition she suggested that the teachers and girls be given an opportunity to see it right at the school. We are all very happy to see you and your pictures with us. Micheline, take good care of your neighbor, and offer him some cakes and biscuits. The young lady at your right, Mr. Gibran, is one of our teachers—French by origin. Her name is Mademoiselle Emilie Michel; but we call her simply Micheline. She is everybody's darling and the angel of this school."

"Our principal is so kind, Mr. Gibran, she fashions people after her own image; therefore did she call me an angel. But we, the teachers and girls, call her "The Oak"— firmly rooted in the earth yet reaching upward to the sky. We are but little birds that build nests in her branches and there seek shelter from the sun and storm. Often we are perturbed by many things; she is ever calm. Every day we come to her with problems of many kinds; to her nothing is a problem. We seek her decision in quarrels big and small, but always go away more than satisfied. When we ask her to lay down some firm and fixed rule for one circumstance or another, she invariably replies, 'Let love be your rule. Unless you live in agreement with yourself you cannot live in agreement with the law' ".

"Enough self-praise, dear Micheline; and remember that we are in the presence of a high priest of art. Is not Beauty the basis of all art, Mr. Gibran? What is your idea of Beauty?"

"Beauty is that harmony between joy and sorrow which begins in our holy of holies and ends beyond the scope of our imagination. To the body it is a trial; to the spirit, a gift. It is that power which leads our hearts to the throne of Women which is the throne of God."

"You exalt woman far too high, Mr. Gibran, by making her throne and God's as one."

"Most religions speak of God in the masculine gender. To me He is as much a mother as He is a father. He is both the father and the mother in one; and Woman is the God-Mother. The God-Father may be reached through the mind or the imagination. But the God-Mother can be reached through the heart only—through Love. And Love is that holy wine which the gods distill from their hearts and pour into the hearts of men. Those only taste it pure and divine whose hearts have been cleansed of all the animal lusts. For clean hearts to be drunk with Love is to be drunk with God. Those, on the other hand, who drink it mixed with the wines of earthly passions taste but the orgies of devils in Hell."

"Your style of speaking is so much like your style of drawing. Is it also your style in writing? For you told me that you wrote in Arabic. And why did you choose that style?"

"Perhaps it chose me. Quite unconsciously, I found myself walking that path; and each of us has his path. When I began to draw and paint I did not say to myself, 'Behold, Kahlil Gibran. There are ahead of you so many ways to art: The classic, the modern, the symbolic, the impressionistic and others. Choose for yourself one of them.' I did nothing of the sort. I simply found my pen and brush, quite of themselves, recording symbols of my thoughts, emotions and fancies. Some think the business of art to be a mere imitation of Nature. But Nature is far too great and too subtle to be successfully imitated. No art can ever reproduce even the least of nature's surpassing creations and miracles. Besides, what profit is there in imitating Nature when she is so open and so accessible to all who see and hear? The business of art is rather to understand Nature and to reveal her meanings to those unable to understand. It is to convey *the soul* of a tree rather than to produce a faithful likeness of the tree. It is to reveal the *conscience* of the sea, not to portray so many foaming waves or so much blue water. The mission of art is to bring out the unfamiliar from the most familiar.

"Pity the eye that sees no more in the sun than a stove to keep it warm and a torch to light its way between the home and the business office. That is a blind eye, even if capable of seeing a fly a mile away. Pity the ear that hears no more than so many notes in the song of a nightingale. It is a deaf ear, even if capable of hearing the crawling of ants in their subterranean labyrinths."

The conversation continued brisk and lively for more than two hours; like every conversation round a tea cup it shifted quickly from the most sublime to the most trite—from God to the weather, from art to the price of eggs, from literature to the latest town gossip, from the cedars of Lebanon to Chinatown in Boston. Of that conversation Gibran had the lion's share, expatiating as much on the price of eggs as on the broken arms of Venus de Milo, and speaking always slowly and ponderously. Now and then he would stop to search his memory for a more colorful, more ringing and more mystic word than the first one that came to the tip of his tongue. Encouraged by the attention of the company about him and by the satisfaction quite evident on their faces, he felt he was master of his tongue and the situation. Outwardly he addressed his words to all around the table; inwardly he spoke to two only: the principal of the school and the French teacher. He spoke to the head of the first and to the heart of the second, drawing the while a comparison between the two in his mind:

The principal: A long, lean and fair face with a broad and high forehead, and with soft, light hair combed very simply and tied in a small knot at the back. Two thin eyebrows almost bereft of hair; eyelids with lashes barely perceptible, opening and shutting over two round, blue eyes set deep in their sockets and washed with a fluid which is neither from the well of tears nor from the quarry of laughter; a long delicate nose overlooking two thin rosy lips whose ends reach to the middle of the two cheeks; when shut together they form a straight line; when apart, they reveal a good part of the gums with teeth far from the ideal. A narrow chest with high shoulders out of which grow two long arms terminating in two long, narrow hands with long, thin, tapering fingers endowed with large knuckles.

Her dress is very neat and simple and quite unconcerned about the "latest". Her face can truthfully swear that it loses no love on cosmetics. She does not chew words, her speech flowing confident, direct and unaffected. When she expresses an idea she expresses all of it, not one half or three quarters, and that with simple, well chosen words which make no claim for eloquence or for theatrical effects. Her well-balanced logic speaks of a well-balanced mind. Her clear-cut words speak of a nature loath to say what it does not mean—sincere, trusting and trustworthy; a nature that may be mocked and cheated, but itself will never mock and cheat; it may follow where it trusts, but it may not be driven. All in all the woman inspires confidence and respect. To see her and to hear her is to feel certain that her mind commands her life. What her mind says is good she readily accepts as good. If her soul is clean of anger, hate, vindictiveness or envy it is because her mind sees these things as evil and exhorts her to shun them as such. Tall and very unassuming, she walks without grace, but with a foot that likes the firmness of the earth and grips it very firmly.

There is something in her face and bearing that testifies to her absolute innocence of any passions of men; it also testifies that there is nothing in that face to invite a heart-melting kiss, or to arouse a passion that would set both body and soul on fire. She is an oak, as the teachers and students call her—an oak whose trunk is strong and steady, whose green branches are a feast to the eye, and whose shade offers a welcome shelter to the weary way-farer, but no food to the hungry and no drink to the thirsty. An oak she may be, but not that witching, fruit-laden tree which God planted in the middle of Eden and warned Adam not to taste of it saying, "In the day that thou eatest thereof thou shalt surely die."

Micheline: In her dark hair alone is a sheen that fascinates the eye and electrifies the hands to the extent that the looker can barely restrain the impulse to touch it and stroke it. In her large, black eyes sparkles a light teeming with the budding desires and innocent dreams of healthful, energetic, self-confident youth. In her complexion is an ivory tinge suffused with the red of the poppy. Her smile has the modesty and innocence of a child's smile. Her laughter is the gurgling of a running brook; but she seldom smiles or laughs. Perhaps her twenty years have taught her that equanimity is Beauty's strong shield, while too much laughing leaves Beauty open to many poisoned shafts. At times she prattles like a child; at others she utters things full of poetry and wisdom. She walks as if on springs, or as if her feet had wings.

Out of her heart flow both her good and her evil, the mind having little to do with either. Spontaneous in her acts and feelings, she seldom stops to weigh and calculate. Duty with her is that which she cannot restrain herself from doing; and right is that towards which she feels disposed with her whole heart;

while the forbidden is what her soul would not stoop to touch. She dislikes pain for herself and others, but she is always ready to alleviate another's pain at the cost of pain to herself. In the latter case she would never say to herself, "I have done that which is pleasing to God." God in her life is an image wrapped in mist; and Heaven and Hell, but two words found in books and heard from the lips of ministers and priests.

When she senses kindness and sincerity in her interlocutor she crawls out of her shell like a snail; when she senses the opposite she crawls back. Neither is she haughty, nor boastful. What may strike some as haughtiness in her is but a veil she draws on her innocence to protect it from the offensive ugliness of the coarse and the stupid.

She is beautiful and knows that she is beautiful. But does she know, or does she care to know what two hours of her company have done to Gibran? In his mind Gibran likened her to radium —it burns without being burned. For he began to feel as if the chair he sat on were electrified, and had to use his utmost skill and will to hide from the eyes of the others the frequent shocks that startled his blood and set his imagination on wings. "Perhaps", he was saying to himself, "there are electric wires in her chair as there are in mine; perhaps she sees me as I see her—a radium that burns without being burned."

* * *

That night Gibran consumed much coffee, smoked many cigarettes and tore up many sheets of paper on which he tried in vain to portray in words the burning sensation which Micheline's lips left upon his lips, and the living flame which her breath helped to fan in his heart and in his brain. Just before dawn was he able to lay his head on his pillow feeling that he had met Fate itself in the shape of that strange young woman, so divinely beautiful. He could hardly bring himself to believe that what happened had actually happened; and he blessed in his heart the hidden ways of Life so pregnant with surprises.

— 13 —

"What have you brought me to-day, Kahlil, my darling? A tear or a smile?"

"A smile worthy of your smile. How I wish you knew Arabic, Micheline. I could then read you my poems as I read them to myself thus obviating the necessity for translation which can never equal the original. It would please you to know that the short pieces I publish in a certain Arabic newspaper in New York under the general title "A Tear and A Smile" are widely reproduced and commented upon throughout the Arabic-speaking world."

"And that, of course, displeases you immensely! I'm beginning to fear, Kahlil, that in the future I would need a ladder to see myself in your dreamy eyes; so tall and big you will be. Come now, read me from your fresh "Smile"; but first, you must touch my lips with yours, for they have almost forgotten to smile."

Gibran embraced his beloved with passion, and drawing from his pocket an issue of an Arabic journal called *Al-Mohajir* —meaning the Immigrant—he began to translate a piece entitled "The Companion":

"*The first look:*—It is that moment which divides between the ecstasy of Life and its awakening. It is the first flame whose light penetrates the innermost recesses of the soul. It is the first mystic note struck on the first string of the harp of the heart. It is a short moment that unfolds to the soul the scrolls of days and nights long past, revealing to the inner eye the works of the conscience of this world and the secrets of immortality in the other. . . ."

"*The first kiss:*—It is the first sip from that cup which the gods have filled from the fount of Love. It is the dividing line between the doubt which fills the heart with sadness and the conviction which floods it with bliss. It is the first verse in the epic of the spirit, and the first chapter in the story of the spiritual man. It is the link between the strange past and the bright future; between the silence of emotions and their songs. It is the word uttered by four lips at once and announcing the heart a throne, with Love as king, and fidelity as a crown. . . . It is the beginning of those mystic vibrations that detach lovers from the world of weights and measures and carry them to the world of light and inspiration. . . ."

"*Marriage:*—Here Love begins to render Life's prose into verse, and to pour Life's meanings into canticles to be sung by days and nights. Here our longing draws back the curtain hiding the mysteries of the years gone by, and from the fragments of pleasure composes that happiness which no other happiness can surpass excepting that of the soul upon rejoining God. Marriage is the union of two divinities that a third be born on the earth. It is the alliance of two beings strong in their love against a world too weak in its hatred. . . . It is the determination of two souls to be distrustful of distrust and to be confident in confidence. It is a golden link in a chain whose first link is a look, and the last, eternity. . . ."

"And who is your fortunate companion, Kahlil?"

"Naughty Micheline! You would jest when to jest is sacrilege. When the heart is on its throne, let all the senses fall to their knees and chant in one voice, 'Holy, holy, holy!' "

"Holy, holy, holy. And when shall you be wedded to your companion, Kahlil?"

"I have already wed her before God. Her body and mine have already been joined into one pure temple dedicated to the one pure Love. Her soul and mine have been made an eternal throne for the eternal God. Before God said, 'Let there be light,' I was with her in that light; and before God created Adam and Eve I was Adam and she was Eve in the Eden of God's dreams. You do not know who you are, Micheline. But I know. I knew you before your mother gave you birth. Long before you became a trembling word upon the lips of Life you were a latent longing in the depth of my being. You were life coursing in my veins long before you became living blood coursing in the veins of the Earth. You were a divine beat in my heart before you became a pulse in the arm of the universe. Never did Life separate us except to bring us together again; and never did it bring us together except to see its perfection, unity and eternity in our perfection, unity and eternity. Since my birth have I been looking for you; and since your birth have you been looking for me. Every sound that ever escaped your lips meant but one thing: Where are you, my Kahlil? Every step you have taken had no other purpose but to bring you closer to me. Your relatives and mine—the living of them and the dead—as well as all those we have known whether as friends or foes, and everything we have thought and done and have experienced as pain or pleasure—yes all and everything heretofore were but the foreword to the mystic book which is our love."

"Holy, holy, holy! You have wed your companion before God, Kahlil; when shall you be wedded to her before men?"

"How scant is the gold-dust in your dust, Micheline! Men, men, men!! What do I care about men and what they say and do? Have they ever joined two loving hearts except to sunder them later? Or have they joined two unloving hearts except to crush them both?"

"Kahlil, my darling, my soul; Granting I was all dust before I knew you, your love has turned my dust into gold."

"Not even a thousand loves like mine can turn your dust into gold. Men, and always men. I hate men and their ways. I loathe their likes and dislikes. They are like hens—they have wings but cannot fly; they have tongues but cannot sing; they have claws, but use them only to dig for filth and worms; and they lay their eggs in the dark coops of their dark and gloomy traditions only. Give me but one eagle fledgling and take all the hens in the world!"

"For whom do you draw and paint and write, Kahlil? Is it

not for men? With whose pens and brushes do you write and paint, Kahlil? Is it not with the pens and brushes of men? Whose bread do you eat, Kahlil? Is it not the bread of men? And whose glory do you seek, Kahlil? Is it not the glory of men?"

"You are of them. You, too, are a creature of coops and worms. But I, eagle-like, seek the distant and the wide horizons. I cannot bear to look on life except from lofty summits. An eagle and a hen—what strange company!"

"Yet would you not disdain hen's eggs and flesh as food for your body?"

"For my body, but not for my soul."

"Then I am food for your body, no more, no less. I am an outlet for your passions and a plaything in your hands, and our love is but a lowly chick. Pity that love how many times you dug your eagle's claws into its tender flesh while still a helpless fledgling. Now you seem determined to kill it outright. You seem to care for no one but yourself, and to believe in no one but yourself. I say to you that our love is no longer a secret and that the teachers and students at the school already exchange meaningful glances at my expense. You reply, you care not for people and what they do and say. I say to you, I may be *forced* to give up my position. You turn your back and go away. You read me your poems and chide me severely if I fail to exclaim my admiration for almost every passage. You call me earthly and unable to imbibe the beauty of your soul. Pray, make me first a companion fit to walk with you the ways of the earth before you make me a poet able to soar in the farthest regions of the sky. Make me a happy hen before you make me a powerful eagle. Make me a contented human being before you make me a perfect god. You have filled me with sweet poetry and bitter quarrelling. If your love be a drop of honey in a cup of gall, I should break my cup this very moment. Perhaps the God in whom you trust will not desert me."

"Micheline! I am sick of quarrelling. Have pity on yourself

and me. Forgive a bitterness in my heart which nothing can render sweet save your love. You have been my companion from eternity, and you shall remain my companion unto eternity. We shall be wedded even before men as soon as we have the means. Tell me, does Miss Haskell suspect anything of our relations?"

"She has a third eye that sees everything. I am sure that she knows, but pretends not to know."

"How I wish you knew Baalbek, Micheline. You shall know it some day; you shall know my Lebanon, its white peaks and blue sea. The last few days I have been turning in my mind a fantastic story with glorious Baalbek for a background. The story is about a priest of Astarte in the temples of Baalbek 2000 years ago and a maiden like Micheline. The lovers die and are reborn again to carry on to perfection the holy hymn of love— Kahlil and Micheline. I have already thought of a good title for the story: *The Ashes of the Ages and the Eternal Fire*.* The ages burn and turn to ashes, while the fire of Love burns on ever stronger, ever brighter. What do you think of that?"

— 14 —

"Do not say *Chance*, Mary. Life knows no chance. There are threads innumerable in the world, but they all go to make up the one tissue which is the world. Your life and mine are two threads in that eternal tissue, now running together, now moving apart, but always connected. The connection escapes our eye except when made manifest to the senses. But the weaver behind the loom is conscious of it every instant. The thread does not know the purpose of the weaver; but the weaver knows the meaning, the place and the purpose of every thread. My brother, sister and mother died as they did because it was *necessary* for them to die that death and no other. So did my drawings burn with Day's studio because it was necessary for them to burn when and

---

* Now appears in *Secrets of the Heart* (Philosophical Library, 1947).

where they burned. In that there must be some good for me which I cannot now see."

"Nevertheless, it was a great loss, Kahlil. Yet I'm very grateful that I was moved to buy two of your drawings—'The Dance of Thoughts' and 'The Fountain of Pain'—and thus save them from that awful catastrophe."

"Everything exists for a purpose. When the purpose is achieved, existence is accomplished. It seems that my drawings consumed by fire had achieved their purpose. Sufficient that they were the means for the renewal of my relations with you." And to himself, "And with Micheline also."

"Ever since you embraced the doctrine of Reincarnation you seem to tie all the events of your life with it, even to the burning of your pictures. How you have changed in the four years of my acquaintance with you, Kahlil."

"I was lost between life and death. Whenever I thought of human relations I found me as one walking in the dark and always stumbling on riddles. In Reincarnation I have found the key to the riddles and the lantern to light the hitherto obscure human relationships.

"Consider, Mary, how many steps we had to walk, how many turns we had to make before we were brought face to face with each other; each step was a natural sequel to the one before it and a direct cause of the one that followed it. You were born prematurely—two months before the normal time—weighing about two pounds and 'all head, eyes and mouth', as you say. In spite of that you lived, one of five sisters and four brothers; you overcame the handicaps of birth and poverty and succeeded in securing a college education. You wrung the pennies for your tuition and maintenance from the dish-rag and the heat of the furnace where you had to bake a quantity of bread each day; or from the piano keys when you taught music. And behold. You own to-day one of the best girl schools in Boston. From Columbia, S. C., to Boston; from a child handicapped by premature birth and poverty with barely any claim on life to the head of an institution whose staff and students find shield and shelter in your life. What a long succession of events! Had one small event been different, your whole life should have been different.

"And I—I was born ten years after you. Who at the time of your birth and mine could have detected the slightest connection between Columbia and Bisharri, or between you and me? Yet had I not been born the hour, the day, and the year I was born; had not my parents been in constant disagreement; had I not had a half-brother called Boutros, we should not have emigrated; and had we not had some acquaintances here from Bisharri we should not have picked out Boston of all the towns and cities in the broad United States. Had I not been born with a passion for painting, I should not have painted and drawn the pictures I later exhibited at Day's studio; your friend should not have seen them and urged you to see them. Had I not happened to be at the studio when you came to see my exhibit I should not have seen you; and had you not been alone, I should not have had the temerity to approach you and offer to explain the pictures to you.

"Ah, Mary, Mary! Are all those happenings and myriad thoughts, and dreams and longings that preceded them and accompanied them—are they all Blind Chance?"

"No, Kahlil. They are not; but people find it easy to brand as Chance everything they cannot account for in their lives and the life of the world about them."

"Life does not begin with birth and end with death. We hunger after perfection. We all seek God. And who can find God in twenty, a hundred, or a thousand years? 'You were dead, and He brought you to life. Again He shall cause you to die and shall bring you back to life. In the end He shall gather you unto Himself'—so said the prophet of the Arabs, and so proclaimed many prophets of the East. There are millions in India, China, Japan and the Malayas who believe in the constant renewal of individual human life. Even in our Lebanon there is a small sect called the Druses who believe in reincarnation. To me human life is but a perpetual balancing of accounts. We die leaving behind us many unsettled accounts—some are debits, some are credits; we are debited with all the evil we do, and credited with the good. Therefore are we made to come back to life again and again to pay and to collect. And we shall come and go until God be the only balance of our account."

"Let me hope, Kahlil, that the balance of your account against me is not beyond my capacity to pay."

"It is settlement sufficient for me, Mary, that with you I do not feel that awful spiritual loneliness which I feel with others. I talk to you of every flare of my imagination, of every tint of thought, and feel as if I were talking to myself. I am a stranger in this world, Mary, excepting when I am with you."

"Why don't you write in English, Kahlil? In Arabic you are an outstanding writer, having published so far three works: *Music, Prairie Nymphs* and *Spirit Rebellious.* But, as I understood from you, they all cost you money instead of bringing you some money."

"I am not yet certain of my English. Besides, I doubt if the type of writing I do will find many readers here."

"Your English has improved considerably within the last four years."

"Thanks to you, Mary."

"I shall be only too happy to help you with your English insofar as it lies in my power."

"I should devote myself for the time being to art."

"Would you like to go to Paris to continue your art studies?"

"With my whole heart and soul. But . . ."

"But you lack the means. I am willing to pay your transportation and send you monthly the sum of $75.00. Would you not accept that small gift from me as a token of love and appreciation of your rich talents? I wish I could offer more."

"Mary, Mary, Mary! (His tongue almost slipped and said, 'Micheline, Micheline, Micheline!') You have filled my heart and eyes to overflowing. Let my tears be the answer."

Gibran wept, and his abundant tears seemed to say, "Would that Mary's soul were in Micheline's body."

A DAY OF BIRTH — A DAY OF RECKONING

The sun of December 6, 1908, rose over Paris and, looking into Gibran's room in the Latin Quarter, found him sound asleep. Silently it passed over a canvas poised on an easel and bearing the likeness of a nude young woman. As silently it glided over a table cluttered with papers, books, pencils, brushes, paint tubes and the like with an empty whisky bottle in the centre. In front of the fireplace it came upon a bundle of firewood and a pot with two cups for Turkish coffee. Its morning visit over, it slipped out of the room as softly and silently as it slipped in.

It was after ten when Gibran finally woke up. Throwing the cover to one side he slowly and languidly arose as if the sleep still heavy on his eyelids, and the dreams he was dreaming, drew him back to bed. He went to the fireplace and started a fire to cook his morning coffee; from there he walked barefooted to the window, and feeling the ice-cold floor beneath his feet, he said, "This is a day whose cold bites." Seeing the sun outside he added, "But happily its teeth are of gold." As he tried to open the window to let in some fresh air a glass pane broke, and he heard its pieces crash on the sidewalk below; whereupon he said to himself, "This is a day whose feet are of glass. One must be careful how to walk." When the coffee was done and he poured him a cup, then stooped to light a cigarette from the fire, he spilled some coffee on his foot and burned it which caused him to drop the cup in his hand and caused the cup to break into many fragments. Then he said aloud, "This is a day whose heart is of pitch." He poured himself another cup and sat before the fire smoking and sipping coffee. For no apparent reason he began to feel as if he were not alone in the room. Strange phantoms seemed to be walking back and forth and to be conversing among themselves as follows:

"What is Art?"

"It is to carry two watermelons in one hand without having them touch each other."

"What is Life?"

"It is to run with Day without ever overtaking Night; and to run with Night without ever overtaking Day; and not to break your leg or neck in the running."

"What is Glory?"

"It is to drink cod-liver oil mixed with carbolic acid and not to vomit."

"What is Love?"

"It is to cut your nose to please your eye."

"Who is the one sitting before this fireplace?"

"A piece of wood warming itself over another piece of wood."

The phantoms kept dancing and giggling as Gibran smoked one cigarette after another. When the chimes of Notre Dame announced midday he started as one waking from a nightmare and quickly began to dress. Soon he was out in the Boulevard St. Michel walking towards the Luxembourg and turning in his mind an old Arabic verse, "Life is but a cobweb woven by a spider." Men, women and children that passed him by appeared to him like so many spiders. Looking at the sun he imagined it also as a huge spider whose cobwebs were all the spheres including the earth; himself and other creatures on the earth he pictured as so many flies caught in those cobwebs.

Gibran stood long before the Luxembourg, hesitating whether to go in or not. One voice would urge him, "Go in. Perhaps the ugly phantoms pursuing you to-day will flee before Modern

Art." Another voice would say, "Life is but a cobweb woven by a spider." Again would the first voice make an effort to chase away Gibran's gloom, "Go to the Beaux Arts then. You have lessons to finish there; besides there will be a lecture this afternoon on Michelangelo's David; and you adore Michelangelo." Whereupon the second voice would drone out, "Life is but a cobweb." In the end Gibran left the grounds of the famous palace and went straight to a small grocery store which he knew well; there he bought him a loaf of bread with two oranges and went back to his room. On the stairway he met the postman who handed him a letter from Boston; it was from Mary.

The letter contained a check for $75.00 together with tender birthday greetings and sincere expressions of Mary's faith in Gibran and his future. In addition to that was some local news, part of which was devoted to Micheline. It told of the great change that came over her after Gibran's departure for Paris; she has grown thin and somewhat pale; the charming smile no longer hovers round the corners of her mouth; the twinkle in her eyes has become dimmed; she keeps much to herself, and seldom talks to others except when talking is unavoidable. Before he came to the end of the letter Gibran threw it on the table and began to pace the room up and down with Micheline's name on his lips and her image in his eyes.

"Micheline, Micheline, Micheline! You have gripped me body and soul; even the keys of my imagination are now in your hands. You are the source of my joy and sorrow. Your love has made me taste the wisdom of age and the innocence of childhood. My birthday was just another day in my life until you made of it a fete fit for angels. An exquisite rose, a delicate lily, a box of candy, some childish trinket bought, perhaps, with the last pennies in your purse—what a divine meaning they imparted to the day of my birth when presented by you. The fragrance of godhood, the sweetness of Life everlasting, the beauty of Love unconquerable—all these flowed from every birthday present you brought me, no matter how insignificant in itself. But to-day I wake up with my mind overcast, my heart numb and frigid, and the taste of bitter loneliness in my mouth. About me are the phantoms of your pains and mine. I hear them mock me and grate their teeth in revenge. I have sinned against you and against myself, Micheline. It pleased my vanity at first to humble your pride; the consequence was that I mortgaged my will, my heart, and my imagination to your pride. A distraction in the beginning, you have now become the work of a lifetime. I have tried to take without giving; you gave without any thought of taking.

"Yes, I have sinned against you and myself, Micheline, when I allowed another woman to share my life with you, profiting by her purse and mind while taking freely of your heart, and flesh, and blood. I lied to you when you asked me of the woman subsidizing my studies in Paris, saying that there was no woman, and that I had arranged for a loan from some relatives and friends. Your sensitive heart felt that woman's presence, and it gave the lie to my tongue. How I wish I had declared all things to you; then these black shadows now so thick about me should not have been. Ah, come, Micheline! Come to me, soul of my soul and heart of my heart. Come and say to Kahlil that you have forgiven all his transgressions against you. He is ready to make amends. Come! Else I'll pluck you out of my heart even if my own heart be plucked in the painful operation."

Sad and exhausted, Gibran threw himself on the nearest chair by the table and began to fumble aimlessly the papers scattered all over the table, saying as he lifted or laid down each paper, "What is the good of you? What is the good of you." Finally he came upon a manuscript on whose cover were drawn in careful Arabic letters the words *A Tear and A Smile*. As he turned its pages he would stop long at each heading as if trying to recollect the mental, emotional and material circumstances in which that or the other piece was written; then he would read a few lines of each and talk to himself either in reproach or in admiration:

"*To My Two Friends*. Who are these two friends? Ah! They are my needing friend and my sorrowing friend." " 'Did you but know, my needing friend, that the need which condemns you to misery is the very same force which blesses you with a sense of justice and reveals to you the essence of life, you would accept without a murmur what God has allotted you . . . And you, my sorrowing friend, did you but realize that the sorrow which overcame you is but the power that lights the heart, and lifts the soul from the pits of derision to the heights of esteem, you would accept it in contentment as your heritage . . . ' "

"How clever is your tongue, how obedient your pen, and how true what you preach, Gibran. But, alas! How little you are taught by what you teach. Do you not dislike need and sorrow? Why teach others to love what you hate?"

"*To Those Who Reproach Me*: 'Let me be and teach me not. Tell me not of that which is not meet for me to do. In my conscience I have a judge who spares me any punishment when I am guiltless, and denies me any reward when guilty.' "

"It is your conscience, then, Gibran, which is whipping you so hard to-day; from its shady caverns are these dark shadows. If you do not chase them away once and for all, they shall surely chase peace out of your heart. Begin now—this very minute—this very instant. Cast Micheline out of your heart and Mary out of your mind, and live free in the name of Love unbound to flesh and blood, and in the name of Art which is beyond the colors and the shapes of Earth, and in the name of Beauty which binds the heavens to the Earth with that divine light which passes understanding."

"*Have Pity, My Soul*: 'How long shall you wail, my soul, knowing that I am so weak? . . . Have pity, my soul. In the far, far away you allowed me a glimpse of the fair face of Happiness. You and happiness are upon a high mountain; whereas Misery and I are in the bowels of a deep ravine. How shall heights and depths ever meet? In the stillness of night you steal away to where your beloved is, and you are rewarded with a hug and a kiss; whereas this body is ever torn between its passions and the distances that separate it from its beloved. Have pity, my soul, have pity.' "

"What is that soul, Gibran, which you so beseech for pity? And what is that body which you so wish to be pitied? Does a corpse ever long for a kiss, or tremble at the thought of separation? Rather is it the soul—the source of all desires. The more you gratify it, the greedier it is for more gratification. Did not the Man of Nazareth live in continence and die in continence without enslaving his soul to the passions of the body? Where is your scourge, Gibran? Scourge this soul of yours until it is subdued. Subdue it, and your body is subdued. Scourge without pity. Aye, scourge it well."

"*Encounter:* . . . 'The wise of the earth come from the east and the west to bespeak your wisdom, my beloved, and the meanings of your symbols.' "

"The great of the earth come from many kingdoms, my beloved, to be drunk with the fragrance of your beauty and with the charm of your eloquence."

"The palms of your hands, my beloved, are fountains of overflowing plenty."

"Your arms, my beloved, are springs of life-giving waters, and your breath is a vivifying zephyr."

"Is not that a flagrant imitation of Solomon's Song of Songs, Gibran? Have you not always stood for creators and loathed imitators? How come you behave contrary to your own conviction? But what is Imitation? And what is Creation? Did not the author of the Song of Songs declare in another place that there was nothing *new* under the sun? No, there is nothing new. Everything that men do is an imitation of an imitation. But some imitation is beautiful, and is highly prized as creation; while most is unbeautiful, and is looked upon as something trite and cheap. You imitate the beautiful in a beautiful way, Gibran; and that kind of imitation you call creation. That in your logic is logic, even though it may not be so in the logic of men. But what do you care about the logic of men?"

"*Love's Conversation:* . . . 'Lover of my soul! Do you remember that garden where the two of us stood face to face and each looked deep into the other's eyes? Do you know what your eyes said then to me? They said that your love for me was not the child of pity. They taught me to say to myself and to the world that giving, born of justice, is greater by far than giving prompted by charity; and that love born of passing considerations and circumstances is like water in a swamp.

" 'There is ahead of me, my love, a life which I wish to make great and beautiful; a life which shall dwell in the memory of generations to come and shall command their love and respect; a life which began the moment I met you and of whose immortality I am convinced because convinced of your ability to help unfold the talents God deposited in me as the sun helps to bring out the fragrant flowers dormant in the fields. Thus shall my love remain forever a legacy to me and to the coming ages. It shall be free of narrow selfishness because shared with all; and it shall be above and beyond banality because centered in you' ".

"Ah, Mary, Mary! You are to me a source of boundless amazement and delight. Who were we and where were we before we found each other in this life? Were you to me a mother, and I to you, a son? Or were we a sister and a brother? Or were you a priestess of Astarte or Minerva, and I, a priest, and the two of us offered sacrifices on the selfsame altar? How strange that a touch of Micheline sets me on fire, and I care not if it be a fire from hell or from heaven. Whereas your touch quiets my earthly passions and sets aflame passions uncommon to the earth.

Your love for me is not a child of pity; of that I am certain, as I am certain of the fact that you have no back-thought of 'buying' me with the money you send me. But money has a way of subjecting the receiver to the giver; like a worm it eats into their hearts and minds and ends by hollowing out their otherwise beautiful relations; and as a pinch of salt sprinkled over a goblet of old wine ruins the taste of that wine, so may money change the taste of our love. But need is heartless and pitiless. Therefore do I fool my pride by saying to myself that your giving is *justice* and not *charity*. Yes, it is justice, Mary, though the word be deleted from the vocabulary of money. It is just that the world be not denied the fruits of such talents as are mine. It is just that your pure hand should be the hand to help reveal those talents. I do want my life to be one of *greatness and beauty*, and *I am certain of its immortality*, as I am certain that your pure love for me shall bring out of my talents *great words and deeds* much as the sun brings out of the fields fragrant flowers.

"But what is greatness, Gibran? Shall you solve the problems yet unsolved, or shall you bring a new humanity into being? Shall you paint what no one has ever painted, or write what no writer has yet written? To-day you are an obscure youth in Paris. Shall you become great when people passing you in the streets shall point their fingers at you and whisper to each other: "That is he. That is he!"? Or is it greatness to have people compete for your books and paintings, yet for you to remain, as you are to-day, a prey to dark phantoms, with bitterness in the heart and loneliness gnawing away your hours?

"And Immortality—what is it? Are you not immortal as a man? Shall man's works be more immortal than man himself? Let a man's work, whether a book or a picture, live a thousand years; nay, let it live so long as mankind shall live. But neither mankind, nor the earth are eternal. How then, crave immortality from what is mortal? Furthermore, what have you done till this day that holds in it the promise of immortality so as to give you that *confidence* of an immortal life?

"There are the books you have published so far: *Music, Prairie Nymphs* and *Spirits Rebellious.* What's in them? The first is but a pamphlet containing a very immature hymn to Music. The second and third purport to be stories very naively told, but aiming in reality to be tirades against the despotism of certain social orders—particularly marriage conventions— and against the abuse of religious and temporal power. Though vehement and sincere, they fall far short of the Nazarene's vehemence and sincerity in his tirades against the Publicans and the Pharisees. Yet Publicans and Pharisees still sit in power and majesty in the hearts and minds of men. Why? Because the hearts and minds of men are still void of that knowledge which alone can say to Pharisees and Publicans: Begone! We have no need of your talismans.

"And your paintings and drawings—shall they be your torch to immortality? Many of them were consumed by the fire in Boston. Those you have painted and drawn since have not yet blazed their path into the larger world. What, then, is that greatness of which you dream, and that immortality of which you are so certain? And when will you begin to be great and immortal? Behind you are twenty-five years. Twenty-five years and your name is still unknown except to a limited number of Arab readers. Five and twenty years with greatness and immortality still so far away! Today is your birthday. Wherewith shall you commemorate it?

"Upon a day like this my mother gave me birth. Upon a day like this my mother gave me birth. Upon a day like this my mother gave me birth."

The day was spent with Gibran taking stock of the past and looking anxiously into the future. In his brains and before his eyes danced those words: "Upon a day like this my mother gave me birth." In vain he tried to chase them away, to distract himself with something. The words persisted and distracted him from his distraction. Finally he arose, lighted the lamp, and taking a writing pad and a pen began to write:

"Upon a day like this my mother gave me birth.

"Upon a day like this, twenty-five years ago, Silence laid me in the lap of Existence so turbulent with noise, and struggle, and strife."

*　　*　　*

"Upon this day my Past stands before me like a tarnished mirror. As I peer into it I am able to see naught but the pallid faces of the years and the dim age-wrinkled features of my hopes and dreams. I shut my eyes and open them again only to see my own image reflected in that mirror. I stare at that image and behold in it naught but Melancholy. I question Melancholy, but find it dumb. Yet Melancholy, if given speech, would utter sweeter words than would Joy."

*　　*　　*

"As pauses a mountain-climber half-way to the peak, so do I pause to-day and look backward to see a trace of me which I can point to and say, 'This is mine'; but I find none. Nor do I find for my years any harvest other than these sheets of paper tinted with ink, and other than these strange figures on canvas and cardboard. In these have I buried my sentiments, my thoughts and my dreams as buries a plowman the seed in the ground, but with this difference: The plowman having cast his seed in the furrows of the field returns in the evening to his house with his heart alive with the hope of the coming harvest; while I have scattered the seeds of my heart without the hope of any harvest."

Gibran wrote feverishly till away past midnight. Now and then he would rise from his chair to pace up and down the room, to wipe a tear with the end of his thumb, or to wet his lips, dry from smoking, with some *vin blanc*. The long article he concluded with the following words:

"Peace to you, sun-veiled Spirit, holding the reins of Life. And peace to you, heart, able to dream of peace while submerged in tears. And peace to you, lips, able to speak of peace while you are dipped in bitterness."

Whereupon he took his coat and cane and dashed out to a night restaurant in order to appease his empty stomach. He felt as if a mountain had rolled off his chest. On the way to the restaurant he said to himself, "To-morrow I must send thirty dollars to Marianna."

A CHAPTER BEGINS AS ANOTHER ENDS

In those days Auguste Rodin's studio was the Mecca for art students and lovers from all over the world. Gibran had seen in Paris many of the great master's creations such as *Hugo, The Thinker, The Kiss,* and others. He always marvelled at the grand sweep of the man's imagination and the passing ease with which his chisel and his brush made bronze and stone and canvas burst with power, poetry and the will of life to freedom. More than once he stood transported before his *Gates of Hell,* carefully noting each detail from Dante's figure at the top to the multitude of other faces and figures squirming in the eternal throes of hell.

Once, in company with some professors and students of the Beaux Arts, Gibran spent an hour in Rodin's studio which to him seemed like a minute. He was greatly impressed by the old sculptor's simple but dignified appearance and bearing, by his spontaneous and independent speech, and by the many statues, large and small, and drawings in black and white scattered all over the place. Particularly was he impressed by a sculpted hand of large proportions, with strong and well chiselled fingers drawn out and slightly bending towards the palm. So sensitive, so certain of their purpose appeared the joints and the knuckles of those fingers, so powerful and full of taste that one looking at them could easily picture them taking clay and molding of it men, beasts and all the forms of visible life. Gibran knew that Rodin called that hand The Hand of God, and he said to himself, "Is it really God that created Man, or is it the opposite? Imagination is the only creator; its nearest and clearest manifestation is Art. Yes, art is life, and life is art; all else is trite and empty in comparison. The beauty of art is the only beauty; the glory of art the only glory. Rodin's greatness is greatness, indeed. From St. Petersburg to Sydney, from Tokyo to New York, wherever art is spoken of, Rodin is spoken of. From the East and the West people come to be blessed with what life has blessed this man. That is greatness."

The students hurled many questions at Rodin which he answered simply and clearly expounding his philosophy of art and life. Now and then he would say a word, or strike a smile, which would flash through his hearers' minds like a shooting star in the darkness of night. One question led him to speak of William Blake, the strange English poet and artist (1757-1827). He told his visitors something of the man's life and how the muse of art and that of poetry had equally shared his talents making of him a distinguished poet in his art, and a distinguished artist in his poetry. He also told them how Blake saw visions uncommon to the earth, how he translated his visions, now with the brush, now with the pen, in shapes and words abounding with exquisite taste and beauty, but rarely understood by men which led many to think him mad. In truth Blake was not mad, but was a sane man in a company of madmen. What gave his writings that touch of obscurity and unreality was the fact that he tried to express in logic-bound human speech visions, emotions and glimpses which were entirely beyond logic; he treated words as he treated lines and colors. The consequence was that as he advanced in years, and as his visions and prophecies multiplied, his brush became keener, while his pen became more and more obscure. The drawings he made for the Book of Job are surpassing in their beauty of conception and execution; whereas his last writings are such a jumble of words that one attempting to read them may well be excused if he called their author mad.

Gibran left Rodin's studio with Blake uppermost in his mind and imagination. Straightway he went to an English second-hand book shop he knew, and there he found a copy of Blake's works with an extensive biographic study and many reproductions of his drawings. He paid for the book and could hardly wait to reach the gardens of the Luxembourg museum where he sat him on an isolated bench and began to devour the book as devours a hungry man a loaf of bread.

Two hours passed with Gibran oblivious of all things about him excepting William Blake. "How strange," he mused, "that fates should lead me to-day to Rodin who led me to Blake. Truly do they say that things do not happen except in their *due time*. There is a due time for everything. I always thought me a stranger in this world. Now comes Blake to keep me company. I thought me a lonely wanderer; now is Blake with his torch lighting my path. What kinship is there between me and that man? Has his soul come back to this earth to dwell in my body? How beautiful, how peaceful was his life. And his wife—what a wonderful life-companion she was, and how perfect was their mutual understanding. Would that I had that kind of a companion. Perhaps I have her and do not know. What of Mary? Yes, Mary, Mary. What if she be ten years my senior? What if there be no attraction between her body and mine as that which exists between my body and Micheline's? It is enough that our souls feel that attraction. Yes, I should marry her, and the two of us should live a clean married life. I shall be happy when men shall say about me what they said of Blake: 'He is a madman.' Madness in art is creation. Madness in poetry is wisdom. Madness in the search for God is the highest form of worship."

Night was advancing on Paris which fought it with electric shafts when Gibran returned to his room with the volume of Blake in one hand and a paper sack in the other wherein lay side by side a loaf of bread with some cold ham. He was surprised to find on the table a sealed, unstamped, envelope addressed to him, but in a hand quite unfamiliar to him. On opening it he found it to be an Arabic letter from a young

Lebanese girl expressing admiration for his writings and gratitude for the stand he has taken in defense of the rights of "her oppressed sisters in the East". As she chanced to be in Paris, she could not resist the great urge of wanting to touch the hand that wrote those wonderful things. Would he be gracious enough to allot her a few moments of his precious time?

Gibran laid the letter down feeling that the vanguards of the greatness he dreamed of were already in sight. A soft, warm delight trickled into his heart from the simple, outspoken words of the letter. "Who may this young girl be?" he asked himself. "Is she beautiful? Is she rich? Is she an old love speaking to me in new terms? Is she a thread of my life tissue now being picked up by the Great Weaver's shuttle? I am already a torch lighting the paths of people far away. I must see to it that my light be pure. I must be as people picture me to be—clean, upright, transparent, charitable, fair to the oppressed, hard on their oppressors, patient in pain, strong and above all lowly passions. Save me, Lord, from myself. Cleanse me of all my impurities. Forge me in the forge of Your Right."

Like a flash passed through his mind his mother's words, "God save us from the hour of temptation." That very instant he heard a knock on the door. It was the janitor who came to tell him that a lady, who declined to give her name, came to see him in the afternoon, but not finding him at home, promised to come in the evening. After the janitor was gone Gibran scolded himself for failing to ask him of the lady's appearance. Perhaps she was the very one that wrote him the letter. Presently he sat him at the table, opened the volume of Blake and began to read, then reached for the bottle of *vin blanc* and poured a glass, and for the bread and ham and began to eat, thus feasting his soul and stomach at the same time.

Hardly had Gibran swallowed the last mouthful of his supper when he heard a second knock. He jumped to the door, opened it in haste, and his hand froze on the knob as he became like one transfixed. Regaining finally his breath and presence, he shouted at the top of his voice, "Micheline!" and with a burning passion drew the lady at the door to himself burying his face in the folds of her dress between her breasts. She entwined her arms about his neck and laid her head upon his shoulder. Both were so overcome with emotion that for a long space Gibran heard nothing but Micheline's heartbeats and her soft murmurings, "Kahlil, Kahlil", while she felt nothing but his quick, burning breath, and heard nothing but the syllables of her name lightly floating upon that flaming breath, "Micheline, Micheline!"

"You have ordered me, and I obeyed. You called me from across the ocean, and I responded to the call. You see, Kahlil, that you are still my lord and master."

"Not I, Micheline, but Love. It is Love who is lord and master of us all, we are but obedient servants. Whoever disobeys Love, disobeys God. For Love is the only God. Let me now bathe my soul in your sparkling eyes. Let me sip truth from your divine lips. Let me touch life in your exquisite hands. Let me hear my heart beat in your heart. Let me inhale your intoxicating breath.

"Until to-day whenever Happiness knocked at my door, I would say to myself, 'This is but her shadow'; and whenever I heard her footfalls in my house, I would say, 'this is but one of her ladies-in-waiting.' But to-day—Ah, to-day Happiness is fluttering and singing in my heart. To-day she descended on me with the rays of the sun, and entered my room with the morning breeze. To-day she bore me in a palanquin of light. To-day I can swear truthfully that I am the happiest man in the world. Micheline, Micheline! Is this a dream or a reality? This day I came upon a soul who is sister to my soul, and shall be a sister to your soul also. It is a strange and wondrous soul—a unique soul—the soul of a poet and an artist who died ninety years ago and whose name was William Blake. I shall read you his life,

Micheline, and you shall see how beautiful it was; and you shall also see at once that Life has chosen you to be to Kahlil the wonderful companion Catherine was to Blake. I shall show you some of his drawings and read you some of his poetry, and you shall love him as I have come to love him.

"Micheline, Micheline! How generous is God. How beautiful is Life. This is indeed a perfect day such as the fates seldom bestow on mortals. Come beautiful Micheline, tell me of everything—when did you leave Boston? When did you arrive in Paris? When did you decide on coming, and why did you not let me know in time, you naughty, naughty one. This room shall be our home. Though small, it shall be large enough for both of us. Love's dwelling is always as spacious as the universe. Where is your luggage?"

"In the hotel."

"What hotel? Let us go at once and fetch it."

"That is not so necessary now."

"What do you mean? To be in Paris and to have a lodging other than Kahlil's?"

"Let your heart be the lodging for my heart, and I care not where I sleep, and what I eat and wear."

"Wherever my heart is there yours is also. My food and drink shall be your food and drink; my mattress and cover shall be your mattress and cover."

"Ah, Kahlil, Kahlil! I'm willing to be the mat under your feet and the dust on your sandals. I'm happy to be your servant —to wash your clothes, to sweep and dust your room, to cook your meals, to prepare your coffee, but not to be your . . ."

"My what?"

"Your mis . . . your mistress."

"That is sacrilege, Micheline; sacrilege against both Life and Love. What God hath joined together let no man set asunder. And God is Love. It is Love that binds and unbinds. It is Love that tied our souls and bodies from eternity. It is Love that said to us, 'Be!' and we have come to be. Nor men, nor devils can ever tear apart two hearts bound fast the one to the other by the magic thread of Love. Nor priests, nor ministers, nor judges can ever hold together by any laws and incantations two hearts that Love has not chosen to bind in one. Mistress? Many a mistress is nobler in the eyes of Life than thousands of wives whose ties to their mates have been sanctified by the laws of the earth but condemned by the laws of heaven. Love is absolute. It is a law unto itself.

"Everything in the earth lives by the law of its own nature; and from the nature of that law derives the joy and the glory of freedom. Excepting men. For they have bound their divine souls with man-made laws. Their bodies they have subjected to stupid, rigid regulations; their instincts and emotions they have pressed into stifling prison cells; their minds and hearts they have embalmed in silly traditions and buried in dark, damp vaults. Whenever is found a man who dares to flaunt their laws and their conventions, they instantly brand him as a rebel deserving of exile, or as a criminal whose life should be forfeited. I am a rebel, Micheline, and shall remain a rebel to the end of my life. And how shall I not rebel against men who have dragged down God from His throne to place the priest thereon? How shall I obey their laws which would subjugate even Life and Love to the pleasures of the belly and the whims of social decorum? I am a poet and an artist, Micheline, and poetry and art would quickly perish with consumption unless left to roam at will unlimited fields and horizons. Besides—and you know that, Micheline—I'm studying in Paris with the help of some friends and relatives. Should they know that I have taken to myself a wife with the consent and sanction of the state and church—as if God's consent alone were not sufficient—they would surely stop their help."

"Say rather, should *she* know."

"Naughty, Micheline. Don't interrupt me."

"Should your relatives and friends, as you say, know that you live with a woman who is not your wife, would they not cut off their help?"

"That we can keep secret. We are in one continent, they, in another."

"And Life in which you trust, and which, as you say, has eyes and ears that see everything and hear everything—is it also in one continent, and we in another? And your Jesus who said, 'There is nothing hid that shall not be known and come abroad' —is he also in one continent, and we in another? And your new soul-mate William Blake, who was a great poet and a great artist, yet was a good and faithful husband—is he also in one continent, and we in another? It is, rather, Micheline and Kahlil who are in two different continents. You were born for poetry and art which, according to you, are from Heaven. While I, as you once said, am earthy, of the earth. Once I believed in my simple heart that even the earth which brings forth the life-giving corn, the pure lily and the beautiful rose, can also bring forth good art and poetry. How stupid, how idiotic, how blind I was!"

Micheline dashed for the door choking with tears, and descended the staircase in such a hurry that her feet barely touched the steps. Gibran, his face pale, his lips twitching, his eyes staring vacantly, his thoughts and feelings in a whirl, remained in his place. A chill went down his spine; his eyes brimmed with tears; his knees shook. He threw himself on his bed, pressed the pillow tight to his chest and gave vent to his tears. A voice within him would say, "It is the end; it is the end. You have slaughtered your love on the altar of your passions. Yours is a peculiar disease—the disease of words. You think it possible to cover up a weakness in you with sweet and colorful words. Beautiful words have never made ugliness beautiful, and bright colors can never paint weakness as strength. Your saying that Love is God does not make of the bodily passion a god, nor of animal pleasure a law of being." Another voice would reply,

"She will come back; she will come back. She has done that before and returned. She will return."

But Micheline never returned.

* * *

The morning of the following day Gibran received a letter telling of his father's death in Bisharri.

DELIRIUM

Man's life on earth is a constant delirium. Some are delirious of one thing; others, of another; but all are feverishly seeking something that eludes their search. Few only are endowed with that super-imagination which alone enables man to free himself from the grip of worldly delirium. Fewer still are they who having freed themselves can keep their freedom for life, as did Buddha and Jesus. In most cases that kind of freedom, whose other name is ecstasy, is as transient as a sweet dream. It usually visits the soul in those rare moments when the imagination shakes itself loose from the snares of beginnings and ends, of boundaries and barriers, of causes and effects, of good and evil and all the opposites, and roams unhampered in an infinity where the "I" and the "Not-I" are merged into one all-embracing, boundless Self.

From thought to thought, from pleasure to pain, from hunger to satiation, from lowliness to glory, from victory to defeat, from worry to worry—in such goblets men drown their days and nights, believing that they are quaffing the wine of Life, whereas they quaff but delusion. For delusion it is to split life in two halves, and to call one half honey, and the other gall; then to attempt to monopolize the honey and leave out the gall. Yet no one seems to ask, whose share shall be the gall.

Gibran stood alone at the prow of the ship bearing him from Europe to America. The wind played freely with his long hair and sprayed his face with fine ocean spray, while the sun, about to set, was busy painting such fantastic shapes and landscapes as no other brush could ever paint save that of the sun. Taking the wide horizon for an easel, the sky for a canvas, the evening clouds for a palet and its own glow for paint, the sun wrought miracles with breath-taking dexterity and amazing virtuosity: golden prairies where pastured droves of creatures unfamiliar to the earth; snow-capped mountains bearing lakes of fire; domed temples from among whose columns issued wisps of incense smoke and light; caverns teeming with pigmies and nimrods; nymphs dancing in forests of coral; old men and women wailing in cemeteries; dragons with jaws wide open and whales with their tails in the air; thrones with no kings on them; chariots drawn by winged steeds with no charioteers—such was the profusion of things painted in an instant by the sun, and in an instant changed into other things, yet always retaining their freshness and fascination to the eye.

Gibran's eyes were fixed on the distant horizon, but did not see the marvelous work of the sun. He saw instead the slides projected through the lantern of the memory with a speed far surpassing that of the sun. Joys and sorrows of the past, preoccupations of the present, plans and worries for the future crowded his heart and mind. Some traces of the past he wished he could efface, such as his relation with that Lebanese young woman who wrote him in Paris expressing her high admiration for his work and the warm desire to meet him. Some secrets of the future he longed to have revealed to him that very moment; foremost among them was the question of earning a decent living for himself and his sister without compromising his pen and brush, and without any subsidies from any one—even Mary.

He knew that many in America lived by the products of their brush. But he also knew that the brush in the hand of most of them was a lowly maid to the dollar in their neighbor's pocket. Those that did not prostitute their art had fame to bring them money. But Fame is a harlot. To cater to her is to be below her. To shun her is to drive her into another's arms. Can he win her good disposition without humbling at her feet his pride and his art?

And the pen—could he live from the slit of his pen? To be sure, his Arabic writings have attracted wide attention through the Arabic-speaking world, and have elicited favorable comments from a leading magazine which was the first to call them "poetry in prose". But the Arabic-speaking world is a small and a poor world. It pays only those who fill its belly, cover its nudity, and trade in its self-respect. As to those who press their hearts and souls into wine, it turns its back on them unless they offer it their wine in goblets of their own skulls. And even then it pays them no more than words of empty praise, as if praise alone were food sufficient for the writer's bone and flesh and blood.

Here he is after three years of Paris with visits to Rome, Brussels, London and their rich museums, his heart about to burst with emotions which he could well present to men in garments of glowing beauty; his mind and imagination a virgin land touched by the magic wand of Spring and ready to break into grasses, blossoms, leaves and fruits of wondrous colors, shapes, fragrance and taste. How shall he pour his heart in prose and verse when his mind is far astray in the desert of existence, seeking the coy Penny and not finding it? How shall he exploit the fertile soil of his imagination in pictures and poems so long as the landlord does not accept poetry for rent, and the baker, the butcher, the cobbler, the barber, and the light and traction companies refuse to be paid in drawings? Shall the need of the penny stifle his imperious need for self-expression?

There is Marianna with her needle and thread; she is hardly earning her own bare necessities. How long shall he suffer himself to depend on her for his bread and butter? She is now twenty-six years of age, and should have been married but for her great devotion and attachment to him. Shall he mortgage her life and future to the future of his pen and brush so shrouded as yet in mist? What a great shame that men have turned the scales of human values upside down. Some pugilists they would shower with gold and precious stones, while a man of inspiration is left to slay his inspiration with a butcher's knife, or to cremate it in a baker's oven, or to hang it on the hinge of a door because unable to pay the rent for that door! Did men but know the value of inspiration, they should say to all the inspired ones, "Take no care as to what you shall eat and drink, wherewith you shall be clothed, and wherein you shall live. Give us of your inspiration, and all that shall be freely offered to you."

But men do not know the value of inspiration and the inspired ones. How care-free he was in that respect during the years he spent in Paris. The seventy-five dollars he received monthly from Mary more than covered his needs; he was even able to send Marianna some of them. But now, with his studies in Paris over, that help shall surely stop. Ahead of him were days and years of incessant struggle before he can make his mark in the world of art in a land so broad and so hurried as America. Where, then, is the way out?

What of Mary? She loves him dearly, values his talents, understands his ambitions and aspirations and looks condoningly on his weaknesses and sins. She is unlike all women, having not the slightest touch of their jealousy or of their passions for men. One would say she was not fashioned of man's rib, but of his gentleness without his severity, and of woman's purity without her weakness. He loves her, but with a love quite different from his love for Micheline. How he wished he did not taste of any woman's love before he met Mary. He would have reciprocated her pure love with an equally pure love. Would it not be possible for him, even now, to devote himself wholly to his pen and brush under Mary's warm wings and the loving guidance of her clear mind and tender heart? Why not, when his need is so keen for a companion to brighten up his loneliness and to lift the nightmare of day-to-day necessities off his imagination?

And Mary is a careful manager; with her the penny goes as far as the dollar with some careless housewives. She has her school which is a good source of income. Why not tie his life to hers and take her as his legal wife? Let her keep her school until such time as he shall be able to provide for his needs and hers, and let him devote himself to art and literature. For that he had better move to New York where the field is much larger than in Boston. Yes, let things be arranged that way. That is final.

Scarcely had Gibran reached that point in his musings and calculations when he began to feel as one in delirium, or as one who had taken a large dose of a strong narcotic. He rubbed his eyes and shook his head violently as one waking from a nightmare. Before him stretched the great expanse of water like an infinite blue sheet whose ends were tied to shores unseen, with myriads of gay nymphs playing beneath it hide-and-seek, now raising this point of it, now lowering that. He saw the wet cloud-hems set on fire as they touched the hems of the setting sun. He felt as if the wind dishevelling his hair and gliding up and down his face were the breath of all time—past, present, and to come. With an abandon he bared his chest to that wind, and greedily inhaling large draughts of it, he said at each draught,

"You are that same spirit of God which moved upon the face of the waters when the earth was without form and void, and darkness was upon the face of the deep. You are the breath of the heavens and the earth since heavens and earth were established. Ah, fill me up; fill up my chest; fill up my mind and heart with a loving sense of kinship between me and all things visible and invisible. Are they not all in me, and I in them?"

His imagination bit the bridle, as it were, and dashing right and left, up and down, fraternized with everything it came in contact with. Where comes the light in his eyes?—From the sun. Therefore is the sun in him, and he in the sun. Wherewith does he quench his thirst?—With water drawn by the clouds from the sea. Therefore is he one with the cloud and the sea. And his food, and raiment, are they not the gifts of the earth? Can he, then, say, "I and the Earth"? Is he not one with the Earth?

He felt as if a veil had slipped off his inner eye, and he beheld himself as a center from which radiated an infinite number of lines connecting his heart and mind with every heart and mind in the boundless universe. And he marvelled at himself, how a few moments before, he allowed the cares of day-to-day existence to gnaw his heart, to cloud his mind, and to hobble his imagination, those same heart, mind and imagination which are now dancing with the nymphs below the magic, blue sheet; or skipping lightly over the hills and dales of the ocean; or ascending the ladders of mystic light suspended from the clouds to the surface of the water! All Time has been pressed into the everlasting Now, and all Space into the ever-present Here. All things move in a circle where beginnings and ends are indistinguishable. There is no beginning and no end to anything. And there is no beginning and no end to the man standing at the prow of that ship—to Kahlil Gibran. Nor is there a dividing line between him and anyone, or anything; nor a trace of enmity between him and the least or the most significant in the world. On the contrary, all things in the wide world seem to call to him, "You are our beloved son."

The gong sounded the call to dinner. Gibran started like one walking alone in a beautiful garden and suddenly hearing a peal of thunder out of a clear sky. The far horizon had already shed the gorgeous twilight robes, and night had begun to tune the star-pegged strings of its harp on which it was making ready to play its eternal melodies of life and death.

Slowly and reluctantly Gibran moved toward the dining salon; and as slowly and reluctantly moved his thoughts to the tavern of humdrum life there to sip sweet hope and bitter care from the selfsame cup.

MAN PROPOSES

Before she knew Gibran Mary Haskell had but one vineyard
—her School; to it she gave the best in her heart and mind. But
after she came to know Gibran, and especially after she sent
him at her own expense to Paris, she found herself with two
vineyards—her school and Gibran; and the second vineyard
was more to her mind and heart than the first. For a school,
no matter how varied its aspects and cares, remains a school
with fixed courses and routine which seldom change from year
to year: classes, lessons, textbooks, monthly tests, final examina-
tions, commencements, certificates, etc. Generations come and
go, the last pressing the first out. Year in and year out the work
is practically the same. Whereas the vineyard which was Gibran
seemed to teem with promises and surprises which followed no
set course or program. Every time she talked to him and scru-
tinized his face and movements she felt her soul caressed by
tender breezes coming from far away, and her imagination
carried as on wings to magic worlds. His loneliness, his material straits, his rich talents, his inordinate ambitions drove her
heart to him and made it a great pleasure for her to give him
freely of her soul and substance. Was it love? Was it admiration? Was it charity on her part—she never stopped to analyze.
Of one thing, however, was she certain—the absence of any trace
of physical passion in her feelings for Gibran. Until his return
from Paris she never felt herself physically drawn to any man.
She did not know whether to view that as a lack in her feminin-
ity, or as an addition to her virtue; as a blessing, or as a curse.

One thing troubled Mary in her relations with Gibran. Not only was he oversensitive about his personality, but he was also oversuspicious to the extent that he would shut his heart to a sincere friend because of an innocent word which he might interpret as derogatory to his person, and open his heart to a bitter enemy because of a word of praise said, or reported to have been said, by that enemy. He loathed criticism of any kind as much as he delighted in praise from any source. Because of his love for praise and fear of criticism, and because he spoke, and wrote, and painted in metaphors, he drew from words and gestures many meanings where others would draw one; he read many lines where there was but one, and saw many colors where others saw one only.

But she was extremely simple, open and frank in everything —in thought, speech, manner, dress and all approaches to people and things. She would not hesitate to say the truth even when against herself. Her speech was direct and ungarnished with symbols and similes. She spoke her mind with ease and in full, never feigning or equivocating. After she discovered Gibran's failing for praise and his dislike of frankness that dares to contradict or to criticise she began to fear for her relations with him. A well-meant word, a friendly gesture might well put an end to their relations if misinterpreted by him as touching his personality the wrong way. To offer always to Gibran a silk-gloved hand so that he would find its touch soft and pleasant, and to speak to him in sugar-coated words so that he would find them sweet was to change her nature—a thing which she neither wished to do, nor could do if she wished.

Soon after his return from Paris Gibran paid a visit to Mary Haskell. She received him as a conqueror and kissed him with the kiss which in one of his articles he called "the Virgin Mary's kiss." Long did she listen to his narrative of things seen, heard and experienced during his stay abroad. The narrative centered, of course, about his own activities. He told of the great artists, of the men of letters and personalities in high positions whom he had met, of their flattering estimates of him and his own estimate of them; of the works he had finished and works left unfinished; of his Arabic writings and the wide attention they were drawing; of cities and museums he had visited, and of the exhibits in which he had participated. To the glowing side of his activities and relations he added more glow; the less brilliant he presented in words that gave them brilliancy. When his memory swerved to any event or circumstance which he wished to keep hidden from Mary's eye he either brushed it off with silence or quickly passed it up to another which would elicit Mary's approval and admiration.

From the moment Gibran began his narrative a certain word kept boring in his mind and maneuvering to slip to the tip of his tongue. Yet he stubbornly refused it a turn. "Be patient", he would admonish it. "Your turn is not yet. You are, perhaps, the biggest word of my life. I may live to bless you or to curse you. But the ear into which you shall fall shall surely receive you as thankfully and joyfully as the Hebrews of old received the life-giving manna. It is hungry for you without a doubt. Mary shall know how highly Gibran appreciates a good deed when inspired by love, and how highly he prices love which is not born of narrow selfishness. You are a big word that may change the whole course of my life. Be patient till I set for you a stage worthy of your greatness."

Gibran kept talking and watching for the appropriate moment until he reached a point requiring some silence and thought. Feeling that his interlocutor was deep in thought he suddenly put forth his hand, and grasping Mary's hand, he put it to his lips. Then shutting his eyes and speaking with the voice of an oracle, he said,

"Mary! Will you walk with me?"

Startled at the sudden change in Gibran's voice and manner, Mary asked somewhat automatically and without knowing why he put the strange question to her and why she was answering it,

"Where, Kahlil?"

"To where Life calls both of us."

"Do you mean marriage, Kahlil?"

"Yes. Will you walk the road with me to the end?"

With child-like simplicity and frankness entirely unarmed, and therefore able to disarm its opponent, Mary replied with another question, her voice and face still reflecting her bewilderment,

"But are you clean, Kahlil?"

Gibran understood at once what Mary meant by her question. She wished to know if he was free of ugly sexual diseases. But the question turned him at once from a gentle lamb to a wounded lion; from a Seraph chanting sweet hymns before the altar of Love to a rebellious Lucifer whose pride was humbled by God. His face became ashen, his lips began to twitch, his nerves were set on edge, his mind became muddled, his tongue tied. So infuriated was he that he wished his tongue were cut off before he put that question to Mary and before he heard her answer.

In putting that question Gibran had a subconscious wish which he dared not confess even to himself. It was that Mary should say or do something that would be justification for him to make "an orderly retreat", thus avoiding a marital venture dictated by his mind but not so cherished by his blood. In that way his accounts with Mary would be settled to his advantage. If she gave him of her money, he was willing to give her of his soul and to mortgage his life and happiness to her life and happiness. That, surely, would add to his moral stature in Mary's eyes. But he, in his wildest calculations, never expected such an answer from Mary. Although the answer was quite in keeping with his subconscious wish, yet was it a blow to his pride, to his estimation of himself and of Mary's love for him. That love he believed to be utterly self-effacing and willing to

go through fire and mire for the sake of the beloved. He furthermore believed that for him to hint to any woman of his desire
to take her for wife was sufficient to make that woman the happiest creature in the world. And here he is offering to Mary—
"the beloved of his soul"—to make her his life-companion, and
she, instead of melting in joy, confronts him with that chilling
question. Had another woman dared to ask him such a question
he should surely, despite his gentle manners, spit in her face or
knock the teeth out of her mouth. How can any woman dare—
and Mary of all women—to question his "cleanness"? What a
brazen effrontery! What a blow to his pride! What a dumb
calamity!

* * *

Gibran left Mary Haskell's apartment with night in his
heart and a volcano in his mind. If he reviewed his past, its
shadows passed before him gaunt and depressed. If he peered
into the future, he saw its landmarks grim and forlorn. What
took place between him and Mary that evening left him with
the feeling that he had fought the greatest battle of his life and
come out of it beaten and scarred. Over and over he would turn
in his mind their conversation, and each time he would chide
himself for a word said which should not have been said, or
one left unsaid which should have been said. What is to be
done? Should he suffer in silence Mary's slight to his person?
Should he not wound her as she wounded him? Should he break
his relations with her? But how shall he wound her without
wounding himself with the same thrust? How shall he break
away from her unless he breaks away from everything beautiful
in his past, transparent in his dreams and smiling in his future?
He has written to her and of her many lovely things which, if
he were to renounce to-day, would make of him a hypocrite,
and make of his heart a buffoon to his mind. In his article "Baby
Jesus and Baby Love" did he not address her thus:

"Of a certain night; nay, of a certain hour; nay of a certain instant, which stands apart from my life because the most beautiful in my life, the Spirit descended from the highest circle of light and looked at me out of your eyes, and spoke to me with your tongue. From that look and that word Love was born in my heart of which it became the master. . . . That great love enthroned in the manger hidden in my breast, . . . that babe reclining on the chest of my soul has turned all the sorrows in me into joys, and all despair into glory, and all loneliness into bliss. That king on the throne of my inner self has with his voice called back to life my dead days, and with his touch refilled with light my tear-dimmed eyes, while with his right hand he rescued my hopes from the deeps of hopelessness."

How shall he erase to-day what he had written yesterday? Should he not smother Mary's love as he had smothered that of Micheline and crawl back into his melancholy shell? Better, perhaps, to write Mary a long letter of complaint, yet in condescending tones. No. Better not to speak or write, but to keep silent. After a long struggle the council of silence gained the upper hand.

A few days later, his wound healed, his equipoise regained, Gibran was musing over the trifles of existence which swell up at times to the extent that both the inner and the outer eye, however turned, can see nothing but those trifles, as if they were of life its very core and essence and everything else but superfluities. Of such trifles is the invention of an excuse to be offered a landlord at the beginning of the month when he comes to collect the rent, and you—the tenant—have a purse at odds with all forms of acceptable currency. His musings were interrupted by the mailman who came to hand him a letter. At once he recognized the hand. The letter was from Mary and contained a check for $75.00. She spoke to him in the same old, loving vein as if nothing at all had happened to make her change her tone or to stop her monthly subsidy.

By the time Gibran came to the end of the message his emotions flowed in warm tears out of his eyes, and he felt his mind's horizons broaden again and brighten up. In his heart he blessed and glorified life, marvelling at its mystic paths and currents and at the ignorance of men who know nothing of those paths and currents, yet never tire of planning and charting, only to suffer bitter disappointment each time life swerves them from their charted path to sweep them in her broader and masterly laid course. Did he not lay for himself what he thought was a perfect plan for marriage? It was quite possible for Mary to say "yes" to his proposal, or to express her misgivings in a way that did not wound his egotism. Would not his life then have taken an altogether different course? Would he not have bound his life forever to the life of that one woman? But Mary with a simple question, quite innocently asked, changed the proposed course of her life and his. Was Mary free in doing what she did, or was she moved to do it by a force other than her consciousness? Is not the old saying true, "Man proposes, God disposes"?

* * *

A year after his return from Paris Gibran was on his way to New York. In his ears he carried Marianna's sobs; in his eyes, her tears; in his heart, the love and blessing of Mary; in his pocket, a small sum of her money; in his satchel, the manuscript of his Arabic novelette "Broken Wings" together with an English copy of Nietzsche's "Thus Spake Zarathustra."

PART II

Night

THE MOUSE LABORED AND BROUGHT
FORTH A MOUNTAIN

In the year 1626 after the birth of Him who said, "Freely ye have received, freely give" The Great Penny mounted his throne, and calling his counsellors together spoke unto them as follows:

"Ever since men put in my hands the reins of their affairs I have been working night and day to make them happy. One miracle after another have I wrought to lift them out of misery and to spare them pain.

"I heard men complain of the confusion of their tongues, and I invented for them a single tongue which is myself. I am the letter, the syllable and the word. Wherever two or more are gathered in my name they instantly arrive at common understanding even when none can speak a word of the other's tongue. That is my miracle number one.

"I found men torn among too many gods. So I created for them a single god who is myself. I am the weigher and the weight. I am the judgment and the judge. Men worship me with all their hearts, and minds and souls. Whereas their other gods they worship but with their lips. That is my miracle number two.

"I saw that men were feverishly seeking Happiness through innumerable avenues and doors, and I led them into the only avenue to Happiness which is myself, and to the only door which is also myself. I am the way and the goal. I am the entrance and the exit. That is my miracle number three.

"I dwelt in men's dwellings, and sat at men's boards. And I found that their princes would not cohabit with their shepherds; their ladies would not sit at board with their servants; their priests and ministers would not share the same cup with their harlots; and I heard them cry aloud for equality. Then I yoked them all with one yoke which is myself. I am the yoke, the plow and the plower. Under my yoke the prince walks side by side with the shepherd, the lady with the servant, the priest with the harlot. That is my miracle number four.

"I looked into the hearts of men and found them stocked with passions as is the heart of a pomegranate with seed; and I found that men had divided their passions into good and bad, giving the first a free play and setting sentinels over the second. Yet did their hearts, thus split in two, harass me with their cries for Freedom. To free men's hearts I set a value on each passion, that of the bad being twice as high as that of the good. By so upsetting men's values I freed their hearts of their hearts. That is my miracle number five.

"I walked through the earth and found that men had divided it by the foot-rule and yardstick, marking well their divisions and setting the sword a guardian over their boundary lines, so that a neighbor cannot cross his neighbor's boundary without fear of retribution. To give men the freedom of the earth which is their birthright I bridged all boundaries with myself, thus setting at naught their armies and their swords. I am the bridge and the crosser. I pass where the sword dares not shine, and cross where armies dare not tread. That is my miracle number six.

"But the miracle of miracles is that I mixed all men in one crucible making of them one race, one nation whereas before they were a multitude of races and nations. Yea, even more than that—I have made men of one flesh, one bone, and one blood by making one their food and drink, their raiment and their dwellings.

"I am the food and the drink. I am the raiment and the dwelling. As men imbibe water not knowing that they imbibe therewith all mineral, vegetable and animal substances over which it passed, so do they receive the penny and purchase therewith drink, food, clothing and dwelling not knowing what in truth they are drinking and eating, nor wherewithal they are clothing themselves, nor where they are dwelling. I give you of that an instance:

"Yesternight a certain woman sold the passions of her stray heart and the quiverings of her feverish blood for a sum of money. In men's vocabulary that woman is called a harlot, a social fault, a cesspool to be shunned by the clean and the pious. This very morning the woman went to church and bought with part of the money so earned some incense for the church, and donated a part to the priest. The incense was burnt by the priest as praise and prayer to his God; while with the donation he bought himself some meat. Do you suppose that the priest in burning that incense to his God burnt but some sap congealed from some fragrant tree? I say to you that he burnt the blood that oozed and congealed out of a harlot's heart. Or do you suppose that meat he bought and ate was but the flesh of some innocent animal? I say to you it was the harlot's flesh. And which is easier—to eat and drink with a harlot at the same board, or to eat her flesh and drink her blood and thus become one with her?

"And again:

"A robber, having heard that a certain old woman carried a goodly sum of money in a bag tied to her neck, broke into that woman's house and stabbing her with a dagger, carried the money bag away well soaked in her blood. That very night the robber gambled away part of the money. The man who won it bought with it a cloak from a merchant. The merchant paid the money as a tax into the treasury. The treasury paid it as salary to the judge. The judge condemned the robber to death. Do you suppose the judge is less answerable for the woman's blood than the robber? I say to you that he too, though unwittingly, became a robber. The robber spilled innocent blood. The judge drank it.

"So well have I mixed men in my crucible that they became one Man, although they know it not. Seven major miracles have I wrought for their happiness aside from minor ones; yet are they still deep in misery and pain, and their voices knock incessantly at my ears, 'Give us happiness!' To-day I have decided to gratify their wish by a new miracle.

"I have built for men many wonderful cities in the past. Now I propose to build for them a city that shall surpass in wonder and grandeur all cities built heretofore. I shall endow that city with ears capable of hearing every tongue, and with eyes that shall behold all shapes and races of men. Its bowels I shall make more spacious than the space. All lands shall carry to it their goods, and all seas shall bring her of their treasures, yet shall it not be filled. In it shall be a refuge for every one of men's passions. It shall have room for all men's fancies and ideas. Men's gods and satans shall walk in it side by side. Out of the fires of men's hells shall grow the trees of their Edens. The house of worship shall squat on the same plot with the tavern and the house of ill fame. The museum and the school shall be neighbors with the sweat-shop and the dungeon.

"I shall inject the inhabitants of that city with a new serum —the serum of perpetual motion. Their nights shall be as feverish with activity as their days. Thus shall they be distracted from meditating on the sources of their pains and sorrows. They shall be as obedient to me as my fingers, and as attached to me as my shadow. Their gods they shall denounce, but me they shall always honor and revere. Their very souls they shall offer me in sacrifice. The heavier I load them of myself, the louder they shall cry, 'Give us more.' So crowded and congested shall be the surface of the earth with their numbers that they shall be forced to bore tunnels in the bowels of the earth, and to rear high towers in the skies. I shall make their feet food for their heads, and their heads food for their feet. Thus shall they devour each other in utter ignorance of the fact that they are cannibals.

"Behold, my faithful counsellors! The plan is now laid bare before you, and you are called upon to execute it. The site I have chosen for that city is an isle in the New World encircled by two rivers and the sea. It is called Manhattan, and is to-day the property of a red tribe. Hasten to the spot at once and let the work commence without delay. But before you go hence let each re-affirm his allegiance to the throne. And I shall be with you to the end of time."

Hardly had the Penny concluded his discourse when a winged creature of exceeding beauty arose from among the company. About his neck was a chain of gold, and on his eyes a veil of gold. Proudly he walked towards the throne followed by his ten twins, chained and veiled like himself. Falling to their knees and touching the ground with their foreheads, they spoke in one voice as follows:

"We swear by the Great Penny's obverse and reverse that we shall obey him in everything he commands, without any equivocation or mental reservation."

To which the seated on the throne replied:

"You have spoken well, Imagination. Let the best of all your arts and crafts be amply represented in my city."

Then arose an old man, majestic with the weight of centuries and the wisdom of untold generations. About his neck was a chain of silver, and on his eyes a veil of silver. Behind him walked, two by two, his twenty-five twins, all chained and veiled with silver like himself. Move for move and word for word they did and said what those that went before them had done and said. To which the seated on the throne replied:

"You have spoken well, O Conscience. Let the new city bear ample evidence of your fingerprints."

Then arose the figure of a man in middle age with two large

spectacles on his eyes, and with his feet in chains of copper. He hopped on crutches towards the throne, and behind him hopped on their crutches, two by two, his forty-nine twins, all bespectacled and hobbled with chains of copper. Move for move and word for word, they did and said what those that preceded them had done and said. To which the seated on the throne replied:

"You have spoken well, O Reason. See to it that every door in my new city be adorned with such spectacles as those you and your children are adorned with."

Lastly hopped towards the throne a ball of flesh having the appearance of a porcupine; so many needles seemed to pierce it through and through. Word for word it repeated what those that preceded it had said. To which the seated on the throne replied:

"You have spoken well, O Heart. Be of good cheer; for in my new city you shall find many targets for each of your needles."

Thereupon the Great Penny looked to the prime minister at his right whose name was "Greed", and to the chancellor at his left whose name was "Cunning" and said to them:

"This is your day. Proceed at once to the New World where dwells the red tribe that owns the island of Manhattan and buy it at the cheapest price possible."

The Penny was about to adjourn the meeting and to disperse his counsellors when his eye, of a sudden, fell on an entirely naked maiden standing right before the throne. Beauteous beyond words, she turned in her hands a crystal sphere of dazzling transparency and brilliance. Utterly puzzled by the maid's appearance and dazed by her beauty and the brilliance of the sphere in her hands, he mumbled incoherently,

"Whence came you, maid?"

"I was here before you were."

"That is impossible. And who may you be?"

"I am Life."

"That also is impossible, for life has ever been in the hollow of my hand. And what may be the purpose of your coming here?"

"I heard you say that you were seeking Happiness, and I came to lead you to it."

"Of all impossible things that is the most impossible. For no one knows Happiness and the way thereto except me. I am the way and the guide. I am the entrance and the exit. And what is that sphere in your hand?"

"Happiness."

"How most ludicrous! Do you not know that we are to-day breaking the grounds for the new city which shall be the citadel of Happiness? Or are you jesting?"

"I speak in earnest."

"Your earnestness is so amusing, it makes me laugh. Yet the sphere in your hand is truly fascinating. Would you not sell it?"

"Happiness can neither be bought nor sold."

"That is insanity twice insane. In my kingdom everything is bought and sold. Granting, however, that happiness cannot be bought and sold, how, then, is one desiring it to obtain it?"

"Whoever receives me as I am receives the jewel in my hand. Freely I have received, freely do I give."

"What a shameless witch! How dare you stand before me with nothing to cover your shamelessness except your skin? Take this whore and cover up her nudity; then pour molten lead into her mouth, fetter her hands and feet with iron, and cast her into the seventh pit of Hell, and hand me the jewel in her hands."

The guards rushed at the maid, and snatching from her the brilliant sphere, handed it over to the one sitting on the throne. Barely had they thrown one of their garments over the maid when the Penny looked at the sphere in his hand, and, lo! It was a lump of black coal; and at the maiden, and she was a spotted snake; whereupon he shouted in glee:

"Did I not say she was a witch? Crush her skull, and let us be done with her. Go each about his business, and never put off till the morrow what you can accomplish to-day. Go in peace."

And it was as the Penny ordered. His aides bought the island at a price equivalent to $24.00 and started building their promised city. Until this day they dig foundations; they rear and demolish buildings. And in the ruins of buildings demolished, and within the walls of buildings reaching for the sky millions and millions of people look daily and in vain for a trace of the brilliant sphere.

In the fall of the year 1912 after the birth of Him who said, "The kingdom of God is within you," Gibran slipped into the great metropolis to join the millions of seekers after Happiness.

GRAVE-DIGGER

Number fifty-one West Tenth Street is an old brick, three-story building quite indistinguishable from a long line of closely packed buildings filling the block between Sixth and Fifth Avenues on the outskirts of Greenwich Village proper. In that building Gibran rented himself a small studio which served him at the same time as a bedroom, a reception room, a dining room and a kitchen. In that obscure and modest corner of the world he began to lay down the plans for the unfolding of his great talents. His first guide and biggest aid, as well as the most welcome companion of his solitude, was Friedrich Nietzsche. Never did he accompany him on any of his Zarathustrian excursions except he exclaimed from the depth of his soul:

"What a man! What a man! Alone he fought the whole world in the name of his Superman; and though the world forced him out of his reason in the end, yet did he whip it well. He died a superman among pigmies, a sane madman in the midst of a world too decorously insane to be mad. So must men live and die. What an imagination! With one leap it would reach the core of life, divest it of all excrescences, then burn those excrescences and fling their ashes into the eyes of those who brought them into being. So must all imaginations be. And what a pen! With one stroke it would create a new world, and with one stroke it would efface old ones, the while dripping beauty, charm and power. So must all pens be. And what a will! Harder than flint and sharper than steel. It was that will that gave birth to the Superman and charted the path thereto—a will that can truly say, 'There is no god but me. I am the creator and the creation. I am the goal and the way to the goal. I shall carry man beyond man, and I shall lift him above good and evil, and set him free of all creeds and judgments, of vice and virtue and all notions that hobble his feet in his effort to reach his greater self. Therefore do I smash all men's weights and measures for they are so many chains about their Will's neck. I give them instead The Superman. Whoever has such a will let him walk the earth and take account of no man or thing excepting his own self. Let all the weak of will and understanding step aside from his path, else let them be to him as ladders which he shall climb to himself. Should mankind be condemned to extinction in order to produce a single Superman, let mankind perish! So must be every will.' "

Every time Gibran thought of Nietzsche he compared him to the earth which, when shaken with inner fire, finds an outlet for her excessive fire through the crater of a volcano. What a volcano is Zarathustra, spouting in the same breath weal and woe, curses and benedictions! What a plunge it was for Nietzsche's imagination to make into the hoary past, there to stumble upon Zarathustra, to brush the dust of centuries off his features, and then to take him for a mouthpiece through which to speak to men his bold creed and stinging mockery. Not less than a prophet's tongue did Nietzsche choose to speak his mind, nor hands less worthy and less clean than those of a venerable master in which to put the fruits of his imagination.

There is Nietzsche's Zarathustra, thirty years of age, leaving his home "and the lake of his home" and going into the mountains, there to enjoy "his spirit and his solitude". Ten years after, he descends in to the world to reveal to men all the secrets of his heart. Before descending he looks at the rising sun and speaks to it as follows:

"Lo! I am weary of my wisdom, like the bee that hath gathered too much honey; and I need hands outstretched to take it."*

---

* Years later Gibran wrote an article in Arabic under the title "My Soul is weighted with its fruit". It opens with the sentence, "My soul is weighted with its fruit; are there none so hungry as to pluck, and eat, and be filled?"

Zarathustra then meets with an old man "who had left his holy cot to seek roots." The hermit recognizes him and asks him the reason for his returning to the world; to which Zarathustra replies that he loves men and is going back to them laden with precious gifts. The old man tries to persuade him that men do not value hermits' gifts; therefore he had given up his love for men and centered his affections in God alone. But Zarathustra would not be persuaded. When he is done with the hermit and once more alone, he says to his heart: "Could it be possible! This old saint in the forest hath not yet heard of it, that *God is dead!*"

When Zarathustra arrives in the first town nearest to the forest he finds a multitude of people gathered in the market-place to see the performance of a rope-dancer; and he speaks thus unto them:

"*I teach you the Superman.* Man is something that is to be surpassed. What have you done to surpass man?

"What is the ape to man? A laughing-stock, a thing of shame.

"Ye have made your way from the worm to man, and much within you is still worm. Once were you apes, and even yet man is more of an ape than any of the apes.**

"I conjure you, my brethren, *remain true to the earth,* and believe not those who speak to you of super-earthly hopes! Poisoners are they, whether they know it or not.

"Despisers of life are they, decaying ones and poisoned ones themselves, of whom the earth is weary: so away with them!

"Once blasphemy against God was the greatest blasphemy;

** At the end of an Arabic article entitled, "Sons of Gods and Nephews of Apes" Gibran says, "What see you, sons of apes? Have you taken one step forward ever since you issued from the crevices, of the earth? . . . Seventy thousand years ago I passed you by and found you writhing like worms in the dark corners of your caverns. And seven moments ago I looked out of my window and saw you crawling in your filthy alleys with chains of serfdom round your feet, and wings of death a-flutter over your heads."

but God died, and therewith also those blasphemers. To blaspheme the earth is now the most dreadful sin, and to rate the heart of the unknowable higher than the meaning of the earth!"

But the multitudes, craving to see the acrobat's performance more than to hear admonitions, meet Zarathustra's sermon with derision. They pin their eyes on the man walking the rope, paying no heed to Zarathustra and his Superman. The rope dancer falls to the ground badly injured and disfigured. The crowd disperse leaving Zarathustra alone with the dying man. When the man breathes his last Zarathustra puts the corpse on his shoulders and sets out on his way. He finally buries the dead man in the hollow of a tree and sleeps the night beside him "to protect him from the wolves." Thus buries Zarathustra the world—the world of juggleries and trinkets. When he awakens in the morning he feels a new light dawning in his heart. It was the light of conviction that henceforth he should not waste his wisdom on crowds and dead people, but should seek him a chosen company. The harvest was ripe, and he was in need of good harvesters:

"Companions the creator seeketh, not corpses—and not herds of believers either. Fellow-creators the creator seeketh—those who grave new values on new tables.

"Companions the creator seeketh, and such as know how to whet their sickles. Destroyers will they be called, and despisers of good and evil. But they are the reapers and rejoicers.

"Fellow-creators Zarathustra seeketh; fellow-reapers and fellow-rejoicers Zarathustra seeketh: what has he to do with herds and herdsmen and corpses!

"With the creators, the reapers, and the rejoicers will I associate: The rainbow will I show them, and all the stairs to the Superman.

"To the lone-dwellers will I sing my song, and to the twain-dwellers; and unto him who hath still ears for the unheard, will I make the heart heavy with my happiness."

Thus went Zarathustra preaching the Superman, his words now thunderbolts, now lightnings and rainbows. Should he speak of the simplest of things, such as the worth of reading and writing, he would upset the accepted values and contradict the common notions:

"Of all that is written, I love only what a person hath written with his blood. Write with blood, and thou wilt find that blood is spirit."

"It is no easy task to understand unfamiliar blood; I hate the reading idlers."

"Every one being allowed to learn to read, ruineth in the long run not only writing but also thinking."

"Once spirit was God, then it became man, and now it even becometh populace."

"He that writeth in blood and proverbs doth not want to be read, but learnt by heart."

"In the mountains the shortest way is from peak to peak, but for that route thou must have long legs. Proverbs should be peaks, and those spoken to should be big and tall."*

In his discourse on "The Bedwarfing Virtue" Zarathustra makes mock of men and their standards and creeds. Having returned to them after a long absence in his "Happy Isles", he finds them smaller than they were because of *their doctrine of happiness and virtue*:

"I pass through this people and let fall many words: but they know neither how to take nor how to retain them."

"And when I call out: 'Curse all the cowardly devils in you, that would fain whimper and fold the hands and adore'—then do they shout: 'Zarathustra is godless.' "

"And especially do their teachers of submission shout this; —but precisely in their ears do I love to cry: 'Yea! I *am* Zarathustra, the godless!' "

---

* Gibran opens his Arabic article "Giants" with the words, "He who writes with ink is not like him who writes with blood". His love of parables and proverbs is quite evident in his books.

"Those teachers of submission! Wherever there is aught puny, sickly, or scabby, there do they creep like lice; and only my disgust preventeth me from cracking them."

"Well! This is my sermon for *their ears*: I am Zarathustra the godless, who saith: 'Who is more godless than I, that I may enjoy his teaching?' "

"I am Zarathustra the godless! I cook every chance in *my* pot. And only when it hath been quite cooked do I welcome it as *my* food."

"Mine own forerunner am I among this people; mine own cockcrow in dark lanes."*

* * *

Nietzsche's brilliance eclipsed for Gibran almost all the great poets and writers he had known before. Not only did he find in him an inspiring companion, but rarely missed an occasion to recommend him to others as such, as can be seen from the following letter he wrote to Miss Adele Watson, a young neighborhood artist he met soon after he arrived in New York:

My Dear Miss Watson,

Yes, Nietzsche is a great giant—and the more you read him the more you will love him. He is perhaps the greatest spirit in modern times, and his work will outlive many of the things which we consider great. Please, p-l-e-a-s-e, read "Thus Spake Zarathustra" as soon as possible for it is—to me—one of the greatest works of all times.

Do come and see me sometime soon and let us have a talk on Nietzsche.

But Nietzsche, while brightening up Gibran's loneliness in some respects, made it more unendurable in others. He detached him from his past to the extent that everything he had done with brush and pen began to appear to him trite and wan. When he came to put the finishing touches to his "Broken Wings" before turning it over to the press he almost gave up the thought

* The opening sentence in Gibran's "Forerunner" is: "You are your own forerunner."

of having it published. He fancied that the great Nietzsche, if he were to read that work, would pat him on the back as a grown-up pats a little child, and say to him ironically:

"Sonny! Let those whose brains are of mucus and whose hearts are of dough pass their time in recording such tearful confessions. True manhood should not be made effeminate by a woman's love. True manhood should not allow the will of a mere bishop to rob it of its own will. True manhood, furthermore, should be ashamed to parade its failures before men, and to bewail their harsh iniquities. For men are harsh and iniquitous towards the weaklings only. And those whose will is still in the fluid state are generous with tears. Tears become women's eyes; but most unbecoming to a man is a wet eyelash. Be done with tears!"

But Gibran imagined, or liked to imagine, that the story was written with his heart's life-blood, since it was an account of his first romance while still in his teens and a student at *Al-Hikmat* school in Beirut. He packed it with tender sentimentality, sweet melodies and glowing colors of youthful heart-palpitations, together with brilliant sketches of Lebanon's beautiful nature in different poses and moods. To bury all that at Nietzsche's command would be like burying a living piece of his heart. Besides, his conquests in the domain of Arabic literature have not yet reached their limit. This novelette would represent a new conquest, since nothing like it had yet been published in Arabic. Though a trinket in Nietzsche's eyes, it would be a jewel in the eyes of the Arabic-speaking world. Furthermore, it shall be a fitting epilogue to the era of tears and plaints in Gibran's life. Thereafter he would regain his will, hold back his tears, and use his pen and brush as instruments for demolishing whatever had outlived its usefulness of old forms and conceptions to rear in their place newer and more useful ones.

The Broken Wings came out and was hailed as an event of importance by most of the Arabic press. It carried the following glowing dedication to Mary Elizabeth Haskell: "To her who stares at the sun with steady eyelids; who grasps fire with untrembling fingers; who hears the chant of the spirit universal from beyond the din and shouting of the blind—To M. E. H. I dedicate this book. Gibran."

Being yet babes in the art of story-writing, the Arab readers and reviewers were much impressed by the sparkling form at the expense of the substance. Gibran's vanity was quite flattered; but his sense of beauty and value, made riper and keener by his contact with Nietzsche, left his heart desolate. It grieved him to find himself still a stranger among his own people who were impressed more by his forms than by his substance. He longed for a soul of his own tongue and kindred capable of delving into his soul, of knowing its hopes and pitfalls, of taking with it flights into the vast realm of dreams devoid of ugliness and sorrow; a soul with whom he could speak freely and to his heart's content of Art and Nietzsche. It seemed to him that he was doomed to remain a stranger not only to his people, but to himself as well.

Soon after the appearance of *Broken Wings*, Nasseeb Arida, a deep poet and a devoted friend, asked Gibran the permission to publish the collection of his short prose pieces which appeared periodically in an Arabic journal in New York under the general title *A Tear and A Smile*. Gibran replied with a verse from one of his poems:

"Gone now is that era of my life—the era of erotic songs, sighs and plaints." Then by way of amplification, "The youth that wrote *A Tear and A Smile* has long since died and been buried in the valley of dreams. Why do you wish to exhume his remains? Do what you like, but forget not that the soul of that youth has been re-incarnated in a man whose love for will and power is equal to his love for good taste and beauty; who is bent on demolishing as much as on building. That man is at once the friend and the enemy of men."

That same man, however, was so carried away by Nietzsche

that for a long space his greatest pleasure was to mock men, to ridicule their laws and their gods, and to dig graves for them. He who but erstwhile spoke to the poor and the downtrodden in this wise, "Do not lose hope. For behind the clouds—beyond the ether—beyond all things, is a power which is all goodness, charity, affection, love"—that same man now began to speak to his fellowmen with a spade in his hand and with nothing better to offer them than the grave. He became a god unto himself, despising pity as a sign of weakness, and weakness as another name for death, and finding none worthy of life excepting men of his own likeness and image.

This new era in Gibran's life was opened up with a strong article which he entitled *The Grave-Digger*. Had he chosen to put at the end of that article Nietzsche's famous refrain "Thus Spake Zarathustra" the article could pass as a chapter in the German poet's book. In his wildest wanderings up and down the world Zarathustra rarely encounters a shadow so terrible and fantastic as the shadow encountered by Gibran in "The valley of the shade of Life, strewn with bones and skulls." That shadow is no other than the new Gibran "reincarnated in a man who loves will and power" and who makes fun of Gibran of the "erotic songs, sighs and plaints", counselling him to forsake the business of writing poetry because "it neither helps nor hurts," and to make grave-digging his business instead in order to relieve the living of "the corpses heaped about their dwellings, courts of justice, and houses of worship", for men are dead even since their birth, "but finding none to bury them, remain on the face of the earth stinking disintegration."

The Shadow discovers that his interlocutor's name is Abdullah, and that the name was given him by his father, and he says to him,

"The fathers' gifts are the children's bane; and save a man be rid of his fathers' and forefathers' gifts, he shall remain a slave to the dead until he joins the dead."

The Shadow further finds out that Abdullah is married and has three children, and he advises him to divorce his wife, for "marriage is man's slavery to custom." He also advises him to teach his children the business of digging graves, to give each of them a spade, and then to leave them to themselves. Should he, however, be unable to remain single, he should take him a jinnee maiden for wife. "Such a marriage leads by and by to the extinction of dead creatures who tremble in the face of the storm but dare not walk with it."

When the Shadow learns that Abdullah believes in God and honors His prophets, and that he likes virtue and has hope for the hereafter, he mocks him in these words:

"These are words created by the ages past and put between your lips by habit and inheritance. From the beginning man has worshipped naught but himself under many names and forms— now as Baal, now as Jupiter, and now as God."

Of himself the Shadow says that he is his own god; that he is omnipotent and omniscient; that his name is "The Mad God," and that he is not wise "because wisdom belongs to weaklings only." Finally the Shadow takes leave of Abdullah saying, "Farewell. I go to where ghouls and giants meet."

The article concludes with the following:

"On the day after I divorced my wife and married a jinnee maiden, I also gave each of my children a spade and admonished them, saying, 'Go! And wherever you find a dead man bury him at once.' And from that hour till now I have been busy digging graves and interring dead. But the dead are far too many; and I am alone with no one to lend a hand."

How shall he not be alone who sees all men as dead and himself as the only living one? How shall he not be alone who is so busy interring men to remain as the only living monument over their graves?

So drunk did Gibran become at that time with Zarathustra and with the wide fame he had gained in the Arabic world that he began to talk to his own people "as one having authority," and to feel no compunctions at calling them "rotten teeth", or in addressing them in this vein:

"I pitied your weakness heretofore, my mother's children. But pity is useless to life; it augments the numbers of the weak and the indolent. To-day I look at your weakness, and my soul shudders in scorn and disgust. What seek you of me, children of my mother? What seek you of life which no longer counts you among her children?

"I hate you, children of my mother, because you hate greatness and glory.

"I despise you, because you despise yourselves.

"I am your enemy, because you are the enemies of the gods, although you know it not."

Not only that. It became a source of shame for him to own as his birth-place an obscure village like Bisharri, and as his country, a small country like Lebanon. A man like him, he became convinced, must have a mystic birth in a mystic birth-place. And what land is more mystic than India? Therefore he told Nasseeb Arida when seeking of him some biographic data for his magazine *Al-Funoon* (The Arts) that he was born in Bombay, but did not wish the fact to be publicized. The magazine came out with the biographic sketch worded as follows:

"Gibran was born in the year 1883 in Bisharri, Lebanon (and some say in Bombay, India)," etc. The sketch was reprinted in toto in a collection of Gibran's published in Cairo in 1923, and never was an effort made on Gibran's part to deny it, or to correct it.

His war against conventions was a war for recognition. If men would only accept him as he accepted himself, he would willingly condone their frailties. The bitterness the fight engendered in his heart was the bitterness of the warrior unable to wring a word of praise or submission from his opponent. It was quite different from Nietzsche's bitterness.

THE SCATTERED ARE RE-GATHERED

Among my school-mates at the Russian Teachers' Institute in Nazareth, Palestine, were Nasseeb Arida and Abdul Masseeh Haddad, both of Homs, Syria. That was in the early part of the first decade of the present century. In 1906 I was sent on a scholarship to Russia and heard no more of the two mates than that both had emigrated to America and settled in New York City.

In 1911 New York City was my gateway to the New World. I stayed in it two days while on my way to the state of Washington. In those two days my path may have crossed that of Arida and Haddad more than once, but neither they recognized me, nor I them. Perhaps I brushed shoulders with Gibran without exchanging with him even as much as an inquisitive glance for neither of us was conscious of the other's existence.

In the fall of 1912 I entered the University of Washington and applied myself to my studies, feeling very much detached from the Arabic world and its current literature which up to that time was quite empty, apish, rhetorical and offensively redundant. One day I fell by chance upon an issue of an Arabic newspaper published in New York in which was a long article about Gibran's "Broken Wings". The article purported to be a critical review; but like all Arabic criticism in those days it had to be either a eulogy or a tirade. In this case it was such an effusive eulogy that if I were to believe it I should declare the book to be the greatest ever written by any man, and Gibran to be the master of all who ever wielded a pen. But I could not believe it because of its exuberant praise which defeated its own purpose, since it left the reader without any clear notion as to the structure and contents of the book and the qualities worthy of such a praise. Therefore I laid it aside, saying to myself, "Our friends are incorrigible. They still strike the same old anvil with the same old hammer in the same old manner. What have I to do with them?"

Months later the mail brought me another "chance" in the form of a number of an Arabic monthly published in New York. I could hardly believe my eyes. The magazine was brought out in excellent taste—good paper, beautiful type, clean printing, a diversity of materials, some original, some translated, but all readable from cover to cover, the poetry vibrating with life, the prose far from being anemic, and all interspersed with a number of reproductions from the works of some of the greatest masters of art. The name of the monthly was "Al-Funoon", meaning The Arts. The publisher and the editor was no other than Nasseeb Arida!

On the heels of that second "chance" came a third in the form of a copy of "Broken Wings" presented to me by a Lebanese immigrant who had bought it on the strength of the "review" I mentioned believing it to be an entertaining light novel of the kind usually sought by people of primitive taste; but finding it "all imagination," he gave it to me as if to make me share in his disappointment.

After reading the book I was prompted to write of it an article which I called "The Dawn of Hope." The article, which was my *debut* into the literary world, was sent to Al-Funoon and published immediately. In it I bewailed bitterly the stagnation prevailing for centuries in Arabic literature, chiding our poets and writers for wasting their time in word acrobatics and deadly imitation of the old classics without paying heed to the roaring currents of life within them and all about them. As to the book itself I found it deficient as a story, the characters stilted, the action scant and loosely knit together, the analysis superficial;

but as a piece of descriptive writing, so melodious, so suffused with delicate colors and hues, so rich in sentiment, so new in form and texture, it presented a daring and a most welcome innovation. The author I likened to an eagle not yet fully fledged; but I was certain that he will develop strong wings and pinions and ultimately soar high in our literary skies.

The article, as soon as received by Arida, was read by him to several men of letters including Gibran. He later wrote me of the effect it produced on them, particularly on Gibran, who exclaimed, "Where was this man hidden all this time?" and who went on plying Arida with questions about the unknown critic.

The war of 1914 broke out dislocating normal avenues of trade and postal communications. Because of that Al-Funoon was soon dashed on the rocks, its limited financial resources having been quickly exhausted. Its farewell contribution to Arabic letters was the bringing out in decent form of Gibran's collection of short prose pieces which had appeared sporadically in the Arabic press of New York under the general title of *A Tear and A Smile*. An effort was made in 1916 to revive the magazine, with Arida retaining the post of the editor-in-chief, and an enthusiastic friend taking charge of the management. Both men wrote me and feverishly urged me to come to New York and put my shoulder with theirs to the task of rolling the precious load uphill. I needed little urging, for my inclinations had always been towards pens, pencils, papers and inkpots. Having been already graduated from the university earlier in the summer I readily turned my face east, and in the fall of that year was one of the millions condemned to look for the needle of happiness in the mountains of steel, and stone, and brick, and pitch known as New York City. Soon, however, I discovered that the magazine, though much admired by intelligent readers, was unable to cover its expenses. For that reason I did not join its staff, yet decided to remain in New York.

The afternoon of the day I arrived in New York, while at Al-Funoon's office, I saw a young man walk in carrying a round-headed cane the upper part of which was inlaid with fine silver wire. He was pleasant of looks, below the average in stature, well-built, neither stout nor lean, dressed in a simple but neat grey suit, and wearing a black felt hat with a round, flat top. The moment I saw him I said, "This is Gibran." And the moment his eye fell on me he said, "This is Mikhail Naimy". We exchanged warm handshakes and hugs as if we were two brothers coming together after a long separation.

Two or three days later Arida, Haddad and I were invited by Gibran to spend the evening at his studio which was known to the small coterie of his Lebanese and Syrian friends as "The Hermitage" and which I was quite anxious to see. The studio was on the third floor of an old, brick building which gave me, as I entered it, the feeling of entering a monastery. My friends led me through dark passageways and up twisting staircases lighted dimly by a small gas jet, the light casting queer shadows on the walls which seemed to ask a thousand questions and to resent our disturbing their quiet. The old wooden steps squeaked under our feet as if groaning. At the top of the stairs, to the left, we halted before a grim wooden door with an iron knocker in the center. Immediately after we knocked the door flung open, and behind it was Gibran in his working "robe" of cream-colored linen reaching down to the knee and tied with a braided belt around the waist.

I sat down on an old settee, my two companions taking each a chair—the only two chairs in the studio; while Gibran arranged himself on the wooden platform in the center intended for seating models. In front of us, in the middle of the eastern wall, was a small fireplace accommodating a small wood or coal-burning stove for heating purposes. Above the fireplace was a gas jet which was our only source of light that evening.

The "hermitage" was a room of about nine yards in length

and six in width. To the left of the fireplace was an old sofa covered with a blanket and cluttered with cushions of various shapes and colors. That was Gibran's bed. By the bed was a small bed-table on which were books and papers. To the right of the fireplace stood the easel, and behind it a round table with books and writing materials. To my right was another round table, also covered with books, writing pads, pens, pencils and inkwells. Behind were large black folios for drawings.

At the middle of the north wall were bookshelves holding some two hundred volumes of different books. In the north, as in the south wall, were three high windows hung with heavy dark draperies. Similar draperies were drawn across a large skylight in the high ceiling overhead. On the west wall hung a large piece of ancient cloth representing the crucifixion. In the north corner of that wall was a small door leading to a narrow closet containing a small, very much neglected bath-tub, together with some kitchen utensils and shelves encumbered with dusty magazines and newspapers. That same closet served Gibran for a wardrobe also.

That was "the hermitage." It spoke more eloquently of Gibran's poverty and his magnificent struggle against it than of his love for austerity and self-denial. It also spoke more of the storms tossing his heart and mind than of his serenity and contentment in his poverty.

Throughout that evening Gibran was the embodiment of kindness and gentility and good humor. He prepared for us coffee and offered it in red Chinese bowls of teakwood together with cigarettes and some apples. The conversation was most warm and animated with Gibran always taking the lead. The four of us feeling actually like one, rambled light-heartedly from topic to topic, literature being the most inviting and the nearest to our hearts. When Russian literature was mentioned Gibran surprised me by expressing his unbounded admiration for three of the great Russian masters—Turgenev, Dostoyevsky and Tolstoy. Perhaps he wished to please me after he heard me place Russian literature in the vanguard, and Dostoyevsky above all writers of the modern age.

Little did I think as I left the modest studio that night that I shall re-enter it times without number during the following fifteen years; that I shall witness in it the birth of all the important products of Gibran's fertile pen and brush from that night until the night the swift wings of his imagination were folded and stilled by death; and that I shall live to remember it as remembers a seafarer a quiet isle that sheltered him for a space from the storms and turbulence of the sea. Nor did I think then that the joys and sorrows of the man who tenanted that lonely corner in West Tenth Street shall in time sink so deep into my depths as to become one with my own joys and sorrows.

IN THE DARK CAVERNS

In those days Gibran wrote a prose piece under the title of "The Imprisoned King" in which he addresses a lion in the Bronx Zoological Gardens as follows:

"Behold, mighty king, the crowds in front of your prison cell. . . . There is one who is as filthy as a pig, but his meat is not fit to eat. There is another who is tough as a buffalo, but his hide is useless. Yonder is a third more stupid than an ass, yet he walks on two feet. A little further is a fourth, black as a raven, but he crows in temples and exacts a price for his crowing. Beyond is a fifth strutting like a peacock, but her feathers are all borrowed ones.

"Look, imperious sultan, at those palaces and lofty towers. They are stifling nests inhabited by men and women who pride themselves on the decorative ceilings that shut away the skies from their eyes, and on the firmness of the walls that stand between them and the sun. They are dark caverns, those palaces and those towers, wherein withers the flower of youth, the ember of love turns to ashes, and the flow of dreams into columns of smoke. They are damp, dismal catacombs where the cradle and the death-bed, the nuptial couch and the coffin stand side by side.

"Cast an eye, majestic prince, on those broad streets and hemmed-in alleyways. These tortuous canyons are the haunts of thieves, bandits and highwaymen; they are the battlefields where all manner of purposes commingle in a fight of life and death, and where souls dash at souls, slashing, tearing, and devouring but without the help of the sword and the claw; they are the jungle of horrors inhabited by beasts tame of appearance, polished of horn, perfumed of tail, whose laws decree that the foxiest and the craftiest, and not the fittest, shall survive; whose traditions glorify not the noblest and the strongest, but the foremost in cheating and in lying. Their kings are not lions like you, but queer creatures endowed with eagle bills, hyena claws, scorpion stings, and throats that croak like frogs."

But the author of that diatribe worked night and day with his pen, brush and tongue, and worked most feverishly, in order to attract to himself the attention of those "queer creatures", and in order to make "those tortuous canyons" hear his footfalls when he walked in them, and force open the doors of those "stifling nests" when he knocked at them. Never did he make the acquaintance of a man, woman, or a family with some artistic, literary, financial, political, or social prestige except he spoke to me of it with apparent indifference but with much inward pride and satisfaction. To be constant in his professed contempt of worldly appearances and his joy at coming in contact with people "higher up", he would throw a mantle of "something spiritual" over all such connections. He would, for instance, say to me, "I had tea last night at Mrs. Corinne Robinson's." And after a pause, and with evident pride, "she is Teddy Roosevelt's sister." And after another pause, "She is a poetess, Mischa; and you would like her poetry." Likewise he would tell me of an evening spent at Mr. So and So's house who was the president of some important bank and "quite an art connoisseur"; or of a week-end invitation by such and such a family, "one of the oldest, richest, and most cultured families of America, and on intimate terms with the president."

Thus Gibran smote the world with one hand, only to pat it with the other. He rebelled against it when his soul writhed in pains at the sight of ghastly iniquity, wickedness and ugliness so abundant in the earth; but he stretched to it a friendly hand when his soul, so hungry for "greatness and glory" and so burdened with material want, rebelled against him.

Thus was Gibran divided against himself—the conformist against the non-conformist; the seeker after fame, wealth, greatness and glory, against the seeker after light, peace, love, and serenity in the denial of the self. So divided, Gibran groped his way in New York's "dark caverns". Each door he succeeded in opening led him to another door—from art circles to literary circles, to men and women of "importance", whose word had weight, whose voice carried far, whose sympathy and patronage had their value. Some of them wished to be drawn by his hand, or to buy some of his pictures. His charge for pencil portraits varied, as he once told me, from $50.00 to $200.00. No wonder he had to be "nice" to them and to accept their invitations, even when he knew that the host or hostess had no other purpose in inviting him but to diversify their guests by including among them a poet and an artist who had the touch of the mystic Orient about him. That is the least a seeker after fame and glory has to pay in a city like the Babel on the Hudson, and in a country so inflamed with human passions as America.

But Gibran, urged by the incessant calls for enfoldment of the twin sisters lovingly nursed by his soul—Poetry and Art— was far from being content with the small and slow conquests he was making in the world. To the American public he offered his art without his poetry. To the Arab public, his poetry without his art. The English-speaking world could not read his Arabic poetry; the Arabic-speaking world could not understand his western art. The twins must be made to work as one team. For that he must write in English. Has he not hoped all along to make his voice heard outside the Arab world? Did not Mary and most of his American friends share that hope? The English-speaking world is a world of culture, far-flung and rich, incomparably wider, richer and more advanced than the Arabic-speaking world. With the pressure of material need considerably eased by what he is able to earn with his brush, in addition to the monthly subsidy of $75.00 still coming from Mary, there was nothing to hinder him from "trying his luck" in English except the fear of not finding a willing publisher and a ready "market".

One day in the early part of 1918 I walked into Gibran's studio and was struck by the more than usual warmth of his reception. Hardly had we exchanged greetings when he presented to me the first issue of a new American magazine just published under the name of "The Seven Arts". The number was expensively brought out and quite elegant in appearance. Great was my surprise when I found out that Gibran was one of the publishers; and greater was my delight when, looking through the number, I fell upon some proverbs and a piece of poetry in prose by Kahlil Gibran.

I did not ask Gibran where he got the funds to go on such a venture; but I expressed to him my unstinted admiration for his English style which I found more colorful, more pliable and expressive than his style in Arabic. I said to him, "You little devil! How come you hid these jewels from me all this time? If you have more of them bring them out at once." Whereupon he brought one of his brown-covered writing tablets and read me several proverbs and prose poems all of which were later included in his first English book *The Madman*. When he reached the end of one entitled "God" wherein he says to God, "I am thy root in the earth and thou art my flower in the sky, and together we grow before the face of the sun" I asked him:

"What kind of god is this that *grows* with you before the face of the sun? Can God grow when everything that grows is doomed to dissolution? And how is God to grow *before the face of the sun?* Is the sun older and more eternal than He? Or do you mean that your concept of God grows as you grow?"

His reply was that he had recently formed an idea of God all his own, and that he shall expound it to me some other time. But that time never came; for Gibran re-discovered the God that neither grows nor ages, nor increases nor decreases, nor is subject to any change.

The Seven Arts was short-lived, suspending publication in a few months; yet was it of great service to Gibran in carrying his name to some literary circles, among them the Poetry Society which invited him to read some of his works. He read them his piece "Night and the Madman", but came out of the meeting boiling with anger and resentment, for the audience received him and his piece with a coldness that amounted to hissing mockery.

What did Gibran do? He neither despaired, nor relented, nor acknowledged his defeat. On the contrary; he resorted to his pen, his trustiest friend in moments of hardship, and wrote his famous piece "Defeat" in which he turned his defeat into a sharp sword wherewith to vanquish his defeaters:

"Defeat, my Defeat, my shining sword and shield,
In your eyes I have read
That to be enthroned is to be enslaved,
And to be understood is to be levelled down,
And to be grasped is but to reach one's fulness
And like a ripe fruit to fall and be consumed.
Defeat, my Defeat, my deathless courage,
You and I shall laugh together with the storm,
And together we shall dig graves for all that die in us,
And we shall stand in the sun with a will,
And we shall be dangerous."

It was a dose of opium Gibran administered to his wounded pride, to his heart ever-hungry for "greatness and glory," and to his mind ever impatient of men for no reason except that they were in his likeness and image. Had he believed everything he wrote and said, and had he acted as he believed, he should have long ago forsaken the society of men and any effort to speak to them either by words or by lines and colors; since to be understood by men was to displease himself, and to please himself was to be un-understood by men. Are not words, in such a case, an utter superfluity? Is not art a form of insanity? Did he not once write an article on "Speaking and Speakers" in which he said,

> "I am weary of speaking and speakers.
> My soul is overfed with speaking and speakers.
> My thought is lost between speaking and speakers.

". . . Now that I have bared my repulsion against speaking and my detestation of speakers I find me in the position of a physician who is sick, or of a criminal preaching righteousness to criminals. For I have berated words with words and attacked those that speak while one of them myself. Will God ever forgive my sin ere He transports me to the wilds of thought and sentiment where there are neither words nor speakers of words?"

Why, then, was he so feverishly knocking at the ear-drums of men to force on them a certain way of life which he had not yet succeeded in making his own? Why did not the physician heal himself?

But Gibran, though likening himself—on paper—to a criminal trying to correct criminals and to a sick physician attempting to heal the sick, did not, in fact, see in himself any fault or illness. Otherwise he should not have written that beautiful satire which he called "The Perfect World" and at whose end he shouted most sarcastically, "Why am I here, O God of lost souls, thou who are lost among the gods?" The clear tenor of the satire is that this "perfect world" is the most imperfect. The concluding cry should, therefore, be recast in this fashion: "Why am I—a man so perfect—cast into a world so horribly imperfect?" It is a cry hardly justifiable if uttered by an archangel condemned to live with archdemons.

Gibran imagined at that time that he was fighting a cruel enemy called The World. Had he been able then, as he was able later, to withdraw from the narrow circle of his ego and to watch the battle from a distance, he should have realized at once that it rolled between two opponents, both called Kahlil Gibran— Gibran of the "hermitage", and Gibran of the world. The first, looking at men's honors found them as dishonors; their riches he considered as penury, their virtue as slavery, their pleasures as nests of pain and ugliness. Therefore he mocked and chided them. The second craved the honors of the world and the pleasures and the riches thereof; therefore he approached it with a begging bowl. And since the mocker would not be a beggar, and the beggar dare not be a mocker, the war between Gibran in the "hermitage" and Gibran in the world was most inevitable. It was a war whose bitterness flowed in beautiful cascades from the lines of Gibran the poet, and whose pains wove charming veils over the living forms created by Gibran the artist.

Furthermore, had Gibran in those days examined well himself before a mirror, he would have seen that the robes he borrowed from Nietzsche were most unbecoming to him; for they were not cut for his stature since Nietzsche's temper, will and faith were not his temper, his will and his faith. The kinship he found between himself and the German iconoclast did not reach beyond the fact that both had inordinate imaginations which refused to be clothed in commonplace words and colors. Otherwise their worlds were far apart. But Nietzsche's first impact on Gibran was so strong that it carried him off his feet and almost uprooted him from his Oriental soil, leaving him much embittered against the world.

So went Gibran groping in the dark caverns of his soul believing them to be the caverns of the world. He sipped the bitterness dripping from his own heart believing it to be dripping from the bitter hearts of men. Had his soul then been flooded with light, it should not have groped in the dark. Where there is light, darkness can have no foothold. Had his heart been a-brim with sweetness, it should not have overflowed with bitterness. Has honey ever been extracted from gall? That bitterness so clouded his vision for a time that he called Life "a beautiful harlot" saying that those who could "see her filth would detest her beauty." He almost forgot all the things he held sacred in his early youth, particularly love—woman's love. He would now permit a woman to share his bed, but would allow her no share in his heart, mind and soul. He would not have his heart "surrender" to love, and his will to be swayed by a woman's will. "The Witch" of whom he writes in one of his Arabic articles was but a Lebanese lady in New York who had aroused his passions to the extent of self-effacement. Wishing to shake himself free of her grip he offers her peace on the following terms:

"Long have I hung unto the hems of your garments as hangs a babe unto his mother's hems. Oblivious of my dreams, unconscious of the shadows swarming round my head, my eyes glued upon the beauty of your countenance, I followed you like your shadow attracted by the magnet diffused through your body. . . .

"But wait a while, O charmer. . . . Behold, I have regained my strength. I have smashed the chains that ate into my feet. I have dashed to the ground the goblet from which I quaffed the poison once so delightful to my taste. What now do you wish that we do, and what road do you desire that we follow. . . . ?

"Would you be content with the love of a man who accepts love as a companion but declines to acknowledge him as a lord?

"Would a heart that loves, yet refuses to surrender; that cient unto you?
burns, yet would not be consumed—would such a heart be suffi-

"Here is my hand, then, shake it with your beautiful hand. Here is my mouth; kiss it a long, deep, speechless kiss."

* * *

From time to time Gibran's solitude was brightened up by the soft, quiet light issuing from Mary's loving heart. At times that light approached nearer and became warmer and more soothing when Mary came to New York, or when he visited her in Boston finding in her clean heart a welcome shelter for his troubled heart, and in her understanding soul a safe haven for his turbulent ambitions, his impatient dreams, and his rebellious thoughts.

From time to time a voice would strike his ear—a voice so distant, yet so near; it was the voice of that youth whose death he had announced a few years ago saying that he had buried him "in the valley of dreams." The truth, however, was that that youth had never died, but was wrapped in shrouds and prematurely laid in a coffin with his pulse still beating high. The shrouds he was wrapped in were no other than Nietzsche's flowing robes.

THE TWO VOICES

"Pull it out!"

"No. You pull it out!"

With such maneuvers were most of our encounters begun. The usual greetings over, each would ask the other of anything new he may have written whether of poetry or prose, going sometimes to the extent of searching each other's pockets in the hope of falling on some treasure-trove in the form of some literary flower just out of the bud.

On that day of May, 1918, I went to see Gibran, and from his insistence on hearing something new from me I felt most certain that he had something new to read to me. My feeling quickly proved to be correct. No sooner did we light each a cigarette and take a cup of wine than Gibran brought one of his brown-covered books, and before starting to read paved the way as follows:

"This will please you, Mischa. It is a poem in two voices. Don't you agree with me that more voices than one in the same poem helps to give it a wider swing and to hold the reader's attention much more closely?"

Then he began to read affecting a deep and a grave tone unnatural to his voice:

"Men do good only when compelled, while evil rules them even in the grave." And so down to the last verse of the long poem which was quite in conformity with the requirements of Arabic meter and rime.

I listened to Gibran as he read and tried to read him in what I heard:

There was that Gibran "reincarnated in the body of a man who loves determination and power" having a tournament with

145

Gibran the youth who "was buried in the valley of dreams" but who, to his burier's surprise, shed away his shrouds, rolled the stone that sealed his sepulchre, and rose from the dead with the light of a new truth in his eyes and the ember of an old faith in his heart.

The first approaches life through the narrow socket of the human eye reinforced with the telescope of reason. Therefore does life appear to him as so many disconnected, mutually self-excluding links such as good and evil, right and wrong, justice and injustice, freedom and slavery, love and hate, birth and death, and all the other opposites. He finds that men are in constant unrest and turmoil because they are ever trying to weld the disconnected, self-excluding links into one chain, yet never can succeed. And they can't succeed because they don't know how to measure and to weigh the different links. But he knows. Yet he is as stingy with his knowledge as he is generous with his sarcasm. He mocks men's good and evil, but refuses to reveal to them his own good and evil. He satirizes their gods and creeds without deigning to unveil his god and his creed. He pokes fun at their justice but would not give them an inkling into his own justice. He derides their kindness without enlightening them as to what true kindness is. Between salvos of scorching sarcasm and derision he would let fall a few precious jewels of his super-manic wisdom to show men how great an abyss stood between him and them. Of those "jewels" is his pronouncement of Right:

"Right is the property of Might. Strong souls are called to rule; weak ones, to submit."

And that of Love in which he seems to chide himself:

"Love is to be known by the soul, not the body; as wine is to be drunk for inspiration and not for inebriation.

"When Love is led to a couch of sensuality it commits suicide." And that of Knowledge:

"The best of knowledge is a dream which, once attained,

makes of the dreamer a laughing-stock for those immersed in sleep."

And that of Happiness:

"Happiness is but a vision to be sought. Once made corporeal, it becomes a wearisome thing."

And that of Death:

"Death in the earth is the end to the child of the earth. To the ethereal it is but the beginning and the victory."

In general, what does this man, so well initiated into the mysteries of souls and bodies, say to men? He says to them that the links of their lives could never be made homogeneous and forged into a perfect chain because they were not well-fashioned and correctly named. If men would stretch the link of Right and call it Might, then their right would be the right kind of Right. He does not say, however, by what trick or artifice shall Might and Impotence live at peace and go into the making of one chain without exposing the chain to the danger of rupture.

He tells men that the wine of Love should be drunk for inspiration and not for physical gratification; but he points no way of combining Love and Hate in the same chain without causing ominous friction and clanking.

He tells men that Death is annihilation to the earthy, but victory to the ethereal. How shall a finite creature of the earth be turned into an infinite ethereal being—the secret of that he does not reveal. He does not reveal it because he does not know it; and he does not know it because he thinks in terms of weights and measures, believing that men do not know Life because they do not know how to weigh and measure it. Did they but adopt his own weights and measures, they should find Life longer and heavier than they thought. He seems quite unaware of the fact that weights and measures, no matter how varied and accurate, can weigh and measure that only which has a beginning and an end, a weight and a dimension. But Life which has neither beginning nor end; which is nor long, nor wide, nor deep nor high, nor light, nor heavy—how shall you weigh it and wherewith shall you measure it?

Had Nietzsche sensed that truth, he would not have dissipated the immense powers of his marvelous imagination in a fruitless search for new standards, and in a mad fight against those who came to rid the world of the nightmare of finite standards, such as Jesus the crux of whose teaching was that Man and God were one, as the father and the son are one. If Man be as infinite as God, how shall you weigh and measure him?

To that extent was carried by Nietzsche the Gibran who was incarnated into a man of "determination and power."

On the other hand Gibran the youth who was prematurely interred in the "valley of dreams" and is now resuscitated takes the stage in the poem with the light heart of a man whose mind and imagination have broken free from the grip of the despotic senses and all the opposites they create. Life to him is a glorious harmony keyed to a rhythm away beyond that of good and evil and all the progeny of conflicting notions they trail in their wake. The Woods which he roams and of which he sings so ecstatically are not a symbol of Nature in the narrow sense of the word; rather do they symbolize Life universal and all-embracing. The reed flute which he is so fond of blowing is but the instrument through which the Cosmic Spirit communicates his breath to all the lesser spirits. That breath so exhaled over the universe is a symphony unmarred by the slightest dissonance.

A wolf devours a lamb, and men shudder and shout in utter resignation: "Such is the cruelty of Life. It makes of the weak a repast for the strong." But Life all-embracing neither shudders nor shouts; for it feeds itself with itself. Therefore it neither bemoans the lamb's death, nor makes merry at the festival of the wolf. It is alike to a banana tree whether its fruit is eaten by a man or a monkey, and to the oak whether a deer or a porcupine seek shelter in its shade, and whether an angel or a devil warm themselves over a fire built from its twigs. For the man and the monkey, the deer and the porcupine, the angel and the devil are all the children of the same Woods—of Life Universal—which has one purpose and one will in all. Whoever knows that purpose and that will submits to them, thus adopting them as his own. Whoever knows them not opposes them, and is crushed thereby. There are two kinds of submissiveness: that of the ignorant which is slavery, and that of the understanding which is freedom. Of the second kind is the submissiveness of the flute-player in the poem, so fond of his flute and so serene in his woods which lie beyond the bounds of good and evil. His favorite refrain is always the same: "Give me the flute and sing!" Should the first voice intone his belabored views of Right, Freedom, Happiness, Hope, Faith and kindred weighty values, the second would pipe up on the instant that his Woods are blissfully unconscious of such values because unconscious of their opposites. To him the voice of the flute, symbolizing perhaps the harmony of being, is the reality transcending all realities and alone destined to outlast even time itself.

Having passed in review those *processions* of human values as seen by rebellious but ignorant Reason, and by submissive but knowing imagination, it was natural for Gibran, at the end of the review, to indicate where his own sympathies lay. His concluding lines are quite significant in that respect:

"In the Woods only Life is Life.
  Had all days and nights been placed within my hand,
  I'd scatter them no where else save in the Woods."

It was clear that Gibran's heart and soul leaned toward the flute-player. Having begun his song in a major key, he concludes it in a decidedly minor one:

"But", says he in mournful resignation, "Life's purposes have blocked my way to many a wood.

"The Fates would not change their course.

"And men, the frail, too oft fall short of their aim."

The reading over, Gibran began to show me the drawings he had prepared for the poem. Those, to me, were much more impressive processions than the ones he had just paraded before me in glowing uniforms of verse and rime. For those uniforms, though brilliant in places, showed decided signs of great fatigue in the effort spent over making the meter and the rime subservient to the thought; while the drawings looked as though they had drawn themselves. It was evident that Gibran the artist had an eye more amenable to his imagination, and a hand more obedient to his eye than Gibran the poet; at least in Arabic. Moreover, Gibran the poet was very fond of the colors and the music of words; and both he used in abundance giving his poetry and prose the appearance of being over-decorative. Whereas as an artist he always sought simplicity of form and execution which gave his works that intriguing lightness and transparency. It was a classical simplicity which had a firm grasp of the basic fundamentals of art without being conscious of the fact; a simplicity that with a few lines would create many shapes. Far from being boundaries to the looker's imagination those lines were eyes and wings that carried the looker leagues and leagues beyond themselves.

The first drawing Gibran set before me on the easel represented a youth, naked, determined, well built, light of movement, firm of foot, marching forward with a reed flute in his right hand, his eyes fixed on something invisible in the far distance. Behind him was the ethereal form of a woman floating in space, her arms extended forward like two protective wings, her face suffused with something more than men are wont to call love, her eyes peering into the far horizon and beyond as if pointing the goal to the youth and as if saying to him, "March on. Be confident. I am with you." Behind the youth trooped crowds of people who appeared as pigmies in comparison.

That was The Dreamer who had realized in himself the

unity of being and, because of that, had tasted the joy of co-ordinating his individual will with the Will Universal, thus put-ting at naught the dreadful power of that misguided ego that would set him at war with the world. The ethereal shape behind him was his greater imagination—his only guide and pilot. The multitudes were the human herds usually drawn by the man of vision without being able to make his vision theirs.

I was impressed by the drawing but soon realized that it was much below Gibran's peak when those of Religion, of Jus-tice, of Freedom and others were set before me. The one of religion represented a sort of a tower whose top was composed of three heads: Ra, Zoroaster and Buddha. Over Buddha's head in the center was a sphere symbolizing eternity. About the middle of that human tower and over Buddha's chest was the Crucified Nazarene with his arms extended in both directions, the one touching Ra's shoulder, the other Zoroaster's. Below the Crucified's arms and down to the bottom of the tower were many human forms with a serpent twisted about the ankle of one of them. It was the serpent of fanaticism, of religious bigotry, of lowly passions aroused by silly notions of man's servitude to God, and of criminal trafficking for material gain carried on in the name of religion.

The drawing of Justice—human justice—showed a power-fully executed figure of a man, strong and muscular, holding in his left hand a pair of scales and gracefully bending over them, with his right hand in one of the cups making it almost touch the ground; while in the other cup, lifted in the air, was a small human figure bent upon itself. So do the strong of the world weigh out justice to the weak. Around the main figure with the scales was a stream of human forms representing men and women seeking justice only to find that uneven-handedness which the more powerful of the world always mete out to the less powerful. So simple, yet so expressive and so perfectly har-monious was the drawing in structure and conception that one could hardly change the slightest line or shade without damaging the beauty of the whole.

Perhaps the drawing on Freedom was the most impressive of the group. Simple and powerful at once, it evoked thoughts and sensations which haunted one long after one's eyes were lifted from it. You see in it a tall, young man, powerfully built and endowed with two strong wings. He stands with his feet apart, his muscles taut, his gaze fixed and determined, and his wings spread for flight. But he cannot lift himself from the ground. His effort is so intense and so exhausting that you take pity on him and would do your utmost to help him rise in the air. Quickly you realize, however, that all his efforts would be entirely in vain except he first cut the hawsers that tied him to the ground. And what are these hawsers? They are the lusts, the passions, the cravings that hold men in slavery to the earth. It was evident to me that the drawing was a kind of spiritual self-portrait, as it was clear that the following words in the poem were a kind of self-confession:

"The free in the earth build of their cravings prisons for themselves."

* * *

A few days later I bade Gibran and the rest of my friends in New York farewell, donned the uniform of a soldier and sailed with the American Expeditionary Force to France.

When I returned from the great world holocaust a year and two months later I found that Gibran had added to the library of Arabic poetry a new book called "Processions" which he brought out at his own expense in an elegant form; and that he had blazed his path into the world of English literature with a small book which he named "The Madman."

ARRABITAH

One of the "casualties" of the 1914-1918 war was *Al-Funoon*—the beautiful and fragrant journalistic lily planted by Nasseeb Arida, but loved and tended by Gibran and myself as affectionately as by its planter—perhaps more. It was to us and to a small coterie of belles-lettres devotees a silver-toned trumpet through which we liked to blow of our spirits. It was a clean hand into which we gladly put fragments of our hearts and minds to be offered to those who wished to commune with our hearts and minds. Its offices were a Mecca to us; there we gathered almost daily to exchange opinions on all manner of topics from the most sublime to the most ridiculous; there fraternized our joys and our sorrows.

Soon after I returned from France and was demobilized towards the middle of the summer of 1919 I went to the state of Washington to rest and to forget, if possible, the horrors of war and the sweet and the bitter of its experiences. Fearing that my absence will be extensive, Gibran wrote me a long letter in which plans were laid down for bringing *Al-Funoon* back to life. He urged me to return to New York soon and take charge of carrying out the plans, concluding his letter with the following words:

"In brief, the success of the plan depends upon your presence in New York. If it be a sacrifice on your part to return to New York, that sacrifice should be viewed in the light of laying what is dear at the feet of that which is dearer, and of offering the important on the altar of that which is more important. To me the dearest in your life is the realization of your dreams; and the most important is the exploitation of your talents. . . ."

I returned to New York, but *Al-Funoon* did not return to life. The plans laid down by Gibran and Arida looked well on paper, but were impossible of execution. For those whose hearts were full of literary dreams had empty purses; while those who had full purses, had no room in their hearts for literature. To raise the necessary funds one had either to beg or to steal.

Al-Funoon died; but there was *As-Sayeh*, meaning the Traveller—a semi-weekly established six years earlier by Abdul-Masseeh Haddad. To be sure, it was in substance and form not to be compared with *Al-Funoon*, but Abdul—as we called its owner and publisher—was so close to our hearts and souls. Before we realized it *As-Sayeh* became our new trumpet, and its offices our new Mecca. In those unpretentious offices on Washington Street (later moved to Fifth Avenue) we used to while away our spare time, now jesting, now philosophizing, but always mocking the old and hailing the new in literature. We were a small group of like-minded, like-hearted men, with varying aptitudes and talents, of course, but with artistic and literary tastes not far apart and with differences in age amounting to no more than 15 years. Some of us wrote much, some little, while some produced nothing at all. It was natural that within that small group should be a smaller yet group bound by closer spiritual ties than those that bound the group as a whole.

Of that group of ten was organized ARRABITAH. Below are the minutes, as recorded by my own hand, of the first two meetings which gave birth to the organization:

"On the evening of April 20, 1920, at an entertainment given by the publisher of *As-Sayeh* and his brothers at their home, the discussion arose as to what the Syrian writers in New York could do to lift Arabic literature from the quagmire of stagnation and imitation, and to infuse a new life into its veins so as to make of it an active force in the building up of the Arab nations. It was suggested that an organization be created to band the writers together and to unify their efforts in the service of the Arabic language and its literature. The suggestion was met with warm approval by all the poets and the writers present; viz., Gibran K. Gibran, Nasseeb Arida, William Catzeflis, Rasheed Ayoub, Abdul-Masseeh Haddad, Nadra Haddad, Mikhail Naimy. The time not permitting to work out details and by-laws, Gibran invited the company to spend the evening of April 28 at his studio."

"The meeting of April 28, 1920 at Gibran's studio. Present at the meeting were the following: A. Haddad, N. Haddad, Elias Atallah, W. Catzeflis, N. Arida, R. Ayoub, G. K. Gibran and M. Naimy. After a thorough discussion the following points were unanimously agreed upon:

1. The organization to be called in Arabic AR-RABITATUL QALAMYIAT (meaning the Pen-Bond), and in English, ARRABITAH.

2. It is to have three officers: A president who shall be called "Chieftain", a secretary who shall be called "Counsellor" and a treasurer.

3. The members shall be of three categories: Active, who shall be known as "Workers", supporters who shall be known as "Partisans", and correspondents.

4. Arrabitah to publish the works of its own members and other Arab writers it may consider worthy, as well as to encourage the translation of world literature masterpieces.

5. Arrabitah to foster new talent by offering prizes for the best in poetry and prose.

The worker Mikhail Naimy was charged with the final drafting of the by-laws. The present then unanimously elected G. K. Gibran for Chieftain, Mikhail Naimy for Counsellor, and William Catzeflis for Treasurer. . . ."

I drafted the by-laws with a preamble from which I quote the following extracts showing the aims and tendencies of the new organization:

". . . Not everything that parades as literature is literature;

nor is every rimester a poet. The literature we esteem as worthy of the name is that only which draws its nourishment from Life's soil and light and air. . . . And the man of letters is he who is endowed with more than the average mortal's share of sensitiveness and taste, and the power of estimation and penetration together with the talent of expressing clearly and beautifully whatever imprints Life's constant waves leave upon his soul. . . .

"This new movement aiming to transport our literature from stagnation to life, from imitation to creation, is worthy of all encouragement. It is the hope of To-day which shall be the foundation of To-morrow. On the other hand, the tendency to keep our language and literature within the narrow bounds of aping the ancients in form and in substance is a most pernicious tendency; if left unopposed it will soon lead to decay and disintegration.

"Yet do we not aim to break away completely from the ancients. For there be some among them who will remain to us and to those who follow a source of inspiration for many ages to come. To revere them is a great honor. To imitate them is a deadly shame. For our life, our needs, our circumstances are far different from theirs. We must be true to ourselves if we would be true to our ancestors. . . ."

Gibran drew a beautiful emblem for *Arrabitah* representing a circle with an open book in the middle of it and with this quotation from *Hadith* * written across the open pages: "How wonderful the treasures beneath God's throne which only poets' tongues can unlock!" From behind the book can be seen part of the disc of the rising sun filling the upper part of the circle with effulgent light. At the lower end of the book is an elongated earthen vessel whose one end is an inkwell with a pen dipped into it making the ink issue as light from the other end. Below the circle is the name of Arrabitah written by Gibran in original

---

* *Al-Hadith* is a compendium of the sayings of the prophet Mohammed, as distinguished from *Al-Koran* which is supposed to be the word of God Himself.

Arabic characters. Beneath that is the name in English followed by the address which was Gibran's address.

With that was concluded all the preliminary work necessary for the launching of the new organization. So far only, and no farther, did Arrabitah resemble a regularly constituted society. In all other respects it was a self-created team, conscious of its work irrespective of forms and formulae. Rather was it an *esprit de corps* to which we gave a name. It was work that counted; and that went on spurred by the frequent spontaneous meetings and the lively heat and enthusiasm they generated.

Soon after *Arrabitah* was launched, with active membership limited to ten only, its members' literary contributions began to appear in *As-Sayeh* with the name of each always followed by the words "a worker in Arrabitah". At the beginning of each year *As-Sayeh* would issue a large special number to which each member was honor-bound to contribute something original. All would take an active part in the selection of paper, cover and illustrations for that number, even to deciding on the page-setting and the format. The appearance of any special number was an event anxiously awaited and widely commented on in the Arabic literary world. Much of the material was reprinted by the press both in the old world and wherever Arabic-speaking colonies were found in the new. Much of it went into new anthologies and school-books. Thus the name of *Arrabitah* spread wide and far becoming tantamount to renaissance, to rejuvenation in the minds of the younger generations, and to iconoclasm and hot-headed rebellion in the eyes of older and more conservative ones. The lines of battle were clearly drawn; the issue was never in doubt. So quickly was the tide turned in favor of *Arrabitah* that those who hailed it were no less puzzled than those who opposed it. They did not know how to explain its breathtaking success. Some would see the secret in the influence of American literature upon its members, which was wide off the mark. Others would insist on finding it in the American "atmosphere", which is yet wider off the mark. Others still would ascribe it to the great distance separating Arrabitah members from their native lands which permitted them to be more liberal in the strict rules of Arabic prosody and grammar and syntax— an explanation which is wider still off the mark than the previous two. The truth is that no one knows the "secret" save that hidden power which brought the members of Arrabitah together at a certain spot, in a certain time, and for a certain purpose entirely irrespective of their conscious planning, endowing each with a flame that may be more, or less brilliant than that of another, but all coming from the selfsame fireplace.

Once a certain Arab journalist in New York, his heart eaten with envy, began to publish ugly things against Arrabitah and Gibran in particular. In his attacks he included as a member of Arrabitah a man who was not a member. Chancing to meet that journalist I told him that the man he named was not one of Arrabitah. Thinking that that would amuse Gibran, I told him of my accidental encounter with that journalist and what I had said to him. To my great surprise Gibran looked at me with flaming eyes, and with lips twitching and dripping poison, said to me:

"Had I met that man, Mischa, I would have acted quite differently."

"What would you have done?" said I.

"I would have spit in his face and then wrung his neck. A dog like him deserves nothing but the stick."

Knowing Gibran's temper and his great zeal for Arrabitah and his deep concern for his own reputation, I quite condoned such an outburst of rage on his part. But I thank God that he never went so far as to wring that poor journalist's or anyone's neck, and that Arrabitah in its turn broke no necks except the neck of that idol which most of the Arab readers of those days worshipped under the name of Literature.

TEMPESTS

When Gibran's book "Tempests" came out in 1920 I wrote an extensive article in which I studied the author's literary personality, his bitterness of soul at that time and the melancholy permeating that bitterness. The article was in my pocket when I stopped to see Gibran on my way to *As-Sayeh*. As usual, he asked me if I had anything new to read him, to which I replied:

"I have something which I cannot read you unless you can hear it as if you were not Gibran Kahlil Gibran."

"You ask me a most difficult thing, Mischa," said he smilingly. "Is it something about Gibran Kahlil Gibran?"

"About his Tempests."

"Allright, Mischa," said he half in jest and half in earnest, "I shall try to do now what I have been trying all my life to do; namely, to forget myself. I'm afraid of you, Mischa. You have an eye that sees into my depths, and a pen that can easily tear the curtains which I draw between me and the ignorant and blind. Read on."

I began to read with Gibran listening most attentively. The article commenced with a brief prelude in which occurred the following passage: "Some day the affluent of us and the indigent, the mighty and the impotent, the overfed and the famished, the noble and the ignoble shall sink into oblivion with their petty politics, their petty joys and sorrows. Time is sure to wreck whatever towers we have builded, political, economical and the like. The beautiful only, the true and the eternal in us shall remain. Who is there to tell of the beautiful, the true and the eternal in us except the artist, the poet and the writer?"

Then I ask of the artists, poets and writers who shall inscribe the name of the present generation in the scrolls of Time, who they are and where they are. I do not find them among the many "nightingales of the Nile and the warblers of Syria and Lebanon", but among the few "whose lips and hearts have been touched by a new fire. Of those some are still within the womb of Creative Silence; some are breathing the air we breathe, and treading the ground we tread. Of the latter—nay, leading the latter—is the poet of Night and Solitude, the poet of Loneliness and Melancholy, the poet of Longing and Spiritual Awakening, the poet of the Sea and the Tempest—Gibran Kahlil Gibran."

At that point I heard what sounded like sobbing. Lifting my eyes from the paper in my hand, I saw tears trickling down Gibran's cheeks. He was crying like a babe. I quickly folded the article and put it back into my pocket. My amazement at watching Gibran weep was so great, I could not utter a word. Finally he wiped his eyes and said, the salt of tears still diffused through his voice:

"Forgive me, Mischa. Forgive me, my beloved brother, and don't ask me to explain my tears. Tears can never be expressed in words. They flow when words are of no avail. But you can understand my tears because you, too, are lonely; you, too, are companionless; you, too, are burning with the same fire I am burning with. You must, then, know the joy of encountering a soul capable of understanding your soul. How difficult it is to live with men and be compelled to talk to them in their own language which, to them, is the only language. When you talk to them in your own language, they stare at you, not understanding a single syllable. What can you do then but keep your peace, or else play the school teacher by teaching others the ABC of your language? How great, therefore, is your delight when you come upon one who knows your language as you know it. We understand each other, Mischa. Read on, please."

I excused myself from reading further and said:

"Is it right, Gibran, to blame men before blaming ourselves? Are we not of them? Is it fair to demand of them what you do not demand of yourself? You would have men understand you. Perhaps they don't understand you because you don't understand yourself. Are you sure you understand yourself?"

"No, I am not sure, Mischa; yet do I speak as one sure."

"Perhaps, that is the vacuum whence issue the storms that sweep your loneliness; the bitterness that drips from your pen, and that rebellion which you are proud to take for a bow and shield. How often we rebel against others not knowing that, in truth, we are rebelling against our ignorant selves. How often we are whipped by storms which sweep away the clouds from our spiritual horizons, yet believe those storms to be coming from outside of us to cloud our spiritual horizons. Do you not see with me that that which we reveal with our pens is but the foam on the surface of our lives, while our silent depths are actually beyond the reach of our pens?"

"That is true, Mischa. There are times when I look upon everything I have written as upon so much effort wasted. But I feel that there is a word on my lips which I have not yet uttered; and I shall have no rest till I utter it. Perhaps I am attempting the impossible when I attempt to pour the quintessence of my life into a word, or a book. Yet I feel that someday I shall dip my pen to the very bottom of my silent depths, and shall make it speak a part—if not all—of the things that live in my depths. What else can I do? I am like a pregnant woman who must be delivered of the burden within her, whatever it may be. I know that bitterness is not a beautiful thing. But I shall remain bitter so long as there is the taste of bitterness in my mouth."

"You shall remain bitter, Gibran, so long as you are a wheel turning to the right among many wheels all turning to the left, as you say in your story 'The Tempest'. But I notice that you have already begun to change your course. For at the end of that story, having poured out all your bitterness against the ways of men and their civilization, you stop to reason with yourself in this fashion: 'Aye, to be spiritually awakened is the only aim worthy of man. Is not this civilization, with all the ugly things encrusted thereon, a stepping-stone to that awakening? How can we question the reason for anything existing when its very existence is a sufficient reason for its right to exist? The present civilization may not be more than a passing symptom. But the eternal law has made of symptoms ladders to truth absolute.' In that you seem to offer men an olive twig, whereas you offered them before but the sword; you seem to be willing to turn with them to the left, whereas before you stubbornly refused to turn in any direction but right."

"Look at the stars, Mischa. Each has its orbit, yet all turn round larger and larger suns forming a single, perfect universe. We all turn in our orbits, but always within the infinite orbit which is Life."

"How arbitrary, then, of us, Gibran, to move in our orbits while denying the others the right to move in theirs. Is not any man's motion a part of your motion and mine?"

"Very true, Mischa. It is stupid of us to see our road as the only straight road. When our road is straight, then every other road is straight; for all roads lead to one. But youth must have its way. It is more impetuous than wise, and quicker to rebel than to judge fairly. Until to-day I have been more impetuous and rebellious than wise and fair. What about a glass of whisky with some soda? I bought a case yesterday from a smuggler for $35.00—cheap in comparison; but like all the present day whisky it is a diabolic concoction whose component parts are known to those only who concocted it. Curse with me the Pharisees who are always concerned about the outside of the cup. This is a land of hypocrites and Pharisees. They have prohibited intoxicants in the belief that God will not admit into His heaven anyone not cut after their pattern—clean on the outside, but full of impurities within. Their prohibition turned out to be a marvelous net for hauling tremendous profits."

He poured two glasses of whisky. Unable to drink mine because of its unpleasant taste, I laid it aside and said,

"I am surprised, Gibran, that you are able to drink such whisky; it is poisonous."

"Not so bad as all that, Mischa. Besides, it is better than none at all. Such is the will of the holy servants of God."

"Enough of whisky and the holy servants of God. Tell me, how far are you now in the 'Forerunner'? Have you added to it any new material?"

"I haven't added anything to what I showed you before. The book is now in the publisher's hands, and will soon be out. You still find it inferior to the 'Madman'?"

"The 'Madman' is delightful in its bitter sarcasm, while the 'Forerunner' is neither bitter to the end, nor sweet to the end. What of the new book to which the 'Forerunner' is but a pathblazer?"

"I am working on the first piece of it, but shall not read it to you until it is finished. That book, Mischa, fills now all my soul. I eat and drink with it, and sleep and rise with it."

The following day Gibran left for Boston. Having there read my article in *As-Sayeh* of his "Tempests," he wrote me saying,

"I have just read your article about the 'Tempests.' What shall I say to you, Mikhail?

"You have put between your eye and the pages of my book a magnifying glass which made them appear much more important than they really are. That made me ashamed of myself. You have laid a great responsibility upon my shoulders. Will I be able to live up to it? Will I justify the basic idea in the views you express of me? It strikes me that you wrote that precious article with your eye on my future, not on my past. For my past has been so many threads, but not a cloth; so many stones of various shapes and sizes, but not an edifice. I picture you looking at me with the eye of hope, and not of criticism; which makes me regret much in my past and, at the same time, dream of the future with a new enthusiasm. If that be your purpose in writing that article, you have achieved it, Mikhail."

Gibran was right in saying that I looked more to his future than to his past. For I had begun to feel from my many talks with him that he was on the verge of a new dawn. The violent storms which Nietzsche had unleashed in his soul, and which almost uprooted him from his eastern soil and left him suspended between earth and sky, were beginning to subside. Slowly his old faith in the wisdom and justice of Life and his resignation to her eternal will were returning to him, imbued with a new meaning and new force. Besides, the millstone of poverty which he carried about his neck ever since he lost his brother, mother and sister—that stone was slowly being transformed into a chain of gold. Gibran could now sleep without thinking of the morrow with its incessant calls for mere necessities. On the contrary, he was now able to put away some money in savings accounts. The $75.00 from Mary Haskell continued to come monthly and regularly. The gaslight in the studio gave way to electricity; the wood-stove to a gas-stove; the telephone being the last touch of new material comforts.

As to the "glory and greatness" which his soul coveted since early boyhood, Gibran began to taste them from the lips of people who read his books or admired his works of art. No longer was it becoming of him to accept praise from people's lips and, then to cauterize those lips with the fire of sarcasm. He did his utmost now with tongue, pen and brush to justify people's estimates and expectations of him, and even to surpass them. The more he succeeded in that direction, the keener became the struggle between his outer and his inner selves—the self he exposed to people, and the self he jealously guarded from all eyes except the ever vigilant eye of his own spirit.

FALSE ALARM

One spring morning of 1921 I awakened from sleep quite perturbed by a dream whose details stood fresh and vivid before my eyes. In vain I tried to chase them away; they clung with tenacity. I saw me standing on the edge of a round, deep well in which there was no trace of water, or even moisture. On the bottom of the well stood a dead tree with a slender trunk and a few branches entirely denuded of leaves and fruit. Beneath the tree lay a man on his right side, his elbow dug in the ground, and his head resting on his hand. Slowly and laboriously the man arose, rubbed his eyes, and like one in a trance, began to scan the tree and the smooth walls of the well as if trying to find a way of escape. His sallow, pain-veiled face was spotted with black, green and yellow. I pictured him as one fighting his last battle with death. So forlorn, so utterly despairing he looked to me that I shouted at the top of my voice, "Gibran!" My own voice and the picture I saw so frightened me that I awoke with my heart beating loud in my ears.

I could hardly wait to see Gibran that day in the hope that my waking eye will give the lie to my eye asleep, and that Gibran's radiant countenance would efface from my memory the picture of his face as seen in my dream. Without saying a word of the dream I began to inquire about his health. He must have noticed my unprecedented concern about his physical well-being, and the anxiety that betrayed itself in my voice; for he said,

"You surprise me, Mischa, with your anxious questions about my health as if you sensed the disorders I have begun to feel of late in my body and of which I have not yet spoken a word to anyone. I always thought me a man of iron; but this marvelous machine we call the body is subject to many disorders like any other machine made of so many parts. Its disorders may be but some of those parts. Of late I began to feel heart palpitations the like of which I never experienced before. The palpitations are so severe at times that I almost choke and am hardly able to climb the stairs to my studio."

"Have you consulted a physician about that, Gibran?"

"I have little faith in medicine and medical men. To them the body is but a collection of so many parts or organs; they would treat this part or that not knowing that the illness of any part is the illness of the whole, and that its cause may not be always in the physical but oftentimes is to be sought in that which is non-physical. How can you treat with drugs what is beyond all drugs? Nevertheless, I shall consult a physician. Perhaps he knows my body and its ills much better than I."

"You overwork your heart, Gibran; therefore the palpitations. Treat it fairly if you would have it treat you fairly. You drain it pitilessly with your pen and brush. You pry out all its secrets to lay them bare before men. You steal each beat of it to make of it a note in a song, or a line in a picture. Night and day you stalk your heart, now goading, now eavesdropping. Furthermore, you overwork it with the excessive quantities you consume of coffee, tobacco and alcohol. Slack up a little."

"Haven't you noticed that I gave up coffee almost entirely? Smoking I shall reduce. As to alcoholic drinks, I think they are bracing and beneficial to the heart. But the illness is much deeper than that, Mischa. You have touched some of the causes. What is there to do? Shall I give up my brush and my pen which are the two main pillars in my life? Shall I, wilfully and consciously work for the miscarriage of the 'Prophet' which is yet an embryo in my soul, and the best my soul ever conceived? I shall go on with it till I finish it, even if it finishes me forthwith.

But tell me, Mischa; what makes you speak so much to-day of my health? Have you noticed anything unusual in my face?"

I told him that I had dreamt a disquieting dream, but gave him no details; which led us to talk on dreams in general. He believed that in sleep many memories and pictures pass in review before the soul's eye. Some may be racial memories such as flying which takes man back to the time when he lived a bird's life before he became a man. Others may be shadows of suppressed desires. Others still may be pictures of things and events already fixed and recorded in Time where the future and the past always meet in the eternal present; or a confused mixture of the things past, present and to come. In most cases dreams come clothed in symbols which need explaining. Rarely are they exact pictures of things and events, as when we dream of a person or a place, then pass by that very place and person a day or more afterward.

I recounted to Gibran a long dream I once had in Russia. It was still as vivid in my memory in all details as if I had seen it but a moment before. I explained the symbolic significance of each detail as I was given to understand it, saying that the dream as a whole was but a chart of my life in its broader aspects rather than in small particulars. Said Gibran:

"I, too, remember very clearly a dream I had many years ago. The mere thought of it makes me shudder even now. I saw me sitting on a great rock in the midst of a wide, foaming, turbulent river both banks of which were devoid of any signs of life. Although I knew I could not swim, I had no fear of the river; rather was I thankful that the foaming waves were powerless to do me any harm. In my heart I wondered how I reached the rock and how I shall swim back to the bank. As I mused on that problem, my eye caught sight of a huge snake crawling out of the river and up the rock on which I sat. The very sight of it made me tremble. I tried to kick it back into the river, to choke it with my hand, but all to no avail. It kept creeping higher and higher winding itself all the while about my body until my ribs were almost crushed, and my breath was about to desert me. Mustering the last ounce of energy, I shouted for help, and forthwith awoke, my heart beating furiously against my sides, and drops of cold perspiration on my forehead."

"What is your explanation of that dream, Gibran?"

"Explain it as you like. To me it is a chart of my life, as yours was a chart of your life."

Little attention did I pay to Gibran's dream at the time, and I doubt if it crossed my memory even once afterwards during his life. But since he died I hardly think of him and the meanings of his many-sided life without thinking at the same time of that startling dream. The foaming, turbulent river now seems to me to symbolize the world with its sham honors and glories; its parades and masquerades; its passions and ambitions; its pleasures and pains, ever tossing, churning, raging and dashing headlong. The rock in the river is the Truth of Being, firm and unshaken in the midst of rushing worldly passions. Gibran had reached that rock with his powerful imagination and made of it a refuge for his soul. The great serpent coming out of the river is the failing he always had for a substantial share of the world's pleasures and "greatness and glory". It was that failing that muddled his serenity of spirit, disturbed his ecstasy of imagination, and strangled his greatest hope— the hope of conforming his life to his convictions, and of making peace between his inner and outer selves.

The summer of that year, towards the end of June, Gibran, Arida, A. Haddad and myself decided to spend a short vacation in the country. Upon Arida's recommendation we chose a hamlet called Cahoonzie, situated some hundred miles from New York. The hamlet nestled in a small pocket of a large forest extending for miles and miles, and rich in lakes and running streams. We put up at a large, two-story farmhouse, located on the top of a most pleasant hill. In that solitude so saturated with peace, so fragrant with silence, so bubbling with beauty we spent ten days which passed like ten minutes. We were like four birds escaped from their cages; or like four schoolboys relieved of the necessity of going to school and of enduring the threats and the orders of their teachers and parents. We always walked together, ate together, went to sleep and rose from sleep at the same time; so much so that the people of the hamlet and the other vacationists in it nicknamed us "The Big Four"—a title which was current yet in the press and on many tongues and which was given to the main authors of the Versailles treaty: Wilson, Lloyd George, Clemenceau and Orlando, the resemblance between us and them going no further than the number.

Arida, having discovered that lovely spot years before, was our guide on all our jaunts. One day he proposed to take us on an "expedition" to a waterfall several miles distant from the hamlet. No quicker did we reach it than it made us forget all the hardships of the road, whether of heat or of aching feet. We found ourselves at the bottom of a valley so thickly shaded by trees on all sides that even the sun could hardly peep into it. Hermit-like, it chanted its prayers night and day, knowing no rest or sleep. There was the roar of thunder in those prayers, the deep-throated majesty of solitude, and the awesome grandeur of speaking face to face with the Eternal.

We approached the bottom of the waterfall as closely as it allowed us to approach it, and there we stood for many minutes charmed and transported. Like ground diamond, the thick spray danced in the air alight with all the hues of the rainbow. The enormous volume of water, rushing from a great height, tumbled into a large pool, churned about, and then flowed in our direction, foaming, singing, joyful at the prospect of ultimately joining its mother—the sea. Our voices attempting to give vent to the feeling of wonder that possessed us were swallowed up in the roar of the tumbling waters. Trees on both sides swayed back and forth, now lowering, now raising their heads; while the grasses among them were in a constant tremble.

At last we began to look for some place to sit down. In the middle of the stream, not very far from the churning pool, we saw a rock whose top was flat and dry. It was the ideal place, as though specially prepared for men like ourselves so hungry for an hour of abandon in the company of singing waters and in a spot so charmingly solitary as that spot. To reach the rock from the bank was impossible; so we began to throw stones into the foaming water, thus making the jump to the rock possible.

We arranged ourselves on that rock with our faces towards the waterfall. And even though not one of us had a voice for singing, we all began at once to sing. We should have felt ashamed of allowing our rickety voices to rise at the same time and in the same chorus with the voice of the waterfall; but the waterfall itself was to blame. Had it not been for its rich, deep tones none of us would have dared to lift his voice in song. We sang old folk-songs of Syria and Lebanon, Gibran's contribution being one that he professed to like best. As I remember it, it began like this:

"O beauteous one! I have strayed off the path of love
  Since I surrendered to you my heart.
  So lonesome am I for you, and the distance is so far.
  Ah! Had we but said good-bye! . . ."

What heightened our spirits the more and made us forget our dissonant voices was, perhaps, the little *arak* we drank mixed with the spray of the waterfall. When that and our repertoire gave out we took off our shoes and descended to the stream allowing its waters to caress our feet and hands, and feeling as if all the burdens of existence had fallen off our shoulders, and as if the pure waters were washing away all our sins of the past and our fears of the future.

At last the hour of returning was at hand. Reluctantly we

bade the waterfall farewell, carrying its prayers in our souls, and the beauty of its temple behind our eyelids. We retraced our steps to the hamlet along twisting, thickly shaded, narrow paths. Arida and Haddad were in the vanguard, while Gibran and I brought up the rear, the distance between us and our companions being enough to prevent us from hearing them, and them from hearing us. Gibran and I, as was our wont when speaking of things metaphysical, literary or artistic, talked in English. The conversation led us, among other things, to an English piece Gibran had recently read to me saying that it shall be the first link in a chain of similar pieces which he proposed to incorporate into a book to be called "The Prophet". I had already expressed to him my admiration for that piece on "Love" and my satisfaction at seeing him switch from the camp of the "rebellious" to the camp of those who would delve into human life lovingly and understandingly in order to bring out whatever it contained of the beauty that emanates from the reservoir which is Life Universal. The conversation reached a point where silence was more expressive than speech.

We walked a distance to the time-beat of our silent thoughts, and to the accompaniment of the breeze murmurs among the leaves to the right and to the left of us. The road was like a magic carpet to our feet.

Suddenly Gibran stopped, struck the road with his cane, and called aloud, "Mischa!" I, too, stopped. Looking at my companion I was abashed to see the change in his face. The glowing picture of the waterfall and the hours we spent with it had entirely evaporated from his eyes. Instead there was a cloud of bitter sadness.

"Mischa!" he called again, "I'm a false alarm." Saying that, he bent his head and fell silent.

Of all the touching and dramatic moments I had with Gibran during the fifteen years of our comradeship that was the most touching and dramatic. Of all things he said to me from the time we met till the time we parted nothing shook me as those four words spoken in the woods of Cahoonzie.

What made Gibran pose as he posed and say what he said? Was it the hours we spent listening to the canticles of the waterfall? Was it the spirit of the vine we tasted mixed with the spray of the falls? Or was it the breath of naked truth so permeating the skies overhead and the woods all about?—I could not tell. I was given to feel very keenly that the soul of the companion at my side was writhing in agony and calling for succor. Perhaps the soul of Nature so open, so clean, so unconscious of any shortcomings it wished to hide away—perhaps that soul so overpowered his own with all its charms of naked verity and beautiful submissiveness; perhaps it lighted in a twinkling of an eye all the shady corners of his soul thus making him ashamed of every weakness he clothed in garments of strength, and every ugliness he painted in colors of beauty, and every gluttonous passion he presented in the form of chastity or fast. Therefore he saw himself as a false alarm—as one estimated by his friends and admirers for more than he was really worth. And it saddened him to be such an alarm in the presence of guileless, sinless Nature. It saddened him more that the companion walking by his side was one of those deceived by the alarm. How to atone for that but by an honest confession? And what confession can best cleanse and rest the heart than one made to a friend? What better witness of that confession than pure and truthful Nature?

As it frightened Gibran to picture me among those deceived by his appearance, it frightened me to have him go on with his confession, scourging his proud soul before my eyes and leaving it naked and unarmed. Besides, who am I to accept another soul's confession even if it be a sister to my soul? Perhaps mine was in a greater need of confessing than his. And who of us, after all, is not a false alarm in one way or another? Therefore, I changed the subject and quickened my pace.

The evening of that day, just as twilight was wrapping the woods and all the countryside about in fantastic shadows, we went out for a stroll on the main highway. We were in a gleeful mood, and our conversation was as brisk as our step; it flowed naturally and easily, the slightest pun causing us all to laugh light-heartedly and even uproariously. One suggested that we compose extemporaneously some colloquial verse. When a pause intervened, I chanted out an extemporaneous verse in literary Arabic. The verse ran something like this:

"Sing me, silence of night, a tune of the Silence Eternal."

Another took up the challenge and added a verse. More and more verses were added, all the four taking part, now with a line, now with a rime. Before we knew it we had composed a readable poem of some twenty-six verses.

* * *

We left Cahoonzie and returned each to his appointed yoke. Gibran went to Boston to spend the balance of the summer with his sister Marianna, as was his custom every summer and every Christmas and Easter. The last thing I said to him on bidding him good-by was, "Take care of your heart, Gibran."

PART III

Dawn

MIST BECOMING CRYSTALLIZED

"Brother Mischa,

Since I arrived in this city I have been going from one specialist to another; from one thorough examination to another still more thorough. All because this heart of mine has lost its meter and rime. And you know, Mikhail, that this heart's meter and rime were never in conformity with the meters and rime of other hearts. But since the casual must follow the constant as the shadow follows the substance, it becomes fixed and determined that this lump of flesh within my chest should harmonize with that trembling mist in the space which is myself —my *I*.

"Never mind, Mischa. What is to be shall be. But I feel that I shall not leave the slope of this mountain before the break of dawn. And Dawn shall cast a veil of light and glow on everything." (From a letter written to me by Gibran from Boston toward the end of the summer, 1921.)

"I" — the alpha and omega of existence. Whoever knows it, knows all things; whoever knows it not, knows nothing at all. To know it is to know how to distil pleasure from pain and how to taste the ecstasy of the spirit even in the most trying moments. Not to know it is to be drunk with pain even when quaffing pleasure. The basic difference between any two men is not one of looks, possessions, prestige, talent, fame and the like; it is in the circumference, of the "I" in each.

The Circumference of the "I" in one who says, "Whosoever shall smite thee on the right cheek, turn to him the other also" is infinitely broader than that of the man who says, "An eye for an eye, and a tooth for a tooth." The first has come to realize that every self proceeds from the All-including Self, and should be as all-including as its mother. In that Self the smiter and the smitten are but one. Whereas the second would detach his self from every other self and build around it illusory walls avenging himself on anyone that may dare to make a breach, no matter how trifling, in his walls; he does not realize that in doing that he is but avenging himself on himself. Inspiration, therefore, is the in-flow of the All-Self into the individual self; the wider the inlet, the greater the flow, the greater the flow, the broader the shores of the individual self and the keener its sense of unity with all things. By and by it begins to feel itself as infinite as the All-Self, embracing like it life and death and stretching from eternity to eternity. What we call Fate, becomes then the will of all in all and for all, and quite beyond our limited notions of good and evil. Predetermination becomes that which the individual invites on himself so long as he clings to the mist of separateness which we call "I".

But the overwhelming majority of people, engrossed in the trifles of existence, have their souls shut to the flow of Universal Self; therefore is their "I" so misty, and everything proceeding from it is but so much mist; therefore is their life a constant trading in pleasure and pain. Whereas the few who have come to see themselves in every self, *and whose lives were in keeping with their vision,* were rightfully called the teachers of mankind and its guides to Truth. Little wonder they are worshipped by many; for they have uncovered God in Man.

Like all men of strong imagination eagerly seeking the Absolute, Gibran experienced moments of Inspiration. Such moments can be glimpsed in some of his pieces written before he surrendered to Nietzsche, and included in his book *A Tear and A Smile*. But after his infatuation with the author of Zarathustra, and his rebellion against men he almost drowned in the foam his rebellion raised, or choked with the dust his battles kicked up without drowning a single man or choking one of men's traditions and conventions. During that period of his life he seemed to be fighting more than one war. On one front he fought poverty; on another literature and art to make them yield to him the "greatness and glory" which he thought were his due; on the third his heart and the women who occupied it for a time, or tried to occupy it. Being so engrossed in his many fights, it was natural that the quest for the universal and the absolute should either be suspended or turned in another direction.

So soon, however, as Gibran won the first round with poverty, and felt himself secure in his art and literature which were winning more and more readers and admirers; and so soon as his heart was emptied of all women but one, he went back to his soul in search of new spiritual comforts. He threw its windows open to the in-flow of the rays of the All-Soul. His soul did not disappoint him. Lovingly it began to teach him and to crystallize the mist he called "I" into a jewel of pure light reflecting in itself every self, yet remaining clear, transparent and beautiful:

"My soul taught me and convinced me that I am neither superior to the dwarf, nor inferior to the giant. But before my soul taught me I treated all men either as weaklings to pity or to deride; or as mighty ones to follow or to rebel against. Now do I know that I, as an individual, was formed of the same elements as the whole race. Their clay is my clay, their soul is my soul, their inclinations and their goal are my inclinations and my goal. When they sin I share in their sin and when they do good I glory in their deeds. When they march forward I march with them; and when they slink back I also slink with them."

Deep is the gulf between the words above and Gibran's words to his own people written a few years before: "I loathe you, children of my mother, because you loathe glory and

greatness." Yet both passages, though vastly contradictory, are
but two waves from the same sea. For Gibran that loathes men
contented with less than "glory and greatness" is the same
Gibran that sees himself a partner in every sinner's sin, in every
weak man's weakness, and in every slave's slavery. The first is
Gibran in the world of externals; the second is Gibran in the
inner world. The first is mist shutting off the light; the second
is light dissipating the mist. The first is the shell; the second,
the kernel.

Thus died down the rebellion of the man who liked to call
himself and to be called by others a rebel. Are not all rebellions,
after all, a temporary boiling over?

Never did the self of any man so broaden out as to become
one with the Self Universal except he felt him compelled to
relinquish all thought of barriers and limitations of any kind.
To the man that passes beyond bar and boundary all human
standards of value become mere toys and playthings. Such a
man sees the result in the cause, the end in the beginning, and
vice versa. In other words, he sees circles and spheres where
others see but straight or broken lines, or three dimensional
shapes. His logic, therefore, becomes entirely illogical to men,
and his thought incomprehensible to their thoughts. They speak
to him in terms of induction and deduction; he speaks to them
in terms of imagination flashes that reveal in an instant worlds
beyond the reach of sight and reason. Should he see a murderer
and his victim he would say that each of the two was at once
the murderer and the murdered. Should he hear one singing
and another wailing he would say that both were singing and
wailing at the same time.

It is to marvel at, indeed, that this imagination of the East
would not be contained within bounds, but ever seeks to pass
from beginnings to beginninglessness, from the finite to the
infinite, and from that which is material to that which is non-
material. All the creeds of the East, so numerous and so ap-

parently conflicting, meet in that immensity where the cause and the effect are one and the same. A man with a daring, free imagination is bound to reach that region soon or late. But woe to the one whose imagination is much stronger than his will. Such a one is like a kite flown by a child. No quicker does it taste the freedom of the freer space than it is pulled down to the earth and the bondage of the earth. Even death cannot liberate such a man from bondage to the earth. That was the case of Gibran with his imagination and will. On the other hand, all glory to those whose will is as powerful as their imagination. Such men, though, walking on the earth, have their hearts in the skies. They conquer death even before they die. Few, very few are they in the long trek of human history.

*   *   *

"Mischa, Mischa! God save us from civilization and the civilized, and from America and Americans; and we shall be saved. We shall return to the white peaks of Lebanon and to its peaceful valleys. We shall eat of its grapes and figs, drink of its wine and oil, sleep upon its threshing floors, talk to its scintillating stars, and dream to the accompaniment of its brooks and the flutes of its shepherds. Why don't you smoke? Light a cigarette; the smoke would not hide your face, from me. Turn to the left a little. There, there. Now the light is perfect. I shall be through with you in less than two hours. Drawing a portrait and writing a poem have very much in common. Once the subject takes hold of you, the proper form suggests itself without much seeking, and the poem appears as though it had written itself. When you feel drawn by something in the person or picture you are drawing, then the pencil in your hand becomes a living part of your hand, and the tip of each finger an eye, and all those eyes see through one pupil. Then the portrait or the picture practically draw themselves. Rest a little if you are tired."

I sat in a chair on the wooden platform. Not far from me

was the easel. On the easel was a white-faced cardboard of about 17" x 21" on which Gibran was making a pencil portrait of me. His movements as he drew me were fascinating to follow. He would squint at me out of the corner of his eye, then rush to the easel and work for a space over the cardboard with his pencil which was no longer than four inches. Every now and then he would stare at me, then at the board; he would retreat a pace or two, again rush at the board, work with the pencil or the eraser which was no larger than a chick-pea and which he rolled between his thumb and forefinger so as to give it a pointed head wherewith to correct a line, reduce a shade, or produce a touch of light. Sometimes he would use his thumb or forefinger to thicken or to lighten a shade here and there. His face radiated with the joy of work; his tongue moved as easily and as fast as his pencil. Feeling his great pleasure in talking, I let him "have the floor," never interrupting him except for the purpose of having him say more.

"Of all the people I draw, Mischa, none give me so much trouble as the ladies. Even the ugliest of them expect to come out on paper more beauteous than Venus de Milo. What I, as an artist, see in their faces is of little moment to them; it is what they think they see, or what they wish to see that decides their evaluation of the portrait. I should be a traitor to my art if I were to borrow my sitter's eyes. The face is a marvelous mirror that reflects most faithfully the innermost of the soul; the artist's business is to see that and portray it; otherwise he is not fit to be called an artist. Any photographic camera can give you an accurate resemblance, but it can never give you those finer and more elusive values that only the keen eye of a true artist can detect. Else the machine should have long ago dragged the artist from his high pedestal. But no machine, however perfected, shall ever be a substitute for man.

"Yes, Mischa. You and I must some day flee this land. To be unknown here is to be of no more value than a rag. To be known is to become everyone's doormat; I am to-day a doormat, Mischa. My soul would regain its self respect; my mind, its freedom; and my body, its rest. These I shall not regain except in Lebanon. If you only knew the "hermitage" I have selected for you and myself in Lebanon, you would this minute take me by the hand and say, 'Let us go!' It is a *real* cloister, Mischa, and not an imitation one as this studio."

"Tell me all about it", said I impatiently.

"It is a small, deserted monastery right near my home town of Bisharri. The name of it is *Mar-Sarkees*. It stands at the upper end of the gorge of Kadisha on the slopes of Cedar Mountain. Its chapel and few cells are hewn into the limestone side of the mountain. The terraced land before it slopes precipitously down to the gorge and is still green with ever-green oaks and grape vines. A more peaceful and beautiful spot for solitude can hardly be found even in Heaven. I have empowered an attorney in Tripoli to buy it for me. There is danger, however, that the monks, once they discover who the prospective buyer is, would refuse to sell. For I, as you know, am an atheist in their eyes. But the attorney is a friend of mine and a capable one. He will somehow fool the monks and arrange the matter.

"There we shall live away from the world, Mischa. There we shall dream our dreams and write to our hearts' content. We shall also buy a printing press and publish our dreams to those who care for our dreams; and we shall make of printing a fine art. We shall also cultivate the land and make the barren of it fertile; even the rocks we shall dress in green. And the winds shall bless us, and the sun shall smile to us, and the gorge shall waft on us its inspiring breath."

Aroused by his enthusiastic description which stirred in me an old dream, I said,

"We are to-day in November, 1922. What say you of meeting the coming spring on the banks of the Saints' Gorge?"

His hesitant reply came like a cold shower. "I have connections here which I cannot liquidate in a month or a year. I also have work which must be attended to, like the publishing of my book 'The Prophet.' "

Said I, "So long as you are here your connections will grow and multiply from day to day. And so long as you have work which cannot be accomplished in Lebanon, you are bound to have more and more. In that case you shall not dwell in *Mar-Sarkees* except in dreams."

"Have patience, Mischa. I shall—rather *we* shall—dwell in that cloister in body and soul. If you be weary of this world of machines and shadows, I am as weary of it as you, if not more. You and I shall not find a better, a holier and a more peaceful refuge than *Mar-Sarkees*. And you shall love that refuge as I love it."

"You have made me love it from this moment. I shall visit it many times in dreams even before my eyes see it and my feet tread its soil. May we be drawn closer to it from now on."

We talked long of *Mar-Sarkees*. The Fates listening to us must have laughed well at us; for they knew that Gibran would not enter that cloister except as a corpse laid in a casket fashioned by those same machines which he wished to flee; and that I would not visit it to give myself up to meditations, but to lay on my comrade's tomb a bouquet of wild flowers my own hand culled from the side of the holy mountain of the Cedars.

ALMUSTAFA*

When Gibran with his powerful imagination came to see the world as a perfect unity and life as an eternal harmony, all the other worlds in which he dwelt before and which he considered spacious and real became to him stifling and unreal. He looked back on those worlds as would a bird on the shell of the egg out of which it hatched; or a river on the rock, and slime and brush it passed on its way to the sea; or as a mountain climber on the hills and dales he crossed before reaching the summit. Wherever he sent his imagination in this new world it brought him back reports of things and beings welded together by the mystic bond of Love too infinite to be contained within bars and boundaries. And he blessed Life, which before he called a harlot, shouting from the bottom of his heart:

"How generous is Life, and how precious all its gifts!

"Would that I had a thousand hands extended towards the heaven and the earth instead of this one bashful hand shut upon a pinch of sand from the shore." He wished he had a thousand eyes to see all the surpassing beauties of Life; and a thousand ears to hear all its witching symphonies. And because he was a poet—and the poet's burden is to put his heartbeats in words; and because he was an artist—and the artist's failing is to express in lines and colors Life's innumerable faces, he began to think of "how" to convey to his fellow-men the charms of his newly-discovered world.

* Al-Mustafa is an Arabic word meaning "The Chosen." It is one of prophet Mohammed's appellations.

This "How" is of paramount importance to the poet and the artist worthy of the name. For it is to poetry and art what the body is to the soul. It is much more than the choice of sonorous words and impressive lines and colors. It is the all-important mold into which sonorous words and impressive lines and colors are to be cast after having been discriminately chosen. A good poet, or a good artist, will give as much attention to the mold as to that which he proposes to cast into it of his own soul. Being both an excellent poet and an excellent artist Gibran sought long and carefully the mold into which to cast his impressions of the dazzling beauties of the world he had recently discovered with his imagination. What was the mold he finally settled on?

He created a mouthpiece called "Almustafa" endowing him with a soul so enlightened that his hearers called him "prophet of God." The very name "Prophet" impresses with dignity and inspires reverence. A word said by a man clothed in prophetic majesty carries much more weight and magnitude than when said by a common man. Thus with that one word "prophet" Gibran the artist raised to the dignity and height of prophecy what Gibran the poet had to say, even before he said it.

But Gibran the artist knew how to cast the mantle of prophecy on his Almustafa. He presents him as a stranger in a city called Orphalese where he spent twelve years of his life awaiting the coming of the ship which was to carry him back to the "isle of his birth." He takes him up to the top of a hill outside the city where he sees his ship coming in the mist. Then he opens up before you the stranger's heart and lays bare his conflicting emotions of joy and sorrow—the joy of an exile set at liberty and turning his face homeward; and the sorrow of that same exile at the prospect of tearing his heart away from his fellow-exiles whom he had come to know and to love, and who had come to know him and to love him dearly. Having thus "presented" his prophet, Gibran takes him down to the city where the people, realizing that he was about to leave them, desert their fields and all their labors and congregate about him begging him to stay with them. He meets their warm supplications with stubborn silence and tears. Finally he walks with them to the great square before the temple. Out of the temple comes a seeress whose name is Almitra. Almustafa looks upon her "with exceeding tenderness, for it was she who had first sought and believed in him when he had been but a day in their city."

Almitra, knowing how deep was Almustafa's longing "for the land of his memories and the dwelling place of his greater desires," does not urge him to stay, but simply asks him: "Now therefore disclose us to ourselves, and tell us all that has been shown you of that which is between birth and death." Her first request was that he speak to them of Love. Thus does that seeress open the door wide for others to ask questions and for Almustafa to speak to the people on the many ties that bind them together, and how those ties should be seen and understood in the light of the spirit and not as casual material connections. Altogether he delivers twenty-six sermons on twenty-six different facets of human life on earth; then bids the people a touching farewell and departs for "the isle of his birth."

That was the mold Gibran chose into which to pour the quintessence of his contemplations of men and their lives. The mold, as you see, fits well the substance, and the substance, the mold. But, alas! It was not all of Gibran's making. Much of it is fashioned after Nietzsche's Zarathustra. It seems that Gibran who had been able to set his mind and imagination free of the influence of Nietzsche's mind and imagination had not been able to free himself from the great German's style and form. Perhaps he was quite unconscious of the fact.

Nietzsche takes for a mouthpiece a prophet called Zarathustra. Gibran, a prophet called Almustafa.

Nietzsche's Zarathustra walks a stranger among men giving them now and then of his wisdom; when tired of his exile among them, he retires to his "Happy Isles." Gibran's Almustafa is also a stranger among men; when weary of his exile he returns to the "isle of his birth."

Nietzsche's Zarathustra on bidding his disciples farewell towards the end of the First Part of the book says to them in part, "Now do I bid you lose me and find yourselves; and only when you have all denied me, will I return unto you." Gibran's Almustafa bids his friends farewell and says to them among other things: "But should my voice fade in your ears, and my love vanish in your memory, then I will come again."

Zarathustra at the beginning of the Third Part, while preparing to leave his Happy Isles for the world, ascends a high mountain, and in ascending reveals the burdens of his heart. Looking at the sea in the distance, he addresses it thus: "Ah, this somber, sad sea, below me! Ah, this somber nocturnal vexation! Ah, fate and Sea! To you must I now *go down!*" Almustafa ascends a hill outside Orphalese, and after speaking long to his heart, looks at the sea and says, "And you, vast sea, sleeping mother, who alone are peace and freedom to the river and the stream. Only another winding will this stream make; only another murmur in this glade, and then shall I come to you, a boundless drop to a boundless ocean."

As Zarathustra is Nietzsche in another form, so is Almustafa Gibran under a borrowed name. Both are subjective creations, veiled with symbol and metaphor sufficiently to hide their authors' identities from the ordinary reader. To one, however, who knew Gibran as I knew him the veil appears quite thin and transparent. The twelve years Almustafa spent in waiting for his ship are the twelve years Gibran had lived in New York up to the writing of the prelude to the *Prophet.* The city of Orphalese is no other than New York. Almitra "who had first sought and believed in him" is Mary Haskell. "The isle of his birth" is Lebanon. His promise to return to the people of Orphalese is but a re-affirmation of his old belief in re-incarnation which

holds that those who leave the earth with their accounts unsettled, whether with men or things, must be reborn again and
again until they break their last bond with the earth. Viewed
from another angle and in a broader light Orphalese may be
taken to symbolize the earth, and Almustafa's exile in it to
refer to the detachment of the individual spirit from the All-
Spirit during its earthly pilgrimage. The "isle of birth", then,
would be the bosom of the All-Spirit, or the centre of Life
Universal. The author leaves the margin wide for the reader's
imagination; and therein lies one of the secrets of his art.

Though close and striking is the kinship in form and style
between "The Prophet" and "Thus Spake Zarathustra", the two
books are far apart in substance. For that substance Gibran
is indebted mainly to his imagination which was able to tap
the ever bubbling springs of the Spirit Universal where all
thirsty spirits must slake their thirst. If you, therefore, are
struck by the great similarity between Almustafa's sermons and
the outgivings of many prophets and *sufis* of the East, be slow
to accuse Gibran of giving you borrowed ideas. Say rather that
he culled those ideas, bravely and independently, from the same
garden where men with an imagination unshackled of weights
and measures have always culled theirs. The ideas may not be
new, to be sure. Is there anything new under the sun? But they
are put forward in words which look and sound almost new;
so rhythmic are they, so palpitating with life, so bright of color
and so graceful of line, and yet so few in number, that only a
pedant, or one color-blind, or one deaf to music, can really find
any major fault with them. In this book, more than in any other
of his books, Gibran's style reaches its very zenith. Many metaphors are so deftly formed that they stand out like statues chiselled in the rock. To some they may look like riddles—enigmatic
and incomprehensible. Such readers must blame their own eye
and ear, their poverty of spirit, before they blame the author.

In *The Prophet* Gibran's imagination, looking at life, found

it to be of one and the same essence—Love. It also found all
men to be equal partners in that essence, the only difference
being in the realization and application of that truth. Love is
ever revealing itself to all without discrimination; but some
have their soul's ears plugged with the maddening hubbub of
the world, therefore cannot hear; or have their soul's eyes thickly veiled with sensory delusions, therefore cannot see. While
those who have purged their souls' ears and eyes of worldly
lusts and passions are given to hear and to see Life's purest
essence which is Love. Therefore are they incapable of loving
one part of Life and of hating the other; rather do they accept
it and obey it as an indivisible oneness.

Therefore does Almustafa exhort the people of Orphalese:

"When you love you should not say 'God is in my heart',
but rather, 'I am in the heart of God.' "

How can one who is in the heart of God feel any barriers
between himself and any other man? Would he not feel all men
dwelling in himself, and himself dwelling in every man? Can
one so unified with all creation ever say, "I have given so much
to my neighbor, or have taken so much from my neighbor"?
Does he not become a taker when giving, and a giver when
taking? Then the desert of one that gives is the same as the
desert of one that takes—no more, no less.

When one is in the heart of God, one can no longer sit in
judgment over one's fellow-men. To judge, then, a sinner with
his sin is to judge God Himself. Is God a sinner and the source
of sin? Man alone is capable of sinning because unable yet to
comprehend his greater, or his divine self. In that respect all
men are sinners:

"And as a single leaf turns not yellow but with the silent
knowledge of the whole tree, so the wrongdoer cannot do wrong
without the hidden will of you all . . .

"You cannot separate the just from the unjust, and the good
from the wicked . . . And if any of you would punish in the

name of righteousness and lay the ax unto the evil tree, let him
see to its roots; and verily he will find the roots of the good and
the bad, the fruitful and the fruitless, all entwined together in
the silent heart of the earth."

When a man is in the heart of God, he can no longer set up
any lines of division between himself and anything even down
to the things he eats and drinks.

"Would that you could live on the fragrance of the earth,
and like an air plant be sustained by the light.

"But since you must kill to eat, and rob the newly born of
its mother's milk to drink, let it then be an act of worship . . .

"When you kill a beast say to him in your heart, 'By the
same power that slays you, I too am slain; and I too shall be
consumed . . . Your blood and my blood is naught but the sap
that feeds the tree of heaven.' "

To such spiritual heights does Almustafa lift his hearers,
his speech sparkling with poetic similes drawn from nature in
her various moods, and closely modeled after the Bible even
to the extent of borrowing bodily certain expressions such as
"You have been told . . . but I say unto you"; or "Verily I say
unto you," and others. But the language flows so smoothly, so
naturally, and carries the reader so readily to its goal, that he
overlooks all borrowed forms and turns. Hardly can he lay the
book down without feeling that his heart has been enriched by
the experiences and contemplations of Almustafa's heart, and
that his soul's eye has been opened up unto the truth and beauty
of the Universal Soul.

Gibran had twelve drawings prepared for his *Prophet*—
ten done in wash and two in black and white, the latter being
Almustafa's face at the beginning of the book, and the "Creative
Hand" at the end.

Taken as a whole Almustafa's face is, perhaps, the loveliest
and the most impressive ever drawn by Gibran, not excluding
that of Jesus done a few years later. The large, dreamy eyes seem

to look away beyond the present moment and the immediate circumstance. Sorrowful and penetrating, they speak eloquently of a most sympathetic heart and a soul suffused with loving understanding. The mouth, though thick-lipped and passionate, is rich in sensitiveness, patience, forgiveness and delicacy of taste. It is the mouth of one who has tasted the pleasures of the world and found them bitter, and would no longer soil his lips with a drop from that fountain. The effect of that delicate veil of sadness drawn all over the face is broken by the barely suggested circle of hair forming a halo of light. Framed within that halo are eternities of painful struggle against all the things that keep man chained to the earth and make of his life a tug of war between good and evil, birth and death. Though the struggle be yet going on, and the wounds it caused be yet bleeding, the issue is not in doubt.

The "Creative Hand" represents an outstretched hand, sensitive, powerful, graceful, beautifully sculpted, and with an open eye in the middle of it that seems to see all things. Around the eye is a cyclone-like whirl of wings. Around the whirling wings is a dark abyss heaving with chaotic shadows and fringed with a chain of human bodies. That is the hand of God. It sees as it touches, and imagines as it sees. It imagines forms before it creates them; then touches chaos and out of it makes all forms to issue as by magic. In drawing that hand Gibran's memory may have carried him back to the hand of God by Rodin. The two may have something in common in so far only as the basic idea of creation is concerned; but they are vastly different in conception and execution.

The rest of the drawings in the book are either interpretive of some thoughts, or represent new thoughts not expressed in words; but are all deeply symbolic and very delicately executed, the delicacy in some cases being almost tantamount to effeminacy. Though lacking in the touch of masculinity, those drawings, without exception, bespeak the grandeur of the imagination that conceived them and the wonderful sensitiveness of the hand that gave them form. An example of that is the drawing of "Pain". It represents a woman crucified on the chests of two men whom she loves equally and by whom she is equally loved. Neither can she divide her heart between the two, nor would either of the two be content with less than her whole heart. What greater pain can there be than the pain of love becoming a cross to the lover? On the other hand, what joy can be greater than the joy of Love leading to the cross, and from the pains of the cross to the bliss and emancipation of Love triumphant?

A month, or two, before he turned *The Prophet* over to the publisher Gibran gave me a typewritten copy of it with the tacit hope that I will write an exhaustive study of the book to be published upon its release. A similar copy was sent to Mary Haskell who was Gibran's confidential editor of all his English books. Not that she ever made any major corrections, or changes; but here and there she would come upon a misused word or usage and suggest the more correct ones. Knowing how extremely subjective Gibran was in everything he wrote, it was not easy for me to decide whether he had meant *The Prophet* to be an expression of his deeper longings for final spiritual emancipation, or whether he had meant it as a representation that he had actually reached that emancipation. In the latter case he would be holding himself out to be a prophet in *thought and in deed*. I doubt if Gibran, who had called himself a false alarm, intended to parade before men in a prophet's mantle. Yet that was precisely what the book conveyed to some readers—at least to those who had inscribed above his tomb the following words in Arabic:

"Here lies our prophet Gibran." Evidently they were called to account for the pronoun "our"—to whom did it refer? therefore was the sentence, by the simple shifting of dots, made to read thus: "Here lies *among us* Gibran." That was the version I read when I visited the tomb in the summer of 1932.

SHARE IN HEAVEN AND SHARES IN EARTH

In the fall of 1923 *The Prophet*—a small, black book, neat but unassuming—made its appearance on the overcrowded New York book-market. Like all the children of the prolific modern press it had to struggle for a foothold on the slippery path of Time where millions of books go dashing to an early doom and eternal oblivion, publicity notwithstanding. Clever publicity can make a "best seller" even of a mediocre, or a bad book; but only for a space. It cannot cheat Time. It can help a worthy book along; but cannot give worth to an unworthy one—cannot breathe life into the lifeless.

The Prophet, though helped along in the beginning by some publicity, was not of those books that depend for their life on publicity alone, or that are still-born and cannot be made to live by the magic of any publicity. It contained of pure thought, of the fire of the spirit and the imagination more than enough to insure for it a life rich in undulating years and reverberating echoes. For Gibran knew how to make of it a perfect plant with roots buried deep in the soil of human life thus assuring it of constant sustenance. So long as men experience birth and death; so long as they eat and drink, love and hate, marry and beget children, laugh and weep; so long as men are men, just so long will they seek the meanings of birth and death, of love and hate and all the other relations that bind them to each other and to the nature about them, and who will find comfort in Gibran's interpretation of those relations. The style of the book may some day fade, or become out of date as many other styles have faded and become out-dated; but the essence of the book will neither fade, nor become outmoded.

One would think that Gibran, having delivered himself of *The Prophet,* should have sighed a sigh of relief and said in his heart, "Now I have uttered *it*," meaning that word which he had always felt to be on the tip of his tongue and which he would not utter until absolutely certain that he had put into it the very quintessence of his spiritual experiences and his final answer to himself of Life—its meaning and its goal. That life he had come to see as One Whole, indivisible, immeasurable, unconfinable in time and space, reflected in the drop of water as in the ocean, and in the grain of sand as in the mountain, boundless, infinite even in the least of its manifestations. He must have been thinking of all those things and of his rebellious attitude towards life, when he wrote his excellent aphorism,

"When God threw me, a pebble, into this wondrous lake I disturbed its surface with countless circles. But when I reached the depths I became very still."

Having *reached the depths* Gibran should have become *very still*. Yet far from becoming still, he went on making more and more circles, because he had reached the depths *with his imagination only*, his heart and will lagging far behind. Like Moses, he was allowed to see from afar the Promised Land, but not to live in it; to taste its milk and honey in hope, not in fact. Or like a sea diver who touches the bottom for few fleeting moments and is then pulled up to the surface with a rope. The ropes that tied Gibran to the ever turbulent surface of life were too sturdy for his will to break. It was those ropes that kept cutting into the joints of his days and nights, thus frustrating all his efforts to make a lasting peace between his inner and his outer selves to the end of his life.

A word, once spoken, becomes a witness for or against the speaker towards his fellow-men. The testimony stands until vitiated for good or ill by the speaker's own conduct. In *The Prophet* Gibran gave of himself a testimony which is almost perfection itself. One so testifying of himself must renounce his individual self to find it in the infinite All-Self. He must not hate any man, for he becomes all men; nor must he own anything, for all things are his; nor must he flee from pain, for pain is the way of deliverance from the separate self; nor must he judge anyone lest he be judging himself; nor must he covet any worldly glory, for all worldly glory is vanity. Any other conduct would render the testimony false.

Gibran was well aware of all that. He fully realized the truth of the Imam Ali's saying: "Whoever would be a teacher of men let him begin by teaching himself before teaching the others; and let him teach by example before teaching by word. For he who teaches himself and rectifies his own ways is more deserving of respect and reverence than he who would teach others and rectify their ways." Feeling the weight of all that, Gibran was always dissatisfied with himself because unable to create a perfect team of his will and imagination. He consoled himself by the thought that in a future rebirth he should be able to accomplish what he failed to accomplish in this birth.

The Prophet was yet in manuscript when a tremendous wave of speculation in real estate spread all over the United States. In those days one would constantly hear of lots or buildings bought in the evening for so much and sold the following morning for double the amount. Gibran was swept by the mighty current. In company with a certain Syrian friend he bought a building in Boston, paying $10,000 down and giving a mortgage on the balance of $40,000 or thereabout. Almost immediately the partners were approached by a woman who proposed to rent the entire building for several years and make of it a sort of women's club on condition that certain repairs and alterations be made to make the building answer the purpose. The rent agreed upon was sufficient to pay for the alterations and repairs, to cover the interest and to redeem the mortgage even before maturity. The lease was signed; the alterations and repairs made.

Both partners were elated with the prospects of quick and ample profits. Gibran began to taste beforehand that financial independence of which he had been dreaming all his life.

In a few months, however, the lessee defaulted in payment, her excuse being that the proposed club proved a failure which was heart-breaking to her since she had staked all her hopes on the success of the venture. As her hopes were her only assets, the partners were unable to collect any money from her. As the building, after having been altered to suit that particular club, became unfit for any other purpose, Gibran and his friend were unable to find for it any new tenants. Their capital had already been used up by what they paid of the price and expended on repairs and alterations. The result was foreclosure.

Just about that time I received a letter from Gibran written in Boston. I quote from it the following:

". . . God knows that never in my past life have I spent a month so full of difficulties, trials, misfortunes and problems as the last month. More than once I wondered if my *djinnee,* or my *follower* or my *double* has turned into a demon who delights in opposing me, in making war on me, in shutting the doors in my face, and in placing obstacles in my way. Since my arrival in this crooked city I have been living in a hell of worldly problems. Had it not been for my sister, I would leave everything and go back to my hermitage, shaking the dust of the world off my feet.

". . . The reasons that have kept me in this city, and shall yet keep me for ten more days, have nothing to do with what I have written or read, or what I shall write and read; they have to do with things stupid, wearisome, filling the heart with pricks and gall, and pressing the soul with an iron hand as rough as steel files".

It was a staggering blow to Gibran. It meant the loss of hard-earned savings over a period of years. It shook his soul, scattered his thoughts, shut the avenues of his inspiration and quickened the march of the disease in his body. But like the brave man he was, he received it in hopeful patience and with a stout heart, and went about repairing the damage it had done to his financial independence. Giving up writing for a while, he applied himself to drawing portraits. The royalties on his books, though still insignificant, together with the $75.00 coming monthly from Mary, helped to rebuild the shattered financial structure. In two or three years his pocketbook regained its health. He re-gathered his thoughts, found the keys to the treasures of his inspiration, and went back to his pen and papers. Three years had passed, and no new book had appeared under his name. It was a long pause, especially in a country like America, for a writer who did not wish to be forgotten by the public in his own life-time.

He bethought him, therefore, of some aphorisms and proverbs he had written in Arabic at different times. He collected them, translated them into English, added to them, and had them published in 1926 under the title of "Sand and Foam." He told me at the time that he felt very much as king David felt when his beloved son, begotten of Bathsheba the wife of Uriah, died. It is told of David that he fasted and was grief-stricken during the boy's illness which lasted seven days. When on the seventh day he was informed of the child's death he "arose from the earth, and washed, and anointed himself, and changed his apparel, and came into the house of the Lord, and worshipped; then he came to his own house, and when he required, they set bread before him, and he did eat . . . And he said, While the child was yet alive I fasted and wept; for I said, Who can tell whether God will be gracious to me, that the child may live? But now he is dead, wherefore should I fast? Can I bring him back again? I shall go to him, but he shall not return to me."

Likewise he—Gibran. Before the case of the building in

Boston was settled once for all he had hopes of retrieving all, or part, of his loss. When that hope was dead he cast it out of his heart and mind, and went back to his pen and brush.

Not many years later Gibran was able to buy forty shares in the building where he had his studio. The transaction proved so profitable that it more than doubly covered his loss sustained in the Boston building.

THE HOAX

One of the members of *Arrabitah* was Rasheed Ayoub, a delightful poet and a remarkable wit. He and Abdul-Masseeh Haddad whom he called "The Master Fox" were our best entertainers in hours of relaxation. Many a somber situation was made to ring with hearty laughter when tackled by their sparkling witticisms; many a minute whose seconds crawled in fetters of care and heaviness of heart was given wings of joy and hilarity.

Saturday afternoon was usually the time when most of the "gangsters"—as the members of *Arrabitah* liked to nickname themselves—were likely to congregate in the offices of *As-Sayeh*. On one such afternoon, soon after luncheon, I walked in on Abdul and found him alone and deeply immersed in work. He was getting one of the "specials" out, and had just returned from the pressroom as the ink stains on his fingers testified. Most of the material for the number had been set up and printed, the last being a poem by Rasheed Ayoub which he—Abdul— had read me the day before, and which I liked so much that I immediately read it on the telephone to Gibran who also praised it highly.

Abdul was telling me of his exhausting labors in arranging the various materials, in supervising the setting and the printing, in proof-reading and similar work which he had to do all by himself. On the desk before me was a heap of Arabic newspapers and magazines that had just been received from Egypt, Lebanon, Syria and South America. Ferreting that heap out I came upon a number of a Damascus newspaper in which about

two thirds of a column were left entirely blank, the censor having deleted the "dangerous" material. As I commented on the
stupidity of censors and censorship in general, while staring at
that blank space, it occurred to me that it held out excellent
promises for an unusual hoax to be played by Abdul on Rasheed
Ayoub. I hinted to Abdul of what transpired in my mind. Reflecting for a moment, he jumped to his feet, snatched the paper
from my hand, and shouting gleefully, "I have it", rushed out
of the office. In a few minutes he was back smiling maliciously
and patting himself on the shoulder. "Behold!" he said slyly
and boastfully as he handed me the paper. "What an unusual
opportunity the Damascus censor gave us."

I looked at the paper and was most amazed to see that the
white space in the censored column was filled in with neat, black
lines; the lines were no others but Rasheed's verses which he
had composed for the annual special number of *As-Sayeh*. Abdul
had them printed and captioned as selections from the works of
an ancient Arab poet who lived more than a thousand years
before. The eye of an expert only could detect the difference in
type and ink between the freshly printed lines and the rest of the
material in the paper.

Rasheed was in the habit of taking his daily after-luncheon
"cat's nap" in a certain chair in the office of *As-Sayeh*. A friend
who was not a member of *Arrabitah* was initiated into the plan.
He was to take a seat opposite Rasheed's and to fumble through
the near-by waste basket where the Damascus paper in question
was to be placed with many others. He was to take up that paper
most casually and look through it quite disinterestedly until he
came to the "selections" from the ancient Arab poet. Then he
was to upbraid Abdul for throwing such precious poetry into
the waste-basket instead of reproducing it in *As-Sayeh* which
often reproduced ancient verse but seldom of such a high caliber.
He then was to read the poem aloud just as Rasheed was about
to fall asleep.

The friend acted his part perfectly. When Rasheed, about to doze off, heard the "hot" argument and the first two verses of his poem, he suddenly straightened himself up in his chair, opened his eyes wide, threw his spectacles up from his nose to his forehead, and despite his fifty years, made one long leap towards the man, snatched the paper from his hand, and looking at his verses in the strange journal, stood for a moment pale and transfixed not knowing what to think, or what to say. Though it lasted but a short moment, the spectacle was at once most pathetic and most humorous. From the smiles and suppressed giggles of the men about him Rasheed, very much puzzled, realized that the affair was a well-staged hoax. Putting back his spectacles on his nose, and grinning broadly, he looked at Abdul and said, "You master fox! This is your work!"

Just then Gibran telephoned saying that he was coming down. All those present instantly agreed that the hoax should be played on him also. It fell to my lot to play the major part.

Contrary to our habit we received Gibran coldly, with long drawn faces, sad and very much perplexed; excepting Rasheed who remained his usual self pretending that he knew nothing of our plan. Presently Gibran's face also became worried and puzzled. Taking me to one side, he asked me in a whisper, "What is the matter?" I made no reply, but took him by the hand and led him into an adjoining room, carefully shutting the door behind me as if to make sure that those outside could not hear us. With the stage thus set I laid the Damascus paper before Gibran and said to him in a whisper, "Read." Then I sat me to one side and went on observing his movements and the changes that came over his face as he read the poem. Finally he lifted his eyes from the paper, and looking at me in utter bewilderment, said,

"Are not these Rasheed's verses that you read me yesterday over the telephone?"

"Word for word."

"How strange, Mischa, that Rasheed should plagiarize this poem when he has already produced so much poetry of even superior quality. Is it not possible that he has written this poem sometime ago and mailed it to this paper in Damascus?"

"That is quite impossible, Gibran. We all know that Rasheed has never published anything in that paper before. He knows, furthermore, as we all know that all the material going into the 'special' should be fresh and original. Besides, he told Abdul and me that he wrote this poem but two days ago."

"Shall we say, then, that the same theme and form, by some queer coincidence, suggested themselves to two poets more than a thousand years apart? Or shall we suppose that Rasheed had learned that poem in his youth and forgot that he learned it; and when he came to compose a poem for the 'special' the theme and the form floated out in his memory quite unconsciously on his part and he believed them to be his own?"

"Such far-fetched explanations are an insult to your intelligence and mine, Gibran."

"I never thought that Rasheed would commit such a crime."

"Now that he has committed it, what is to be done to cover it up? What shall we say to the Arab world when the 'special' is out and the readers discover that a member of Arrabitah plagiarized an old poem from the first to the last syllable? Will there be enough soap in the world to wash that blotch off Arrabitah's name?"

"Let us tell Abdul to drop it from the special number."

"But it has been already printed, Gibran; and there is no way of dropping it except by destroying the whole print. Besides, what shall we say to Rasheed when the number is out and his poem is not in it? Shall we tell him that we discovered him to be a plagiarist and, therefore, dropped him?"

"A thousand times No! We'll simply tell Abdul to drop it from the 'special' and to publish it in one of the ordinary numbers. The latter have not the same standing in the readers' eyes as the special numbers which are supposed to carry original material only."

"Thus we end where we began exactly, with the stain on the name of *Arrabitah* unwashed, and with Rasheed Ayoub a plagiarist. No, Gibran; such an excuse is worse than no excuse."

"Then let the poem appear in the 'special' under Rasheed's name, and let Abdul announce in the following regular number that Rasheed's name was erroneously attached to the poem."

"In that way we will be like one making an ink stain on his clothes worse by trying to rub it off. As to Rasheed we will, in that case, be dipping him in a barrel of pitch. No, Gibran. Give me a better solution."

At this point Gibran fell silent. I could feel how hard he worked his brains for a possible way out. I could feel his thoughts dashing back and forth like fishes caught in a net and beating vainly in search of a way of escape. Meanwhile Abdul kept coming in and out. He would open the door very slowly and shut it behind him very slowly as if he were walking in on a secret consultation which was to settle the destiny of the world. If he said anything at all, it was to aggravate the situation and give it the appearance and the proportions of a real calamity. Finally Gibran admitted that he had reached his wits' end, and looking at me with supplicating eyes, said,

"But what's your solution, Mischa? This is indeed a blind calamity."

"Frankness is the only solution, Gibran. Any other solution, even if successful, will smear us with shame. I propose that you, as chieftain of *Arrabitah*, speak openly to Rasheed." He started as one stung and said,

"I! No, by God. If I know that Rasheed knows that I know, never would I be able to look at him again. You had better talk to him, Mischa. You are the counsellor of *Arrabitah*."

"That is cowardice, Gibran, to shift the responsibility from your shoulder to another's; and I never knew you to be a coward. If Rasheed be your friend, he is my friend and my townsman also."

At that moment Abdul walked in on tiptoe, and I turned to him and said,

"What is your opinion, Abdul, of this ugly situation? Isn't it the chieftain's duty to talk frankly to Rasheed about it before Rasheed and the rest of us become embroiled beyond reprieve?" Abdul's reply came naturally in the affirmative.

When all avenues of escape were shut before him Gibran became very pensive. A cloud of restlessness and dumb sadness spread over his face, and his eyes moistened with tears. Without saying a word he arose from his chair, opened the door, walked out into the room where other members of *Arrabitah,* including Rasheed, and some friends were sitting, put on his overcoat, took his hat and cane and was about to leave without bidding anyone of the company good-by.

At that moment Rasheed could no longer hold back his laughter. With him laughed another person who was not a member of *Arrabitah.* Gibran looked at him angrily out of the corner of his eye as if to say, "How dare you, a mere stranger, laugh at such a tragic moment?" At that juncture I came out of the "Inquisition" room smiling broadly. Behind me was Abdul laughing merrily. Gibran was abashed and struck dumb for a while. Finally, realizing that the whole matter was a hoax, he smiled half-heartedly and striking the floor with his cane said,

"You devils! You have cut my life shorter by ten years. Who is the author of this masterpiece of a hoax? Until now I cannot understand it. Where is that Damascus paper? Or am I blind and stupid? Come, explain to me how Rasheed's verses were published in Damascus forty days ago when he composed them but the day before yesterday? And where did you dig up that ancient Arab poet? What a hoax! What a masterpiece!"

THE LADY WITH THE BEARD

Man has been talking of Life ever since he learnt to articulate words; he has been writing of it ever since he learnt the art of writing; and has been portraying it with the voice, the string, the brush and the chisel ever since he learnt to sing, to play musical instruments, to paint and to grave images in wood and rock. Yet Life has remained a shoreless ocean, too vast to be contained in any word; too deep to be plumbed with any voice or string; too free and too elusive to be caught in a picture; too volatile to be frozen in a statue.

To reach Ultimate Knowledge is, perhaps, to realize that the meaning of Life, once revealed to the heart and the soul, can never be broadcast by the tongue and the hand. Silence induced by that realization would then be the acme of eloquence. It may be that mankind, quite unconsciously, is moving towards the goal of silent self-expression. Were it but possible for any man to retrieve from the ether everything he had said in his lifetime, he should be struck dumb with amazement at having repeated so many millions of words so many times without wearing his tongue away and without approaching an inch nearer to that knowledge which is knowledge indeed. He should stand aghast at the sight of his soul and mind burdened with so much prattle without being crushed—a prattle which, if carefully sifted, would leave no residue to which he could point and say, "This is the essence of me."

But much speaking, while a common human disease, is a vocation with writers. No sooner does one of them write the last chapter of a book than he begins the first of another, his excuse always being that he has something *new* to offer to the world. Often is a writer forced by his readers to write more and more even when he feels that he has nothing to add to what he has already said. For the readers expect of a writer to be a tree growing by the wayside and always laden with luscious fruit. And as a fruit tree continues to bear even after it has given the most exquisite of its fruits, so does a writer continue to write even after he has produced his very best and utmost.

When Gibran wrote the *Prophet* he felt that he had poured into it the very best of his heart, his mind, and his art. Once the book was off the press and on its way in the world, Gibran began to think of writing another. He must have decided in his mind that *Almustafa* did not express *all* of that *word* he always felt on the tip of his tongue. The book may have given utterance to some syllables of it only; another book would possibly give utterance to the word complete. He did not know that in seeking to utter the word *complete* he was seeking the impossible; for that *word* which is Life will ever defy expression. Therefore he said to me once after *Sand and Foam* was out:

"This is a stop-gap only between the *Prophet* and the next book. It is now three years since I have had a book published. The *Prophet* is a strange little book, Mischa. Many compliment me on it very highly. But it is only the first leg in a tripod— one of a trilogy. It deals with the relations of man to man. I have now in mind a second in which I shall speak of the relations of man to Nature; that I shall call 'The Garden of the Prophet'. The third shall be concerned with the relations of man to God; its name shall be 'The Death of the Prophet.' What do you think of that?"

Soon thereafter, however, he surprised me with a new announcement. When I asked him how far he had gone with the "Garden of the Prophet", his reply was:

"The *Garden* is still in my mind. But what do you say of a book on Jesus? Jesus has been haunting my heart and my imagination for some time past. I am sick and tired, Mischa, of people who profess to believe in him, yet always speak of him and paint him as if he were but a sweet lady with a beard. To them he is beautiful, but lowly, humble, weak and poor. I'm also weary of those that deny him, yet present him as a sorcerer or an imposter. Still more weary am I of 'the scholars' who are ever digging into antiquity to produce lengthy and stupid arguments either for or against the historicity of his personality which is the greatest and most real personality in human history. What shall I say of the senile juggleries of theologians which make of Jesus a sort of a hybrid, half-God and half-man? My Jesus is human like you and me. A certain American writer was even so brazen as to portray him as a clever business man whose deeds and teachings had nothing else in view but cold material profits. Just think! To me he was a man of might and will as he was a man of charity and pity. He was far from being lowly and meek. Lowliness is something I detest; while meekness to me is but a phase of weakness."

Making no comment on his opinion of Jesus I simply remarked,

"Jesus is indeed a topic inexhaustible. No matter how many books have been written about him, there is always room for a new one. But how do you propose to write your book, Gibran?"

"The *how* has already been decided in my mind; and you will like it, Mischa. Once that is found, the book is as good as written. I propose to have a number of Jesus' contemporaries speak of him, each from his own point of view. Their views combined will bring out the portrait of Jesus as I see him. The scheme will be in perfect harmony with my style."

Thus began Gibran to bring the dead back to life and to record their views and impressions of Jesus. In fact he was recording but his own views and impressions and working his mind and heart day and night in doing the recording. Many a night he would sit up until dawn prying into the soul of Judas the Iscariot, Caiaphas, Pontius Pilate, Mary Magdalene, Mary the mother of Jesus, any of the apostles and others. He would try to transport himself into their days and problems, to see things with their eyes and to weigh them in their scales. While at his studio in New York, or with his sister in Boston, he would roam the hills of Galilee, the plains of Judea, the shores of the Dead Sea and the Lake of Tiberias, the Jordan valley and other holy places, following the footsteps of his Jesus, listening to his teachings in temples and beneath the open skies, and endeavouring to put in words the gist of those teachings and to bring out that magic power in them which wrote them in letters of fire athwart the brows of twenty centuries.

Meantime the disease within him kept fortifying itself and tightening its grip on his heart. Perhaps he was blissfully unconscious of the fact. Perhaps he fully realized the hopelessness of overcoming the disease and, therefore, set him at a race with it aiming to finish his new book before being forced to relinquish the pen forever. The fates were still on his side, and he finished the book and had it published the fall of 1928. In October of that year he wrote me from Boston:

"The book on Jesus has absorbed all my summer, with me now ill, now well. Yet I confess to you that my heart is still in it despite the fact that it has been already published and 'has flown out of this cage' ".

How does Jesus look as drawn by Gibran's pencil?

A beautiful and a noble face delicately veiled with something expressive of pity gripping the heart, rather than of sorrow crouching in the soul.

In the sensitive mouth is a firmness too gentle to wound, and a self-respect too proud to be meek. In the nose is the sweetness of poetry, the harmony of art and the symmetry of architecture.

The eyes look through and far beyond whatever material objects they may seem to fall upon. They are inspired, but not serene; and hopeful of ultimate victory, but not yet victorious.

They speak of loneliness unsoothed by Love, and of solitude uncomforted by its own light.

The slightly knitted eyebrows seem to speak of a mind straining after a secret not yet revealed, or an aim not yet attained. They suggest that the man has reached the threshold of that secret whose door remains locked in his face.

In his high and broad forehead is an aloof majesty. The soft hair brushed back from the brow and the temples and descending to the shoulders is eloquent of purity, immaculate and unsoiled.

On the whole it is a face suggestive of many meanings, the most pronounced of them being a will that has not yet conquered, but is determined to conquer.

And how does Jesus look as painted by Gibran's pen?

The answer to that must be drawn from seventy-seven human mouths (Gibran's being one of them). They are the mouths of the disciple and the neighbor; of the friend and the foe; of the man clinging to the earth, and the woman reaching for the sky. For Gibran has chosen to speak of his Jesus through the mouths of his contemporaries some of whom are mentioned in the New Testament, and some invented by the author's imagination. When you have heard all that those have to say—and they all talk in Gibran's poetic style—stop to compare Jesus of the Gospel with Gibran's Jesus, and you shall find a considerable difference between the two:

Jesus of the evangelists was born supernaturally of a virgin in Bethlehem. Jesus after Gibran was born a natural birth in Nazareth.

Jesus of the New Testament weeps and suffers pains. Gibran's Jesus laughs and is above tears and pain.

Jesus of the Gospels beatifies the poor in spirit and the meek. Gibran's Jesus sees nothing beatific in meekness and the poverty of the spirit. On the contrary; he often emerges from Gibran's pages a sort of a Nietzscheesque Superman as witness the following words of Nathaniel: "I am sickened and the bowels within me stir and rise when I hear the faint-hearted call Jesus humble and meek, that they may justify their own faint-heartedness; and when the downtrodden, for comfort and companionship, speak of Jesus as a worm shining by their side. Yea, my heart is sickened by such men. It is the mighty hunter I would preach, and the mountainous spirit unconquerable."

Jesus of the Gospels is not ashamed to cry from the height of his cross, "My God, my God, why hast thou forsaken *me*?" for he had not yet overcome all the weakness of the flesh. Whereas Gibran's Jesus is made to say, "Why hast thou forsaken *us*?", as if ashamed to admit any individual weakness.

What is more startling is that Gibran, in his endeavor to bring out a Jesus who was more than "a lady with a beard", went so far as to make some changes in the text and purport of the Gospel, while adhering more or less to the main narrative of the great, old book. Thus he paraphrases the Lord's prayer and the famous Sermon on the Mount in a way that robs both of much of their majestic simplicity, their sanctity and their incomparable depth and beauty. Some miracles and some events in the life of Jesus are related by Gibran with important details purposely omitted or changed, or with new details added as if to correct the faulty original.

Some justification may be found for Gibran in that he writes of Jesus not as a historian or as a scholar, but as a poet and an artist. You may bridle a historian's pen; but wherewith shall you bridle the poet's and the artist's imagination? Furthermore, Gibran writes of Jesus with a heart full of admiration, love and reverence; for Jesus to him had always been the very noblest and the very loftiest human ideal. Nevertheless, and regardless of the feeling of sanctity attached to the canonic text of the Gospels by millions of Christians throughout the centuries, it is of doubtful taste for any artist or poet to tamper with that text when that very text offers a virgin field for their muses. It is specifically said by St. John at the end of his Gospel that "there are also many other things which Jesus did, the which, if they should be written every one, I suppose that even the world itself could not contain the books that should be written." Is not this an open invitation to any imagination to try its wings in exploring new horizons instead of meddling with things already said and piously accepted?

It is quite permissible and intelligible for so many Christians to have so many notions or pictures of Jesus. But it is hardly permissible for anyone to take his Jesus out of the Gospels, and then to change the text of the Gospels so as to make it fit one's own notion, or picture of Jesus.

That is not to say that Gibran does not write most beautifully and most reverentially of Jesus. Listen to him speak of his Jesus through the mouth of Malachi, the Babylonian astronomer:

"In Jesus the elements of our bodies and our dreams came together according to law. All that was timeless before Him became timeful in Him."

And hear his explanation of Jesus' miracles through the same mouth:

"They say He gave sight to the blind and walking to the paralyzed, and that He drove devils out of madmen.

"Perchance blindness is but a dark thought that can be overcome by a burning thought. Perchance a withered limb is but idleness that can be quickened by energy. And perhaps the devils, these restless elements in our life, are driven out by the angels of peace and serenity."

Hear again what he makes the disciple Andrew say of his Master when the latter saved the harlot from being stoned and said to her, "Neither do I condemn thee: go, and sin no more". Says Andrew:

"And I wondered then whether He said this to her because He Himself was not without sin.

"But since that day I have pondered long, and I know now that only the pure of heart forgive the thirst that leads to dead waters."

In this book, as in all his books, Gibran scatters with a lavish hand a multitude of brilliant figures of speech, and draws many word pictures that sparkle with life and beauty. I cannot help but quote a few:

"At dawn she was still standing among us like a lone banner in the wilderness wherein there are no hosts." The reference is to Mary after her son's betrayal.

"Woman shall be forever the womb and the cradle but never the tomb."

"Women travel not save when led by their children."

"A seed hidden in the heart of an apple is an orchard invisible."

"Even now Jerusalem holds the basin and Rome the ewer, and betwixt the two a thousand thousand hands would be washed to whiteness."

Not less brilliant is Gibran's sarcasm. In the following passage he seems to be defending himself as he defends Jesus against those who accused him of being confounded because he did not know his own mind:

"Many indeed are the owls who know no song unlike their own hooting. You and I know the jugglers of words who would honor only a greater juggler, men who carry their heads in baskets to the market-place and sell them to the first bidder. We know the pigmies who abuse the sky-man. As we know what the weed would say of the oak tree and the cedar."

And these words of Jesus addressed to Judas:

"My kingdom is not of this earth, and my seat is not builded upon the skulls of your ancestors.

"If you seek aught save the kingdom of the spirit then it were better for you to leave me here, and go down to the caves of your dead, where the crowned heads of yore hold court in their tombs and may still be bestowing honors upon the bones of your forefathers."

As pungent is his upbraiding of the rich by the mouth of one of them, and of the conservative men of power and position by the mouth of Caiaphas. Even St. Paul, the apostle of the Gentiles, does not escape his biting sarcasm. For the great man of Tarsus, according to Gibran, has vitiated the Nazarene's teachings by what he added to them of his own teachings.

* * *

All the drawings in the book are rich in symbolism and exquisite delicacy. Particularly effective is that of Jesus used as a frontispiece; and that of Mary Magdalene which seems to justify in full Jesus' words of the reformed adulteress as reported by Gibran: "But I see in you a beauty that shall not fade away, and in the autumn of your days that beauty shall not be afraid to gaze at itself in the mirror, and it shall not be offended", and those of the apostles Peter and John. Likewise are the two colored drawings, one representing a youth kneeling upon a cloud and encircled with a ring of floating human bodies; the other representing "The Tree of Life" with human roots, a human trunk, boughs endowed with wings, and fruits ripening in the sky. Both drawings are symphonies of color and poetry.

* * *

Mountains of books have been written about the prophet of Galilee since he began his mission over nineteen centuries ago. Some have flatly denied his existence; some, while conceding him existence, called him a charlatan; others represented him as a lunatic or a visionary; some believed him to be a god; some accepted him only as a man; while others would have him God and Man in one. Is not that fact alone proof convincing that the man was a most magnificent manifestation of Cosmic Unity? He is far too great to be hemmed in between the two covers of any book. Those who would enter his "kingdom" must not only *understand* his words, but must, above all, *do the will* of his Father in Heaven.

Yet, if unable to do the Father's will, we atone to some extent for our inability with laying bare our longings to walk in His Son's footsteps. In that respect Gibran's book should be viewed as the sacrifice his heart offers at the feet of his Greater Brother—Jesus The Son of Man.

PEACE

Fortune has always been said to be fickle. It seems to joy in wearing masks which are the very opposite of the face they hide. When the mask smiles, the face beneath it snarls.

After *The Prophet* and *Jesus The Son of Man* Fortune began to smile on Gibran. Every day added more and more to his admirers, especially in feminine circles. His revenues increased, and his surplus money was well invested through the help of a banker friend. *The Prophet* had been translated into several foreign tongues. A lecture bureau offered to take him on a reading tour. He moved his sister Marianna from the Chinese quarters in Boston to a new house he purchased in the suburbs of the city. His colleagues in *Arrabitah* commemorized the silver jubilee of his literary activity with a large banquet in one of the best New York hotels. Rarely a day passed when the mail, the telegraph and the telephone did not bring him fresh testimonies of appreciation and admiration. Once he told me with the deepest satisfaction—yet in a manner pretending the utmost indifference—that Queen Mary of Rumania wrote to a lady friend in New York thanking her for the copy of *The Prophet* she had presented her with, and requesting her to give her best regards to the author for the pleasure she had derived from reading his book. He once showed me a letter from the president of Colorado College asking his permission to have the following saying of Almustafa inscribed on the master bell of a set of chimes installed in the belfry of the college chapel:

"Yesterday is but Today's memory, and Tomorrow is Today's dream."

216

But Fortune has a way with those that trust her not unlike the way of the cat when playing with a mouse. The mouse is nearest to perdition when released from the cat's paws and made to believe that it has escaped with life and liberty. No quicker does it taste that momentary freedom than it finds itself once more between the jaws of death.

The fiercest kind of poverty is, perhaps, the poverty that bites with teeth of diamond sunk in gums of gold; and the worst sort of hardship is the hardship dressed in ermine and silk; and the cruelest loneliness is the loneliness that speaks with the tongues of admirers and well-wishers.

Gibran, having lived to see many of the dreams of his youth bud forth and come to fruition, began to feel himself afflicted with a poverty, a hardship and a loneliness much more cruel than those he suffered before. Despite the fact that women flocked about him like moths about a lamp, his heart was void of love. Fame with all it brings of the incense of praise and admiration may anesthetize the heart for a day—for a month; it cannot quench its thirst, appease its hunger, and light up its loneliness when it wakes up in the deep hush of night or the broad glare of day. What if it be the heart of a poet and an artist, and an ill one to boot?

For several years Gibran tried to think of his illness as if it were a minor disorder which could be remedied with dieting and orderly living. But far from diminishing, the disorder seemed to grow. Now he would feel it in his joints and think it rheumatism; now in his respiratory channels, and believe it to be a kind of bronchitis. At other times it would grip his heart with iron fingers, and he would imagine it some sort of a heart disease. As to physicians, some prescribed strict dieting; some, complete rest; others, drugs and radium or electric treatments. He tried all of that with no definite results. Between attacks which came at varying intervals he would find himself almost normal. His hopes would revive; his energy would recover its tempo; and he would rush back to his pen and brush to imprison in word and line the thoughts and shadows that besieged his bed, and walked and sat with him in the street and in the parlor.

In the end the X-rays revealed to Gibran the nature and the seat of his illness. But he kept the matter a secret from me and the rest of his friends, and would have kept it a secret from himself if he could. A physician in Boston advised an operation. Gibran acquiesced. On the day appointed for the operation he dressed, bade his sister good-by and descended the staircase on his way to the hospital. At the bottom of the stairs he changed his mind, retraced his steps to the house and informed his sister that he had decided to let the fates do what they pleased. There was a will and a courage in that decision. Neither before nor after did Gibran make any bitter complaints of his illness. Never did the pain paralyze his hand, or the fear of death hobble his imagination.

With pain reinforcing its armies and increasing its pressure against him Gibran could no longer see *The Garden of The Prophet* with the same clear eye with which he had seen it before. He had visualized it a Garden where the insect and the plant, the light and the darkness, the man and the animal coexisted in perfect harmony in the bosom of Cosmic Unity. Everything was peace, beauty and loving understanding. He had already drawn a few word pictures of that harmony of being during the intervals when he was in a state of truce with pain. Now that those intervals became shorter and shorter, that Garden was no longer the same. Pain was playing havoc with its plants, its clear skies, its peaceful atmosphere. Gibran, therefore, turned his mind away from it hoping all the while to go back to it when he retrieved that ecstasy he tasted while writing *The Prophet*. But that ecstasy never came back.

How often in those days did Gibran seek refuge from his pains in his pen, only to hear his pen say: "Let me be, and go back to your heart. For in the heart only is the light of truth and salvation, 'Blessed are the pure in heart: for they shall see God' ". How often he sought relief in his heart, only to hear it exclaim: "Pity me, Gibran! You have fed me much, and you have watered me much. Yet am I hungry for food that decays not, and for drink that gives no rise to new thirst. Behold me alone in this hermitage, with no sister-heart to assuage my pains, a loving eye to watch over me, or a tender hand to feel my pulse."

One day Gibran received a message of admiration from a young girl who was a total stranger to him. The message breathed more understanding and enthusiasm than any he had received before. It contained the sender's address and telephone number. He called her up and thanked her for her beautiful letter. When she expressed the desire to pay him a visit she was told that she would be most welcome.

The girl went to see Gibran, having read of all his books *The Prophet* only. Stammering with an influx of many emotions, but in words overflowing with pure sincerity, she told of the deep impression the book made on her and how she found in it the greatest prop for her ideals and the surest friend of her own convictions and aspirations. She left the studio drunk with the wine of Gibran's words and feeling that she had found in him the personification of human perfection.

Other visits followed. Gibran had been feeling an emptiness in his heart and his need for a woman to share with him the bitter and the sweet of existence. Before he realized the serious nature of his illness his solitude was too dear to his heart to let any woman disturb it for long. It was the fountainhead of his inspiration, and the cradle for his muse's children. But after he discovered how serious his plight was he began to fear his ill solitude, or his solitary illness. Reviewing in his mind all the women close to him, he could find none after his soul and heart excepting Mary Haskell. Once he proposed marriage to her; and the issue was what it was. She remained a bright star in his firmament; but has recently married one of her rich relatives, a man many years her senior; the two were living in Savannah, Ga. She had consulted Gibran about her marriage, and he advised her to marry and blessed her decision.

Now comes this young girl stranger. Is it that Fate has sent her to him to brighten up his loneliness, to assuage his pains, and to share in his sorrows and his longings? Is she the "destined" one whose name was written from eternity in the mysterious scrolls of the earth? Be that as it may; the fact remains that the girl is a bright, warm ray; she is healthy, vigorous, and her devotion to him is akin to worship.

But flesh is flesh, and ah, how weak! And passion is passion and ah, how strong! This time also Gibran forgot his beautiful verse in *Processions:*

"When Love is led to a couch of sensuality it commits suicide." The excuse he offered to himself and to the girl was, "That is my life." It was an excuse which, if it satisfied Gibran, did not satisfy his young visitor who came to him with a soul vibrating with *The Prophet's* deep tones, and went away with regret and disappointment gnawing her heart and pressing on her mind. She felt as if a wondrous jewel in her hand had suddenly turned to dust; or as if the earth had slipped from under her feet. Upon reaching home she wrote Gibran a long letter in which she bitterly upbraided herself and gently chided him. She had believed when she "discovered" the author of *The Prophet* that she had discovered the ideal man—the man whose beautiful life and spirit would atone for all the ugliness still permeating the souls and the lives of the majority of men. But she found him like any other man—preaching what he did not do, or doing what he did not preach. Is life, then, worth living? Is not straining after perfection a delusion, and clinging to chastity and purity a sheer madness?

The impact of that letter on Gibran was so great that he at once took his soul to task, and stripping it naked of all deceptive cloaks woven by earthly desires and passions, began to wash it with all the water of goodness still bubbling in his heart, and to anoint it with all the perfumed oil of beauty still seeping from his spirit, and to bury at her feet all his shortcomings and transgressions one by one. He felt as if his soul had been far away, and now came back; as if it had been a stranger and an enemy, and now became a kin and a friend. And he embraced it and made peace with it, that very peace which he had been craving all his life. He then called the young girl back to him, asked her forgiveness and pleaded with her not to give up her faith in Life, and not to judge God by the fault of one of His creatures, even if that creature be Kahlil Gibran. He also said to her what he once said to Mary Haskell—"Will you walk the road with me?"

Little was Gibran aware of the fact that, with a few months left him, his road was almost at an end, and that he had to walk it alone to that end.

CLOUD-FILTERED RAYS

In surrendering himself to the will of Life Gibran did not think he was surrendering to Death which he fought stubbornly to the last breath. In one of his last letters to me from Boston he spoke of his ailment in the following vein:

"My ailment is seated in something much deeper than muscle and bone. I have often wondered if it were not a state of health instead of illness. It is a state, Mischa, whether of health or of illness. . . . It is one of the seasons of my life; and in your life and mine there are winters and springs; and you and I do not know *in truth* which is the more preferable."

For that reason, and because he disliked all manifestation of weakness, I never heard him ouch or whimper. Night after night and day after day he fought his pains alone. Seldom would he call a friend to his side except when his pain and his loneliness became insupportable. No doubt that his great power of endurance was sustained by his firm faith in the purifying touch of pain.

Once, in the early part of 1931, I telephoned inquiring of his health. His reply was, "Come and see." I found him in bed with his face showing signs of fatigue and pallor such as I had never noticed in it before. He reassured me, however, that what kept him in bed was nothing more serious than a "severe cold," and that it was almost at an end. I scolded him hotly for neglecting his health to that extent, saying that his living by himself was no longer permissible; that he should allow me, or any other of his friends, to sleep with him; else he should send after his

222

sister to come and live with him. He assured me that nothing of that was necessary, and that the janitor's wife was very kindly and quite able and ready to give him all the service he needed. As to his sister, her coming to New York would necessitate hiring an apartment in addition to the studio, which involved considerable extra expense. Besides he would not exchange the simplicity and the disorder of the "hermitage" for any apartment no matter how large, how orderly and how comfortable.

"And Mar-Sarkees, Gibran. Is it not time you discharged your vow? Believe me, if it were in my power, I should 'ship' you this very day to Lebanon. Your staying here, writing and drawing continually in your present state of health is suicide."

"My vow to Mar-Sarkees shall be discharged, and soon, God willing. But to stop writing and drawing is to become a cabbage. What is my life without writing and drawing? And you, of all men, Mischa, counselling me to give them up! You saying that? I can hardly believe my ears. Must we choke the poetry and the art in us in order to spare the breath in our nostrils?"

"Art is not what we paint or draw, Gibran. Nor is poetry what we compose of rhythmic sentences. Art is the realizing of the harmony of being in our own spirits and of translating that harmony into aims, thoughts and deeds which leave no room for friction in our souls between good and evil. And poetry is the finding of the proper measure and rime for our days and nights. So long as we pass through states which so crush the heart and muddle the mind as to cloud our sight, and turn the honey in our mouths into gall, and disjoint our joints—what is the good of a beautiful picture we draw, or of a ringing poem we write? Can we draw Beauty unless it draws us first? Can we utter Truth before Truth has uttered us? Did we but live a beautiful life, we should do nothing but the beautiful; and then we should have no need of drawing Beauty. Did we obey the Truth in our thoughts, we should be able to utter nothing but the Truth; and then we should have no need *to preach* the Truth."

"Is it not true, Mischa, that every time we draw Beauty we approach a step nearer to Beauty? And every time we write the Truth we became one with it? Or do you propose to muzzle poets and artists? Is not self-expression a deeply seated need in the human soul?"

"The soul is bound, freely and naturally, to radiate its secrets. So soon, however, as we try to give expression to those secrets whether in word or in line, we invariably disfigure them by either adding to them or subtracting from them; they are never the same when expressed as when unexpressed. Often, consciously or unconsciously, we pass up what we consider unbeautiful in us in order to put the beautiful in relief. The beauty which must be extricated from the nets of ugliness is not beauty. The ugliness that cohabits with beauty cannot be ugliness. And man, ever at pains to sift the beautiful from the ugly in life, had better say to the Creator of Life, 'You ill govern Your creation. You have confounded the true of it and the false, the beautiful and the ugly. Descend from Your throne, and I shall show you how to winnow all things and gather the beautiful and the true unto the beautiful and true, and the ugly and the false unto the ugly and the false.' Is not God beyond our notions of beauty and ugliness, and above our right and wrong?"

"He is, Mischa, He is. Perhaps we are nearer to Him each time we try to divide Him and find Him indivisible. Yet do I say that art, through drawing a line between the beautiful and the ugly, is the nearest way to God. Pure meditation which you seem to stress is another way. But it leads to silence and to self-confinement. You are right—silence is truer and more expressive than speech; and the hour shall come when we shall be silent. But why muzzle our tongues before that hour has struck? There is your friend Laotzu; he became silent, but when? After he gave to the world the gist of his faith in words. Yea we shall be silent some day, Mischa. But now let us speak. Here's a bundle of words; read them and tell me what you think of them."

Whereupon he handed me the manuscript of *The Earth Gods* and asked me to read it aloud.

The manuscript was a long prose poem in which three voices, representing three gods, air their views on Man and his destiny. Says the First God, weary of his godhood to the point of desiring annihilation:

"Weary is my spirit of all there is. I would not move a hand to create a world, or to erase one. I would not live could I but die; for the weight of aeons is upon me, and the ceaseless moan of the seas exhausts my sleep. Could I but lose the primal aim and vanish like a wasted sun; could I but strip my divinity of its purpose, and breathe my immortality into space, and be no more; could I but be consumed and pass from time's memory into the emptiness of nowhere!"

The second is a god who delights in playing with things on the earth, and with men and their lives in particular. He would not be content with annihilation, but would "choose the hardest way" which is:

"To raise man from the secret darkness, yet keep his roots clinging to the earth; to give him thirst for life, and make death his cup-bearer; to endow him with love that waxes with pain, and exalts with desire, and increases with longing, and fadeth away with the first embrace; to girdle his nights with dreams of higher days, and infuse his days with visions of blissful nights, and yet to confine his days and his nights to their immutable resemblance; to make his fancy like the eagle of the mountain, and his thought as the tempest of the seas, and yet to give him hands slow in decision, and feet heavy with deliberation; to give him gladness that he may sing for us, and sorrow that he may call unto us, and then to lay him low when the earth in her hunger cries for food; to raise his soul high above the firmament that he may foretaste our tomorrow, and to keep his body groveling in the mire that he may not forget his yesterday."

As he listens to his two comrades' outgivings, the Third God has his eyes glued upon a youth and a maiden dancing and singing to Love in the valley below. In vain does he call his companions' attention to them; they pay no heed at first to his pleadings. In the end, however, he succeeds in winning The Second God to the view that Love is the first and last reality in the world and the only truth of being.

The poem, begun in a minor key, concludes with the following triumphant declaration of The Third God:

"We shall pass into the twilight;
Perchance to wake to the dawn of another world.
But love shall stay,
And his finger-marks shall not be erased.
The blessed forge burns,
The sparks rise, and each spark is a sun.
Better it is for us and wiser,
To seek a shadowed nook and sleep in our earth divinity,
And let love, human and frail, command the coming day."

Now and then I would pause in my reading to comment on some brilliant passage or a striking thought, and to watch the effect on Gibran's face. All through the reading that face seemed bathed in a light like the light of the setting sun passing through a cloud. The cloud was the pain visited on him by life and described in the poem by the Second God. Forgetting that few moments before I had been urging him to quit writing, I could not help but express my unstinted admiration for the glowing style of the poem and the rich imagination that conceived it, regretting that it was not of the same clear metal as *The Prophet*, and that his soul which had found its best expression and ultimate unification in the latter book, became once more confused and divided. In my heart I was certain that pain was the cause of the confusion and division, but my tongue refused to make any reference to that pain.

The reading over, we talked extensively of the poem and its various shades. Then rose Gibran from bed and began to display on the easel before me the twelve drawings he had prepared for the book. The drawings made me almost forget Gibran, myself and the poem whose music still vibrated in my ears. In addition to their lightness of touch, their depth of meaning and their harmony of lines and colors those drawings surprised me with a masculinity, a vigor, a depth and an ease never before so abundant in Gibran's art. It astonished me to see that, as he advanced in years, Gibran the artist was gaining at the expense of Gibran the poet.

"These are all last summer's work. It was a fruitful summer." And after a pause,

"I have remembered you in my will, Mischa."

The last words fell on me like hailstones out of a summer cloud. Violently shaken out of my silence, I felt that my heart had become a jar of tears. The jar would have emptied itself were it not for my fear that a tear falling from my eye at that moment was certain to cause a flood of tears from Gibran's eyes. Haltingly and reproachfully I said,

"I would not hear anything like that from you, Gibran, today or ever. You cannot will me anything more precious than yourself; and that I have without any will. For you shall always be with me as I shall always be with you."

* * *

Two weeks later I told Nasseeb Arida of what Gibran had said to me; and he said that Gibran had made the same remark to him in the same words: "I have remembered you in my will, Nasseeb." Soon after Gibran's death Abdul told me of his last visit to Gibran a few days before his death. Said Abdul:

"It was a rainy day. Gibran called up and asked me to bring him some Arabic newspapers and magazines. I took him an armful of them. He was in bed when I walked in on him; but he got up and ṣat by my side. For the first time I heard the voice of death in his voice, and saw the shadow of death on his face. I tried my best not to let him feel that I heard what I heard and saw what I saw. We talked of many things and most of all of *Arrabitah*. One by one he recalled his fellow-members, giving his frank opinion of each as if wishing to gather them all about him and to bid them the last farewell. He asked me of my family, mentioning each one of the children by name and giving me a small sum of money with the request that I buy with it a bouquet of flowers as a present from him to my wife. He then looked at me and said: 'Have no anxiety about your children's future. If I live I shall see that they get a fair education. Otherwise I have willed them enough. The will is in the drawer of that table!' And he pointed to the small night table by his bed."

But neither Abdul, nor Nasseeb, nor I knew the real ailment of Gibran. We were blissfully ignorant of the fact that he was taking his leave of us, and that the fates were gathering up the threads of his life while we believed them to be continuing the pattern on the loom of time.

DEAD

The rattle deepens in refrain and recedes in distance like the scattered remnants of a storm in the hollow of a deep ravine. The groans sink lower and lower and become far apart. The intern feels the pulse from time to time in expectation of the last heartbeat.

Sitting by the side of the small, white cot I meditate on the heart now throbbing its last—where are its countless throbs from the first to the last? And it strikes me that the Space has a memory wherein are graved indelibly every heartbeat, every desire, every thought, every deed, every murmur, every dream, and every breath; that a day shall come for every man in which his eyes and ears shall be freed from sensory delusions thus enabling him to see and to hear everything he had passed through from the moment he became a separate morsel of palpitating life to the moment he re-discovered his oneness with the One. It even strikes me that that memory is hidden in the depths of man; and that each man, unknowingly, registers his life in himself as voice is registered on a phonographic record. The words of Christ, "For nothing is secret, that shall not be made manifest; neither anything hid, that shall not be known and come abroad" flash through my mind; and I feel the awesomeness and the justice of Judgment, and am persuaded that the Judgment Day is that day in which the inner phonograph shall repeat to us all the details of our lives across the aeons. And I bless Life and pray its forgiveness for all the cruelty and the injustice I and my fellow-men have imputed to it. And I say to my soul: "As you sing, so is sung unto you. As

229

you sow, so you reap. Never have you been oppressed except because you have oppressed; never have you suffered pain save because you have inflicted on others pain; never have you shed tears except because you have made others to shed tears. As you are, so is your life."

And death? Shall the edge of the cot by my side be the limit of the life now flickering away on that cot? Is this cot more spacious than God from Whom that life issued, thus being as eternal as He, and beyond Whom it cannot pass, thus becoming as immortal as He?

And my relations with my friend—shall they stop when his breath stops? And our minds which so often ran together; and our souls so closely fraternal—shall the abyss of death separate them forever? Where is the power that can break a single link in the chain of Time thus breaking the whole chain? Is not the connection between me and my friend a link in that chain and, therefore, unbreakable so long as Time is Time? Is not every link in the infinite chain of Time as infinite as Time? And any two links bound up together in that chain—are they not destined to remain together until the end of Time? If they be out of sight at a certain point of time and space, they must be in sight at another point of time and space, like the sun that "sets" here only to "rise" in another place. Nay, neither on earth nor in heaven is there a power that can sunder a relation which Life has made fast between a man and a man, or between one thing and another. And is there an atom in the world which is not bound fast to every other atom in the world?

How infinite, how beautiful, how just are you, O God! How ignorant are we in detaching ourselves from You in everything we do, and say, and wish, and think, suffering pain in consequence, and moaning and wailing when You draw us back into Your holy presence! How stupid of us to burn away our days and nights seeking any knowledge other than knowing You, and any right other than Your right, and any peace other than Your peace! How very poor are we amassing any riches other than the riches of Your love inexhaustible! How very weak are we buttressing ourselves against *this hour* with all manner of forts except the impregnable fort of Faith in You! And how blind are we in seeking You anywhere save in our own selves!

But why has it been decreed that of all Gibran's friends I, alone, should be called upon to witness his battle with death? More than once have I made efforts to contact Nasseeb or Abdul, but to no avail. He loved them both with a strong love. Perhaps I should try once more.

I rise from my chair near the white cot and hear sobs and wailing outside the door. As I open the door I find that Marianna had just arrived from Boston in answer to an urgent telegraphic call which was the first notice she had of her brother's serious condition. The women in the corridor were leading her to an adjoining room. Her sobs and supplications were heart-rending. I had met her once before when I visited Gibran in Boston, and she knew much of me from Gibran. The moment her eye fell on me she choked with tears and rushed to me as if it were in my power to arrest the march of death and turn the clock of time backwards:

"I beg you . . . I sense Gibran in you. You are his brother and mine. Will Gibran die? Has he died? Please. . . . Will you let him die?"

I go back into Gibran's room with my heart as full of wailing as my ears. The awful gurgling is slowly dying down; the groans are barely audible. My thoughts run helter-skelter. My soul propounds a thousand questions to which I respond with a thousand shades of silence. My feelings become muddled: Should I surrender to sorrow; or should I brace myself with undaunted faith? Should I feel glad for my brother's release from the cares of the earth; or should I grieve over his life, so full of storms, so rich in thought, imagination, hope, light and shade, but now picking up its hems from the earth before having had its fill of the earth?

I feel the deep and awesome mystery Life is fulfilling right before my eyes. To my mind comes the words of Almustafa to the sea:

"Only another winding will this stream make, only another murmur in this glade, and then shall I come to you, a boundless drop to a boundless ocean."

And his last words to the people of Orphalese:

"A little while, a moment of rest upon the wind, and another woman shall bear me."

As the last breath leaves my brother's chest, I feel a power pulling me down to the floor, and I kneel beside the small cot burying my face in the folds of the white spread upon it. Of all the voices that rush into my ears I hear but one. In some tremors of it I hear the prayer of a contrite heart; in others, the hymn of Faith triumphant. It is the great Psalmist's voice:

"Have mercy upon me, O God, according to thy loving kindness: according unto the multitude of thy tender mercies blot out my transgressions. . . . Behold, I was shapen in iniquity; and in sin did my mother conceive me. . . . Purge me with hyssop, and I shall be clean: wash me, and I shall be whiter than snow. . . . Create in me a clean heart, O God; and renew a right spirit within me. . . ."

A momentary trance overtakes me out of which I emerge with the Galilean's farewell words to his disciples upon my lips,

"And, lo, I am with you always, even unto the end of the world."

PART IV

Appendix

GIBRAN'S BODY

It is related of Chuang Tzu, the Chinese sage of the 4th century B.C., that when he was on his deathbed his disciples expressed the intention of giving him a burial worthy of his exalted station. His reply was: "With Heaven and Earth for my coffin and shell; with the sun, moon, and stars as my burial regalia; and with all creation to escort me to the grave—are not my funeral paraphernalia ready to hand?"

"We fear," argued the disciples, "lest the carrion kite should eat the body of our master."

"Above ground," said the sage, "I shall be food for kites; below I shall be food for molecrickets and ants. Why rob one to feed the other?"

But our "enlightened" civilization cannot see eye to eye with Chuang Tzu. Its codes decree more reverence for dust after it is robbed of the breath of life than for that same dust when still a living organism. In addition to sustaining the loss of their dear ones, survivors are saddled with many responsibilities towards the lifeless bodies of the dead.

It was past midnight when I left Marianna at the hotel and went home. The balance of the night I spent wide-awake. To sleep was as impossible as to forget what I had seen and heard that night. The morning of the following day—Saturday—I went down to the studio and found that Marianna and those that were with her had already preceded me there. An obituary notice had to be placed in newspapers; arrangements had to be made to have the body embalmed; a casket had to be bought; non-sectarian undertakers' parlors had to be found where the body could lie in state the major part of that Saturday and all of the following Sunday so as to afford Gibran's many friends and admirers the opportunity of seeing him for the last time before his body is taken to Boston. With the help of some friends all those arrangements were made and smoothly carried out. All day Sunday, and well into the night, a constant stream of people flowed in and out of the parlors where the body lay amid heaps of flowers.

During the day an influential Lebanese journalist of the Maronite faith took me aside and confided to me that the Maronite priest in New York was unwilling to certify to the priest in Boston that Gibran had died a good Maronite; for he had heard from the nun at the hospital what Gibran had said to her when she asked him if he was a Catholic; while he—the priest—was unable to confess Gibran or to commune him. Without the priest's certificate a church burial in Boston would be impossible. I asked the journalist to use his influence with the priest, not for Gibran's sake who cared little for all rituals, but for the sake of Marianna who was in a most pitiful condition being unable to restrain her tears for two nights and two days. The man did not disappoint me.

The following Monday morning the body was on its way to Boston accompanied by Marianna and the two relatives that had come with her to New York, and by most of Gibran's colleagues in *Arrabitah* and two of the American ladies whom I had met at the hospital. In Boston the body lay in state at the Syrian Ladies' Aid Society's quarters until Tuesday morning. It was there that I met for the first time Mary Haskell who came from distant Savannah to take part in the funeral. I was most impressed by her dignified and frank simplicity which was noticeable not only in her features, but even in her dress. Her calm, intelligent face betrayed no sorrow; her voice, no disturbance. She spoke to me then and many times afterward of Gibran as if he were still living. I am indebted to her for much of what is recorded in this book of her relations with Gibran and of Gibran's relations with Micheline.

On Tuesday morning the body was taken to the Maronite church of Our Lady of the Cedars, whence it was carried after the service in a long and a most impressive procession to the cemetery for temporary burial, until Gibran's will was found and opened, and his wish ascertained as to the final resting place he had chosen for himself.

A few months later, though no special provisions were found in the will, Marianna decided to have her brother's body buried at his birthplace in Lebanon which he loved so dearly and to which he had always hoped to return. The body reached the port of Beirut on the twenty-first day of August, 1931, where it was given a reception the like of which Beirut had never before witnessed. From Beirut the body was taken to Bisharri in an unprecedented cortege which grew larger and larger as it passed through the many towns and villages on the way. At Bisharri, after much maneuvering, it came to final rest in a crypt within the chapel of that hermitage to which Gibran and I had hoped to retire, and which Marianna decided to buy.

I visited Mar-Sarkees the summer of 1932, and can find no better words to describe its peaceful solitude than the barely legible inscription above its gate:

OH BEATA SOLITUDO
OH SOLA BEATITUDO

GIBRAN'S WILL

The will of which Gibran spoke to A. Haddad, N. Arida, several of his American friends, of whom I know seven, and to myself did not come to light. The one filed with the court and probated was dated March 13, 1930, a little over a year before his death. A copy of that will was found with Marianna, and the original with Mr. Edgar Speyer. Below is the text of it:

"In the event of my death I wish that whatever money or securities Mr. Edgar Speyer has been gracious enough to hold for me should go to my sister Mary K. Gibran who now lives at 67 Tyler Street, Boston, Mass.

"There are also 40 (forty) shares of the Fifty-One West Tenth Street Studio Association Stock lying in my safe deposit box with the Bank of Manhattan Trust Company, 31 Union Square, New York. These shares are also to go to my sister.

"There are in addition to the foregoing, two (2) bank books of the West Side Savings Bank, 422 Sixth Avenue, New York, which I have with me in my studio. I wish that my sister would take this money to my home town of Besharri, Republic of Lebanon, and spend it upon charities.

"The royalties on my copyrights, which copyrights I understand can be extended upon request by my heirs for an additional period of twenty-eight years after my death, are to go to my home town.

"Everything found in my studio after my death, pictures, books, objects of art, etcetera, go to Mrs. Mary Haskell Mines, now living at 24 Gaston Street West, Savannah, Ga. But I would like to have Mrs. Mines send all or any part of those things to my home town should she see fit to do so."

Gibran's net estate came to $53,196.00. Before the great drop in the stock and real estate prices it was estimated close to $90,000.00.

GIBRAN'S LETTERS

The following letters from Gibran to the author, though personal, are offered for whatever added light they may throw on Gibran's life and personality. Certain outspoken passages in them may hurt the sensitiveness of some readers. Atonement sufficient for that is to be sought in the sincerity and charitable nature of their author. Most of them were left undated; perhaps because coming from Boston to New York—a matter of a few hours. As nearly as possible I have endeavored to indicate the year and the origin of each letter.

Letter 1.—(From New York City to Walla Walla, Wash.)

Sept. 4, 1919.

My Dear Mikhail,

God's peace be upon you. I am back after my protracted absence and have seen our brother Nasseeb and had a long talk with him about reviving *Al-Funoon* and the means of insuring its future. I have had similar talks with many literati and semi-literati in Boston and New York. All those talks would reach a certain point and halt. That point is this: Nasseeb Arida cannot carry the burden alone. It is imperative that Mikhail Naimy return to New York and help Nasseeb in putting the project on working basis before the literati and the business men of New York; for the confidence of those can be gained by the two working together, and is hard to win by one alone. New York is the capital of the Syrians in America, and Mikhail Naimy has influence with the Syrians in New York. A large entertainment should be given in New York, and the proceeds thereof should go to the magazine. How is the entertainment to be a success when the man who is to arrange the various parts of the program, to give it publicity and to see it through is in the state of Washington? A small committee should be formed to carry out the details, with a treasurer known to the Syrians of the interior who shall ask a thousand and one questions before they decide to respond to the circular. And who, perchance, other than Mikhail Naimy can organize that committee?

There are many things, Mikhail, that begin and end with you each time we open the subject of *Al-Funoon*. If you desire the magazine to be brought back to life, you should return to New York and be the "mainspring" in every move, since Nasseeb is unable to do anything at present, and there is no one in New York of all the well-wishers of *Al-Funoon* who is capable of assuming the responsibility for the project. I believe that five thousand dollars would be sufficient to insure the future of the magazine. But I also believe that a circular without an entertainment would not bring even half of that amount. In brief, the success of the plan depends upon your presence in New York. If it be a sacrifice on your part to return to New York, that sacrifice should be viewed in the light of laying what is dear at the feet of that which is dearer, and offering the important on the altar of that which is more important. To me the dearest in your life is the realization of your dreams; and the most important is the exploitation of your talents.

Write me if you will; and may God preserve you for your brother

Gibran.

Letter 2.—(From Boston to New York) May 24, 1920.

Brother Mikhail,

Peace be to your good soul and big heart. And now, *Arrabitah* shall hold its regular meeting to-morrow (Wednesday) evening, with me, to my regret, far from you. Had it not been for a talk I am to give Thursday night, I would return to New York for the sake of *Arrabitah's* eyes. If you consider the giving of a talk a sufficient legal excuse, I should be grateful for your generosity and consideration. Otherwise I shall willingly pay the "fine" of five dollars with something to boot.

In days gone by this city was called the city of learning and art. Now it is the city of traditions. The souls of its inhabitants are petrified; their thoughts are old and worn out. What is strange, Mikhail, is that the petrified has always been boastful and proud; and the worn out and old has ever held its nose high. How often I talked with Harvard professors, yet felt as if I were talking to a professor from *Al-Azhar!** How often I conversed with some Bostonian ladies and heard them say things I used to hear from simple and ignorant old women in Syria! Life is one, Mikhail; it manifests itself in the villages of Lebanon as in Boston, New York, and San Francisco.

Remember me in friendship to my brothers and fellow-workers in *Arrabitah*. May God keep you dear to your brother

Gibran.

Letter 3.—(From Boston to New York) Wednesday Evening. (1920)

Brother Mikhail,

I have just read your article on *The Tempest*. What shall I say to you, Mikhail?

You have put between your eye and the pages of my book a magnifying glass which made them appear much more important than they are in fact. That made me ashamed of myself. You have laid a great responsibility upon my shoulders. Will I be able to live up to it? Will I justify the basic idea in the views you express of me? It strikes me that you wrote that precious article with an eye to my future, not to my past. For my past has been so many threads, but not a cloth; so many stones of various shapes and sizes, but not an edifice. I picture you looking at me with the eye of hope and not of criticism;

---

* Al-Azhar in Cairo is the oldest Moslem theological institution, and is known for its fanatical conservatism.

which makes me regret much in my past and, at the same time, dream of the future with a new enthusiasm. If that be your purpose in writing that article, you have achieved it, Mikhail.

I found the paper you have chosen for the *Arrabitah* stationery most excellent. But the saying "Many a treasure beneath the throne", etc., should, in my opinion, be brought out more clearly. As to the names of officers and members, they should be printed in the letterhead if we wish to produce the desired effect. For every one looking at a letter from *Arrabitah* would naturally ask who its members are. Yet do I prefer to have the names printed in the smallest Arabic type available.

I am very sorry, Mikhail, that I shall not be able to go back to New York before the middle of next week; for I am tied to this detestable city with some essential problems. Had it not been for those problems, I should have gone with my sister to the country two weeks ago. What is there to do?

Go to Milford, and fill your cups with the wine of the spirit and the wine of the grapes, but do not forget your loving brother who is so anxious to see you . . .

                                                    Gibran.

Letter 4.—(Boston-New York) Wednesday Evening. (1920) My Brother Mikhail,

Peace to you and to your big heart and good soul. Now, I would know how you are; and I would know where you are. Are you in the forests of your dreams, or in the glens and dales of your thoughts? Or are you on the summit of that mountain where all dreams become a single vision, and all thoughts a single aspiration? Tell me where you are, Mikhail.

As to me, between my unsettled health and the demands men make on me, I am like an out of tune musical instrument in the hands of a giant who plays on it strange tunes devoid of harmony and rhythm. (God help me, Mikhail, with those Americans). God take us away from them to the peaceful valleys of Lebanon.

I have just mailed to Abdul-Masseeh a short piece for publication. Look it over, brother, and if you do not find it fit for publishing, let Abdul-Masseeh keep it in a dark corner until I return. It was written between midnight and dawn, and I know not whether it be good or not good. As to the basic idea in it, it is not far from the topics we discuss at our evening gatherings. Tell me of Nasseeb and of where Nasseeb is. Each time I think of you and him I feel peaceful, serene and magically tranquil; and I say in my heart, "Nothing is vanity under the sun."

A thousand greetings and *salaams* to our brethren in the spirit. May God keep you, and watch over you, and preserve you a dear brother to your brother

Gibran.

Letter 5.—(The following three letters were sent to me by Gibran while I was away from New York on a business trip.)

New York, Oct. 8, 1920

Dear Mikhail,

Whenever I think of you travelling in the "interior" on behalf of a business concern I feel somewhat pained. Yet do I know that that pain is but a remnant of an old philosophy. To-day I believe in Life and everything she decrees, and I affirm that all that the days and nights bring forth is good, and beautiful, and useful.

We were gathered last night at Rasheed's house; and we drank, and ate, and heard songs and poetry. But our evening was not perfect because you were not wholly with us!

The materials for the Arrabitah's Anthology are all ready, but only in spirit! And all arranged, but only in words! Whenever I make a demand on any of our brethren he replies with either "in two days", or "at the end of this week", or "next week." The philosophy of procrastination, which is of the East, almost cracks my skin. And the strange thing, Mikhail, is that some people consider coquettishness a sort of smartness.

I was glad to hear you say that you will not prolong your absence. Perhaps it is not right for me so to feel.

Come back to us, Mischa, when you wish, and you shall find us as you wish us to be. May God watch over you and preserve you to your brother

Gibran.

Letter 6.—(From New York) Friday Evening (1920)

My dear Mischa,

Good morrow to you, wandering one between the purposes of the earth and the calls of the sky. I have heard your voice calling attention to "your goods" in the marts and squares. I have heard you chant out in a melodious voice, "We have denims. We have muslins"—and your voice sounded sweet to me, Mischa. And I know that the angels hear you and record your calls in the Eternal Book.

It pleased me to hear of your "great success". Yet do I fear that success! I fear it because it may lead you into the heart of the commercial world whence it would be difficult to return to our world!!

I shall see Nasseeb and Abdul at this hermitage to-night, and we shall discuss The Anthology. I wish you could be with us, Mischa. I wish you were with us.

I am these days, with thousand and one things to do, like a sick bee in a flower garden. The nectar is plentiful, and the sun most beautiful on the flowers; but the bee is sick and confused. Pray for me and remain a dear brother to

Gibran.

Letter 7.—(From New York) Monday Evening (1920).

My Dear Mischa,

We already miss you, yet you have barely said good-bye. What will happen to us when you remain away for three weeks?

The Anthology—what shall I tell you of the Anthology?

It is a chain whose links are forged of hesitation and procrastination. Every time I say a word about it to Nasseeb or Abdul-Masseeh the first responds with "to-morrow", and the second with "you are right!" But in spite of procrastination and "to-morrowing" (the word is of my own coinage) The Anthology shall be out the end of the year, *inshallah*.

Write me when you have nothing better to do than writing to me. If your new poem has reached perfection, send me a copy of it. You did not give me a copy of your last poem. May God forgive you. Be as you like, and you shall remain a dear brother to your brother

Gibran.

Letter 8.—(Boston - New York) Friday Evening (1921)

My dear Mischa,

Good morrow and good even to you, and may God fill your days with song and your nights with dreams. I am enclosing herewith a good letter and a check which is better yet from a partisan member of Arrabitah. Will you not answer the first in your usual good taste and clear style, and accept the second as an incense and oil offering?

You say that you have told George* to send me the Spanish magazine and newspaper you spoke of; but George has not done that till now. May God forgive George. And may God darn George's memory with threads of my patience and self-restraint. It seems to me, brother, that George has dumped the republic of Chile into the waste-basket!

The cold in Boston is terrible. Everything is frozen, even to the thoughts of men. But in spite of the cold and the biting wind I feel well and live well. My voice (or my yell) is like the roar of a volcano; my foot striking the ground makes a great dent in it like that made by a falling meteor. As to my

---

* A clerk in As-Sayeh's Office.

stomach, it is a mill whose nether stone is a file, and the upper a rattling tongue. It is my hope that your yell, and step, and stomach are just as you like them to be whenever and wherever you desire. Convey my *salaam* to our brethren reinforced with my love, my prayers, and my impatience to see them. May God keep you dear to your brother

Gibran.

Letter 9.—(Boston - New York) January 1st, 1921.

Brother Mischa,

Good morrow to you and a happy New Year. May the vines in your vineyard be weighted with grapes, and your threshing-floors be heaped with corn, and your jars be filled with oil, honey and wine; and may God place your hand upon the heart of Life that you may feel its pulse.

This is the first letter I write in the New Year. Were I in New York, I would ask you to spend the evening with me in the quiet of the hermitage. But how far am I from New York, and how far is the hermitage from me!

How are you, and what are you writing whether of prose or poetry, and what are you thinking of? Is the Special of As-Sayeh about to come out, or is it still at the mercy of those machines which slow up when we wish them to run fast, and run fast when we wish them to slow up? The West is now a machine, and everything in it is tied to the machine. Yes, Mischa, even your poem "Did The Bramble But Know" is at the mercy of Salloum Mokarzal's wheels!

My health was not good the last week; therefore I did not write anything new. But I have gone over my piece "The Lost One", smoothed some rough spots in it, and mailed it to *Al-Hilal* magazine in Cairo. Remember me, Mischa, longingly and lovingly to our comrades, and may God preserve you dear to your brother

Gibran.

Letter 10.—(Boston - New York) Friday Evening (1921).

My Dear Mikhail,

Peace be unto you. Here is a letter addressed to the Counsellor of Arrabitah from the editor of Al-Barq, the poet Bishara
El-Khoury. As you see, it is short and gentle, and it speaks at
the same time of some pain in the soul of its author. And pain
is a good sign.

What became of the snapshots we took at Cahoonzie? Let it
be known that I want a copy of each. Unless I secure my rights,
I shall file two suits against you: one with the court of Friendship; the other with the court of Ahmed Pasha El-Jazzar.*

Remember me, Mischa, to our brethren and comrades; and
May God keep you dear to your brother

Gibran.

Letter 11.—(Boston - New York) Monday. (1921).

My Dear Mischa,

Here is a sweet letter from Emile Zaidan. Read it, and as
is always your wont, take care of it according to your judgment
and discretion. The heat is oppressive in this city and its en-
virons. How is it in New York, and what are you doing?

In my heart, Mischa, are shadows that move, and stroll,
and spread like mist; but I am unable to put them in words.
Perhaps it is better for me to keep silent until this heart becomes
again what it was a year ago. Yes, perhaps silence is better
for me. But, Oh! How bitter is silence in the mouth of one
addicted to talking and singing!

A thousand *salaams* to you and to the dear brethren. May
you remain a dear brother to your brother

Gibran.

* * *

---

* A well known despotic Turkish governor of the last century.

Once I wrote Gibran teasingly, playing on the Arabic words for "poetry" and "hair" which are written and printed exactly alike, but pronounced differently and distinguished in meaning by their context: "Peace to your heart that beats, and your nose that shines; and peace to what is white of your hair and black of your poetry. Your letter arrived to earn you my scolding rather than my love; for it was brief to the point of unfriendliness." To which the following was his reply:

Letter 12.—(Boston - New York) Thursday Evening (1921)

My Dear Mischa,

And a thousand salaams to your heart that neither beats, nor pities, nor palpitates, nor shines. Now do you taunt me for that which is white of my hair and that which is black of my poetry; and you protest against my brevity in writing and my silence about my state. You even resort to scolding—Allah be my refuge!

I, on the other hand, can see no fault in you whatsoever. You are perfect with the abundant black hair covering your temples and the top of your cranium, and with what overflows of your poetry and prose. Meseems that you were created just as you wished to be created, even while in the embryo state; and that you attained your aim even while a babe in the cradle. From Allah we came, and to Allah we return!

It pains me to be absent with Nasseeb's marvelous *pathe* present. What can I do if the pathe cannot be spread from New York to Boston? It is one of the injustices of life for some to be filled with delicious things while others are hungry even for the grace of God, and are not able to obtain a mouthful of it!

I am glad of Nasseeb's insistence on you to write the preface to the Anthology of Arrabitah. You have undoubtedly written, or shall write, what shall be "a necklace" about the neck of the Anthology and a "decorative tattoo" about its wrist. May you remain "a gem in the crown of literature, and a star in its firmament." (The expressions, common to old Arabic style which Arrabitah fought, are used here in derision.—Author).

My health is better than it was last week. But I am told to remain for three months and longer away from any work, from any thought, and from any feeling if I am to regain my health in full. I say, Mischa, that to abstain from work is harder than to work; and for one accustomed to be active, to rest is the severest of penalties.

I have done my duty towards William Catzeflis and those who are arranging for a dinner in his honor in connection with his trip to the Far East. I sent him and the chairman of the committee a telegram in response to their invitation to the dinner in New York.

May God preserve you and your brothers and mine, and your comrades and mine, and may you remain a dear brother to your brother

Gibran.

Letter 13.—(Boston - New York) Sunday (1921).

My Dear Mischa,

I found the preface very beautiful. What say you of a slight change at the very end. The saying quoted at the end should be as great in its triviality and ludicrousness as is the opening verse quoted from Al-Maarry lofty and profound.

This I offer as a suggestion, not as a criticism. Your brother

Gibran.

Letter 14.—(Boston - New York) 1921.

Brother Mischa,

Since I arrived in this city I have been going from one specialist to another; from one thorough examination to another still more thorough. All because this heart of mine has lost its meter and rime. And you know, Mikhail, that this heart's meter and rime were never in conformity with the meters and rimes of other hearts. But since the casual must follow the constant as the shadow follows the substance, it becomes fixed and determined that this lump of flesh within my chest should harmonize with that trembling mist in the space which is myself— my *I*.

Never mind, Mischa. What is to be shall be. But I feel that I shall not leave the slope of this mountain before the break of dawn. And dawn shall cast a veil of light and glow on everything.

When I left New York I put nothing in my valise save "The Prophet" and some clothes. My old copy-books are still in the corners of that silent room. What, then, can I do to please you and to please the Damascus "Arrabitah"? (Organized after and in imitation of the New York Arrabitah; it was very short-lived.—Author) The doctors have ordered me to leave all mental work. Should anything "seep" out of my pen within the next two weeks, I shall take my sponge and pick up the "seepage". Otherwise my excuse should be quite acceptable.

I don't know when I may return to New York. The doctors say that I should not go back until my health is back. They say I "must" go to the country and there live a simple life devoid of every thought and purpose. In other words, they would have me a cabbage in a garden, or some kind of a parasitic plant! For that reason I propose that you send the picture of our Arrabitah to the Damascus group without my face in it; else you may send our old group picture after you blot out my face from it with ink. If, however, it be necessary that the New York Arrabitah should appear in full force on the pages of the Damascus Arrabitah's magazine, how would it be to have Nasseeb, or Abdul, or Mischa (if that were possible) translate some piece from "The Madman" or "The Forerunner"? This may be a silly—a stupid suggestion. What else can I do, Mikhail, with my health what it is? Whoever is unable to sew himself a new garment must perforce go back to an old one and mend it. Do you know, brother, that this ailment has made it incumbent on me to postpone indefinitely the publication of "The Prophet"?

Remember me to my brothers of Arrabitah. Say to them that my love for them with me in the fog of night is not a whit less than in the broad light of the day. Allah protect you and watch over you and keep you a dear brother to

Gibran.

Letter 15.—(Boston - New York) Thursday Evening (1921).

Brother Mischa,

Having read the last number of the Damascus Arrabitah's magazine, and reviewed the previous ones, I am convinced that between us and them lies a deep gulf; we cannot cross to them, nor they to us. No matter how hard we try, Mikhail, we cannot free them from servitude to literary trinkets. Spiritual freedom comes from within, never from without; you know that better than any man. Do not attempt to awaken those whose hearts, for some hidden wisdom, God has put to sleep. Do for them what you like, and send them what you like, but don't forget that you shall cast a veil of doubt and suspicion upon the face of our Arrabitah. If we have any power, it lies in our independence and aloofness. If we must co-operate with others, let it be with people who are our peers, and who say what we say. I believe that Abbas Mahmoud Al-Akkad—(A well known Egyptian writer.—Author) though one man—is nearer by far to our tastes and literary inclination than anything that came out, or may yet come out, of the Damascus Arrabitah. As a worker in Arrabitah I submit—and submit gladly—to the voice of the majority. But I, as an individual, do not and cannot concur in any literary and artistic agreement with that Damascus group who would weave royal purples out of mucous materials.

I was affected, and very deeply, by what you told me of Saba. (N. Arida's brother.—Author) I wish I could do something for that friendly and loyal young man. "But the eye is far of sight, while the arm is short of reach."

You have done well to stir up Rasheed, Nadrah and Nasseeb a little. If we go on delaying the Anthology of Arrabitah will remain in some pocket of the ether until 1923, or 1924! Send me—and this is not an order—six copies of the anthology and debit my account for the amount; else draw on me!

My health, Mischa, is better than before. The doctors tell me that if I give up all kinds of work and exertion for six months, and do nothing but eat, drink and rest, I should be again my normal self! Allah, help me, Mischa!

So you are on the verge of madness. This is a piece of news magnificent in its fearfulness, fearful in its magnificence and beauty. I say that madness is the first step towards divine sublimation. Be mad, Mischa. Be mad and tell us of the mysteries behind the veil of "reason". Life's purpose is to bring us nearer to those mysteries; and madness is the surest and the quickest steed. Be mad, and remain a mad brother to your mad brother

Gibran.

"A boatload of salaams to the brethren".
Letter 16.—(Boston - New York) Thursday Evening (1921)

Dear Mischa,

Say not that I have found the climate of Boston pleasant and conducive to rest, and therefore have forgotten New York, and my brothers in New York, and the many labors and duties that await me in New York. God knows that never in my past life have I spent a month so full of difficulties, trials, misfortunes and problems as the last month. More than once I wondered if my *djinnee*, or my *follower*, or my *double* has turned into a demon who delights in opposing me, in making war on me, in shutting the doors in my face, and in placing obstacles in my way. Since my arrival in this crooked city I have been living in a hell of wordly problems. Had it not been for my sister,

I would leave everything and go back to my hermitage, shaking the dust of the world off my feet.

When I received your telegram this morning I felt like one waking from a nightmare. My thoughts went back to those delightful hours we used to spend together discussing things spiritual and artistic, and I forgot that I was in the midst of a battle, and that my regiments were in a critical situation. Then I recalled my previous misfortunes and those yet to come, and remembered that I was duty-bound to remain here and carry out some engagements. I am to give two readings this week, the first from "The Madman" and "The Forerunner", and the second from "The Prophet", before a "respectable" audience who appreciate this kind of thinking and this style of writing. But the reasons that have kept me in this city, and shall yet keep me for ten more days, have nothing to do with what I have written or read, or what I shall write and read; they have to do with things stupid, wearisome, filling the heart with pricks and gall, and pressing the soul with an iron hand as rough as a steel file.

I have not forgotten that next Wednesday is the date set for Arrabitah's meeting. But what shall I do when "the eye is far of sight, but the hand is short of reach"? I hope that you will meet and adopt useful resolutions, and that you will remember me with a kind word; for in these days I am in a crying need of good wishes from friends and prayers from the devout. More than that, I am in need of a sweet look from a sincere eye.

The present of our fellow-Syrians in Brazil shall reach the White House, and Wilson shall thank them for their generosity and kind intention.* All that shall be carried out in a beautiful and proper manner. But a wave from the sea of oblivion shall engulf the matter from beginning to end. Yet Al-Funoon is still sound asleep; Arrabitah very poor, and our brethren in Brazil

---

* A finely engraved wooden plaque was presented to President Wilson by a delegation of N. Y. Syrians headed by the author.

neither remember the first, nor feel the presence of the second! How strange people are, Mischa; and what strangers you and I are in their midst!

Peace to you, my brother, and peace to our comrades. May God keep you dear to your brother

Gibran.

Letter 17.—(Boston - New York) 1922.

Brother Mischa,

Saba's passing away affected me deeply, tremendously. I know that he has reached the goal, and that he is now immune to all things we complain of. I also know that he has obtained what I wish every day and every night to obtain. I know all that; yet strange to say that such knowledge on my part is powerless to remove that lump of sorrow now dangling between my throat and my heart. What may be the meaning of that lump?

Saba had hopes he wished to have fulfilled. His share of hopes and dreams was equal to the share of any of us. Is it because he left before his hopes blossomed forth and his dreams came to fruition that we feel that heavy lump in the heart? Am I not, as I sorrow for him, sorrowing in fact for some dream of my spent youth which failed of realization? Are not sorrow, regret and grief but phases of human selfishness?

I must not go back to New York, Mischa. The doctor has ordered me to stay away from cities and city life. For that reason I have rented a cottage near the sea and shall move there with my sister in two days; there I shall remain until this heart regains its orderly course, or else becomes a part of the higher order. Yet do I hope to see you before this summer is over— how, where, and when?—I do not know. But the thing must be arranged some way or another.

Your thoughts on "renouncing" the world are exactly like mine. Since long ago I have been dreaming of a hermitage, a small garden, and a spring of water. Do you recall Youssof El-Fakhry? (The principal character in Gibran's Arabic story "The Tempest".—Author) Do you recall his dark thoughts and his bright awakening? Do you remember his views on civilization and the civilized?

I say, Mikhail, that the future shall find us in a hermitage on the edge of one of the Lebanon gorges. This deceptive civilization has strained the strings of our spirits to the breaking point. We must depart before they break. But we must remain patient and forebearing until the day of departure. We must be patient, Mischa.

Remember me to the brethren and say to them that I love them, and long to see them, and live in thought with them. May Allah protect you, and watch over you and keep you for your brother

Gibran.

Wednesday Evening.

Letter 18.—(Boston - New York) 1923.

Beloved Brother Mischa,

Forgive me my long silence and help me to get the forgiveness of your brethren and mine. Early in the summer the doctors told me to refrain from any kind of writing, and I had to submit after a bitter fight between my will and that of my sister and some friends. The result, however, has proved good; for I am to-day nearer to being normal than at any time during the last two years. Living a simple, quiet and orderly life away from hurried civilization, and near the sea and the woods has changed the palpitating heart to one that barely palpitates, and the trembling hand to the hand able to write you these lines.

I shall be back in New York in two or three weeks, and I shall present myself to my brethren; if they accept me, I shall know how forebearing they are; if they reject me, I shall know how just they are. A beggar should not be exacting; a criminal should make no terms.

A thousand loads of salaams to all; and may God protect you and keep you to your brother

Gibran.

This is the first letter I write in three months.

Letter 19.—(New York - Interior) Monday Evening (1923).

Dear Mischa,

Good even to you. Let me convey to you the glad tidings that our Nasseeb is remaining with us, in us, and of us indefinitely; and that his trip to the Argentine has now become an ancient myth.

No. Arrabitah did not meet the last Wednesday of this month, and that for two reasons. The first is that you are away; the second is the absence of anything special for a meeting. I think that the first reason is sufficient, and is the father of the second one.

I was glad to hear you say that you will be back Thursday. You have prolonged your absence, Mikhail; and in your absence our circle becomes something nebulous, misty, devoid of shape and form.

I did not like your saying, "May Izraeel take Mikhail". (Izraeel in Moslem traditions is the angel of death.—Author.) For in my judgment Mikhail is mightier than Izraeel. The first has power over the second, while the second has no power over the first. There is a mystery in names much deeper than we imagine; their symbolic significance defies our thought. Mikhail has been from the beginning much more powerful and commanding than Izraeel.

Till we meet, brother; and may God keep you dear to

Gibran.

Letter 20.—(Boston - New York) 1923.

Dear Brother Mischa,

Good morrow to you. I am glad to know that your book "The Cribble" is out. But, frankly speaking, I did not like it to come out at this season of the year, although I know that the value of the book which is unique of its kind does not depend on any season or decade. Never mind. What was printed was printed.

I spent long hours with the Archmandrite Beshir going over his translations of "The Madman" and "The Forerunner". Despite my rebellion, I admired the man's enthusiasm and determination. When we were through reading and correcting he said to me, "I shall submit these translations to Mikhail Naimy and Nasseeb Arida and ask them to be outspoken in their criticism." I liked that of him and saw that the man was actually seeking to be benefited.

I have not done anything worth mentioning since I left New York aside from jotting down some notes and brushing up some old ideas. It seems to me, Mischa, that the orderly life in my sister's house makes me least productive and creative. Strange to say that disorderly living should be the best whetstone for my imagination.

I shall joy and be happy to read your and Nasseeb's new poems; but I shall stand before you ashamed of my empty hands. Perhaps I shall not be alone if Rasheed persists in his procrastinating. If he does, I know not how he shall be able to have his collection of poems published.

Give my salaams to our friends and comrades and say to them that life without them is incomplete. May God bless you, Mischa, and keep you a dear brother to

Gibran.

Letter 21.—(Boston - New York) Sunday (1923).

Dear Brother Mischa,

I felicitate you and myself upon the "Cribble". Undoubtedly it is the first living breath of that divine tempest which shall carry away all the dead wood in our literary forests. I have read the book, the old of it and the new, from Alpha to Omega, and I became convinced of the following truth which I have often turned over in my mind, and of which I spoke to you but once: Had you not been a poet and a writer, you would not have reached your present level as a critic, and would not have been able to lift the curtain off the truth of poetry and poets, and writing and those that write. I say, Mischa, that had you not experienced poetry in your own soul, you could not share the poetic experiences of others; and had you not walked long in the garden of poetry, you would not rebel against those who walk only the dark and narrow alleys of meter and rime. Sainte-Beuve, Ruskin and Walter Pater were artists before and after they presumed to criticise the works of others; each of them criticised with the help of his inner light, not the help of an acquired taste. It is that inner light which is the source of everything beautiful and noble. When used for criticism it turns it into a beautiful and a noble art. Without it criticism would be didactic and boring, and devoid of that positive ring of positive conviction.

Yes, Mischa. You are a poet and a thinker before everything else, and your singular power of criticism is but a phase of your poetry and thought. Don't give the example of "the egg", for I refuse to accept it. It may be good dialectics, but points to no positive truth.

I shall be back in New York in ten days *inshallah;* and we shall talk long, and make the drawings for Rasheed's poems, and do many other things; and we shall dream beautiful dreams.

Tell the brethren that I am longing to see them. May God keep you a dear brother to

Gibran.

Letter 22.—(Boston - New York) Sept. 30 (1924).

Dear Mischa,

I have been shut-in in this room for several days, and have just left my bed to write you. You know that I was ill when I left New York, and until now I am fighting ptomaine poisoning in my stomach. Otherwise nothing would deter me from going to the orphanage on the day of its dedication. You know, Mischa, that my work, no matter how pressing, could not keep me from absenting myself two or three days, especially when it is to take part in the dedication of the noblest Syrian institution in the United States. I pray you to offer my excuse to the Archbishop and to let him know the real reason for my failure to come.

Give my salaams and love to the brethren, and may God keep you a beloved brother to

Gibran.

Should my health improve between now and Saturday, I'll go straight to Albany.

Letter 23.—(Boston - New York, 1925).

Brother Mischa,

Peace be to your soul. I have just mailed the design for the cover of the As-Sayeh Special in accordance with your suggestion. And the suggestions of princes are the princes of suggestions! Please, demand of Abdul that he keep the drawing for me after the engraver is done with it.

Did you find in the hermitage some solitude and peace? I was afraid that you might find it cold, and should have told you of an electric appliance which may have helped to warm one of its corners. Anyway, warm hearts do not need heat from the outside!

I shall be back in New York in a week—more or less; and we shall get together and have long talks of things beneath the earth and above the clouds. May God keep you, Mischa, a beloved brother to

Gibran.

Letter 24.—(Boston - New York) Monday night, Oct. 11, 1928.

Dear Mischa,

Peace be to your soul. How good of you and how large of heart to inquire about my health. What I had was a kind of summer rheumatism which went away with the summer.

I learned that you returned to modern Babel some three weeks ago. Tell us, O flower of young manhood, what treasures have you brought with you out of your bodily and spiritual absence? I shall return to New York in a week, and shall search your pockets to see what you have brought with you.

The book on Jesus has absorbed all my summer, with me now ill, now well. Yet I confess to you that my heart is still in it despite the fact that it has been already published and "has flown out of this cage." Convey my greetings, Mikhail, to your brethren and mine. May God keep you to

Gibran.

Letter 25.—(Boston - New York) March 26, 1929.

Dear Mischa,

How good and how affectionate of you to ask about my health. I am to-day in an "acceptable" state, Mischa. The rheumatic pains are gone, and the swelling has turned to something opposite. My ailment is seated in something much deeper than muscle and bone. I have often wondered if it was not a state of health instead of illness.

It is a state, Mischa, whether of health or of illness . . . It is one of the seasons of my life; and in your life and mine there be winters and there be springs; and you and I do not know *in truth* which is the more preferable. When we get together again I shall tell you of what happened to me, and you shall know why I once sent my cry, "You have your Lebanon, and I have mine."

Of all fruits lemon is most beneficial. I take lemon every day . . . The rest I leave to God!

In one of my letters I told you that the doctors forbade me to work. Yet I cannot but work, with my mind at least, or just for spite! . . . What say you of a book consisting of four stories: Michelangelo, Shakespeare, Spinoza and Beethoven? What say you if each of the stories be the inevitable outcome of the pain, ambition, the feeling of detachment, and finally hope ever stirring in the human heart? What say you of a book of this kind? So much for that. As to "The Garden of the Prophet", my mind is definitely set upon it, except that I find it wise to keep away from publishers at present.

My greetings to your brethren and mine. May God keep you a brother to

Gibran.

Letter 26.—(Boston - New York. A telegram dated March 26, 1929).

Deeply touched by your telegram. I feel return of good health will be of slow process. I am told that I must not work for full year. That is more painful than illness. All will be well with me in the long run. My love to you and to all our comrades.

Gibran.

Letter 27.—(Boston - New York. May 22, 1929).
Brother Mischa,

I am to-day better than when I left New York. How great is my need for rest away from society and its noise and problems; I shall rest; and I shall be away from noise and problems. But I would remain close to you and to my brothers in spirit and affection. So keep me close, and do not forget me.

A thousand salaams to you, to Abdul-Masseeh, to Rasheed, to William, to Nasseeb and to all who are linked with us in God's Arrabitah.

May the heavens protect and bless you, brother.

Gibran.

THE MYSTIC PACT

(The poem read by the author at the memorial meeting held at Roerich Hall, New York, April 29, 1931, as "a tribute to the spirit of Kahlil Gibran".)

I chanced upon my Brother's tryst with Death.
Fast were they locked in each other's embrace,
My Brother saying, "Mother of my breath,
Bid it be still, bid it dissolve in space.
It chokes my nostrils with the heavy smells
Of hopes still-born, of putrid days and nights;
And breathless would I dwell upon the heights
And in the depths where breathless Beauty dwells.
"Reach deep, sweet lover, deep into my breast;
Perchance you'll find a fragment of a heart.
'Tis all I have to offer you; the rest
Is mine no longer. Here and there a part
I laid on canvas, melted into song,
Planted in fields unwedded to the plow,
Forged into tongues for all the mute who long
With tongues their silent longings to endow.
Now cleanse me, lover, of the salt and froth
Of earth to sail with you the shoreless sea."
And Death responded to my Brother's plea,
And with the kiss of silence sealed the troth.
As I, a witness to the mystic rites,
Stood dazed, enveloped in a thousand nights,
There spoke a voice exceeding soft and kind:
"What is ahead is already behind."

THE LIVING GIBRAN

The opening address delivered by the author at the Fortieth Day Commemorative meeting held in Brooklyn by the Syrian-Lebanese community, the author presiding:

We have come together on this day not to glorify a dead man, but rather to be glorified in a living one.

Man's only glory lies in his gradual ascent from the human in him to the divine; from the perishable to the imperishable; from the unbeautiful to the beautiful; from delusion to Truth; from Life's dual appearances to Life's inner unity.

We are all on the way. But the way is strewn with aches, furrowed with pitfalls, and shadowed with snarling passions. Yet does the spirit of God hover over it, and the light of God pierce the heavy mist that veils it.

Men differ from men insofar only as they keep, or do not keep, their eyes on the goal; or as they set, or do not set, their hearts on reaching it. Some toddle on the way amusing themselves with pleasures that soon turn into pain. While others march on, knowing that all earthly pleasures are rooted in pain; that pain is the offspring of ignorance; that ignorance cannot be overcome save with knowledge; and that Truth is the only source of knowledge.

We are all vessels for Truth; but we can contain no more of it than we make room for in our souls. You cannot fill with wine a jar you have already filled with vinegar. Likewise the heart stocked with earth passions, unless emptied first, cannot be stocked with heavenly desires.

In other words, we reflect the Truth clearly or otherwise according as the mirror of our soul be clear or tarnished. Whoever has the mirror of his soul disfigured and tarnished, the same will reflect the Truth disfigured and tarnished. That is not to say that he is devoid of Truth; for the moon reflected in a muddy pool of water is the same moon reflected in a clear one; and the sun that peeps at you through a clean window pane and brings you joy and warmth is the self same sun that looks at you through a smoked or dust-ridden pane, and you barely see it.

Gibran Kahlil Gibran's was of those souls that experienced moments of utter clarity in which Truth delights to be mirrored. In that was Gibran's glory. In that was his pain. For the soul that reflects the Truth even for an instant is pained ever afterward each time it reflects non-truth. Vast is the difference between its pain and the pain of tarnished souls! And the eye that glimpses the face of Beauty even for an instant sheds tears of blood ever afterward each time it falls on things unbeautiful. Vast is the difference between its tears and the tears of the eye that beholds earthly beauty alone!

Whoever knows not Gibran's sorrows cannot know his joys. And whoever knows not his joys cannot know the power that made it possible for him to put his joys and sorrows in words that ring with melody, and in colors that stand out as living thoughts and longings, and lines that are ladders between the animal in the human heart and the God enthroned within that heart. In revealing himself to himself Gibran reveals us to ourselves. In polishing the mirror of his soul he polishes the mirrors of our souls. In the same Truth he is glorified we, too, are glorified.

For some purpose unknown to you and to me Gibran was born in Lebanon at the time he was born. And for a reason hidden from you and me Arabic was his mother tongue. It would seem that the all-seeing eye perceived our spiritual drought and sent us this rain-bearing cloud to drizzle some relief to our parching souls.

If any see in that phenomenon a reason for national pride

and boastful self-assertion, let them be proud, and let them boast. As to me I would be too shy to boast of my parched land because of a shower sent down upon it from the sky. Rather would I say, "Make us, God, worthy of this gift that we may be worthy of more."